Backroad Journeys
of the
West Coast
States

Backroad Journeys of the West Coast States

Oregon,
Washington,
and California

David Yeadon

Harper & Row, Publishers
New York, Hagerstown, San Francisco, London

Other books written and illustrated by David Yeadon

Exploring Small Towns of Southern California
Exploring Small Towns of Northern California
Hidden Restaurants of Southern California
Hidden Restaurants of Northern California
Wine Tasting in California
Sumptuous Indulgence on a Shoestring (a cookbook)
The New York Book of Bars, Pubs, and Taverns
Hidden Corners of New England
Hidden Corners of the Mid-Atlantic States
When the Earth Was Young: A Study of American Indian Songs
Nooks and Crannies of New York City

BACKROAD JOURNEYS OF THE WEST COAST STATES. Copyright © 1979 by David Yeadon. All rights reserved. Printed in the United States of America. No part of this book may be used or reproduced in any manner whatsoever without written permission except in the case of brief quotations embodied in critical articles and reviews. For information address Harper & Row, Publishers, Inc., 10 East 53rd Street, New York, N.Y. 10022. Published simultaneously in Canada by Fitzhenry & Whiteside Limited, Toronto.

FIRST EDITION

Library of Congress Cataloging in Publication Data

Yeadon, David.
  Backroad journeys of the West Coast States.
  Includes index.
  1. Pacific States—Description and travel—
1951-   —Guide-books. 2. Automobiles—Road
guides—Pacific States. I. Title.
F851.Y4   1979   917.9'04'3   78-69500
ISBN 0-06-014773-3
  0-06-090672-3 pbk.

79 80 81 82 10 9 8 7 6 5 4 3 2 1

dedicated to
Backroaders—
everywhere

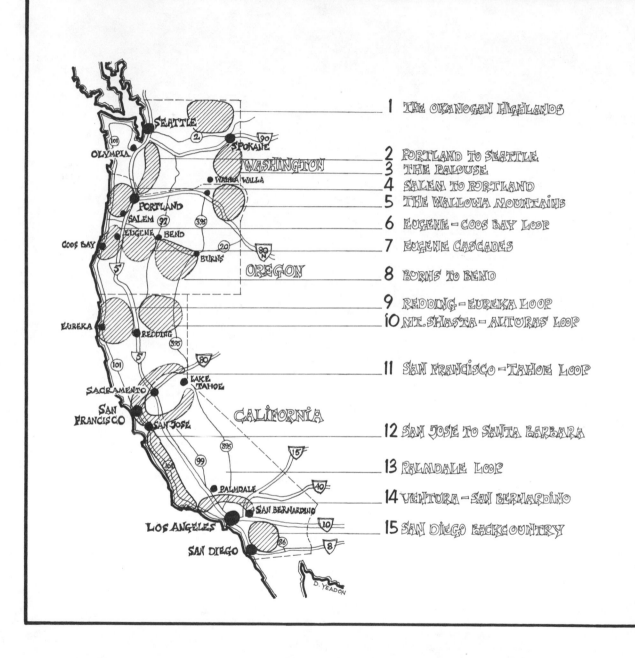

1 THE OKANOGAN HIGHLANDS

2 PORTLAND TO SEATTLE
3 THE PALOUSE
4 SALEM TO PORTLAND
5 THE WALLOWA MOUNTAINS
6 EUGENE - COOS BAY LOOP
7 EUGENE CASCADES
8 BURNS TO BEND
9 REDDING - EUREKA LOOP
10 MT. SHASTA - ALTURAS' LOOP
11 SAN FRANCISCO - TAHOE LOOP
12 SAN JOSE TO SANTA BARBARA
13 PALMDALE LOOP
14 VENTURA - SAN BERNARDINO
15 SAN DIEGO BACKCOUNTRY

CONTENTS

The Art of Backroading

Bid farewell to the superhighways, the motel strips, the junk-food restaurants, and the hullabaloo of a jostling, honking urbanity. Tip your cap to the tourist traps; we won't be seeing those for a while. Forget guided tours, cramped itineraries, advance reservations, waiting lines, turnstiles, tickets, and all the miscellaneous trappings of travel that homogenize experiences and remove the thrills of discovery and surprise. We're off, my backroading friends, to find the real America. We're off to explore parts of the country rarely visited by the conventional tourist, talk with people unaccustomed to strangers, and enjoy new and unexpected adventures. We'll gain a fresh respect for this magnificent country—its land, its people, its communities, and its history. We follow not the easiest routes—just the best routes.

Robert Frost wrote:

> Two roads divided in a wood, and I—
> I took the road less traveled by,
> And that has made all the difference.

Backroaders will understand these lines, both literally and figuratively. Backroading is an art. You are the journey. You create your own perceptions, your own joys. There are no planned events, no prescheduled experiences, no laugh cards. You're on your own.

Actually that's not altogether true. I'm there too, although I hope not intrusively. So—let's go backroading together. We'll discover quiet villages unchanged for more than a hundred years; secluded waterfalls deep in fir forests; old gold-mining towns, creaky and bleached; still lakes said to be the home of mysterious creatures and eerie wraiths. We'll travel across a desert of wheatfields, endless rollings of gold; peer into the deepest canyons in the country, far deeper than the Grand Canyon; while away a warm afternoon by a mountain stream or in a cozy false-front store with the aroma of home-smoked bacon wafting around the wood-burning stove. Ham and his hummingbirds will entice us, Henry will "instigate" all kinds of unusual adventures, Cliff Harthill will show us his odd collection of street clocks, and we'll meet Pauline, who lives in an old mining-town bordello. Then it's off to visit country wineries, bread bakeries, cheese-making establishments, oyster- and shrimp-packing plants, a cranberry festival, a joss temple, quaint local museums, and a salmon hatchery. We'll eavesdrop on conversations in a lumberman's tavern, and we'll meet the wandering Joe and his horse, a young girl at a commune, and representatives of some fascinating religious sects at the base of Mount Shasta. We'll explore undulating sand dunes and the highest ranges of the Cascades; we'll grope our way through spooky talus caves and enjoy the utter silence of the redwoods.

Many times we'll leave the car behind and go wandering along narrow mountain tracks, exploring the quaint streets of a perfect Victorian village, and walking the driftwood-fringed beaches. There are surprises galore. The backcountry comes alive. History flows out fresh in the tales of miners, lumbermen, hunters, and old women with prodigious memories. We'll find the remnants of utopian colonies, an abandoned Irish castle, endlessly eroding deserts, old mineral spas, and a fairy kingdom built by a farmer. We'll lose ourselves in black, brittle lava fields and find ourselves again over a gargantuan dinner in a Basque restaurant.

We'll do all this and much, much more.

If you've never really explored the backroads before, let this book be your guide. If you're an old hand at the game, use the book as a basis for your own improvised ramblings, and stay as far as possible from the freeway. We're off to find peace, silence, excitement, and adventure. Coming?

Backroading Travel Tips

- Before you set off on a backroad journey, it's usually advisable to read the entire text of the chapter and note any warnings about isolated road conditions.
- Use the individual journey maps in conjunction with detailed directions in the text. The journey maps have a simple notation: **the double circle indicates towns or cities offering a range of accommodations and restaurants, and the dotted line is the actual route of the journey.**
- Don't forget, backroading is a leisurely activity. Assume an overall average speed of 20 miles per hour or less. Many of the journeys will take more than a day to complete. Some may need as long as three or four days. Take this into account when planning your route. If you don't have time to follow the whole route, choose the sections that appeal.
- Don't worry about getting lost—it's all part of the fun of backroading, and there's usually someone around ready to help you. However, take extra care with backroads in unpopulated mountain and desert regions. If you have any qualms about routes or the availability of gas, it's best to make advance inquiries at country stores and inns. Also note occasional warnings in the text about seasonal road conditions and obtain prior information where suggested.
- Road conditions vary from smooth tarmac to graded gravel, and most selected routes are perfectly adequate for sedans. There are no routes requiring four-wheel drive vehicles. In cases where road conditions may be a little rough, I've suggested alternative routes.
- Try not to overplan your itinerary. Take the necessary precautions but also allow for the unexpected. If a friendly backwoodsman offers you a meal or even overnight accommodation— accept! If you come across a small-town festival or fancy a few hours of apple-picking or a swim in a hidden mountain lake—stop and enjoy! Surprise is half the fun of backroading.
- Ideally, carry your own camping equipment. Then you can avoid scurrying to the larger towns for overnight accommodation. Alternatively, stay at the country inns and guest houses in smaller communities and eat at their local restaurants (often outstanding).

To summarize: relax, expect surprises, improvise or modify your route as necessary, and relish every adventure.

May you enjoy all your journeys.

D.Y.

WASHINGTON

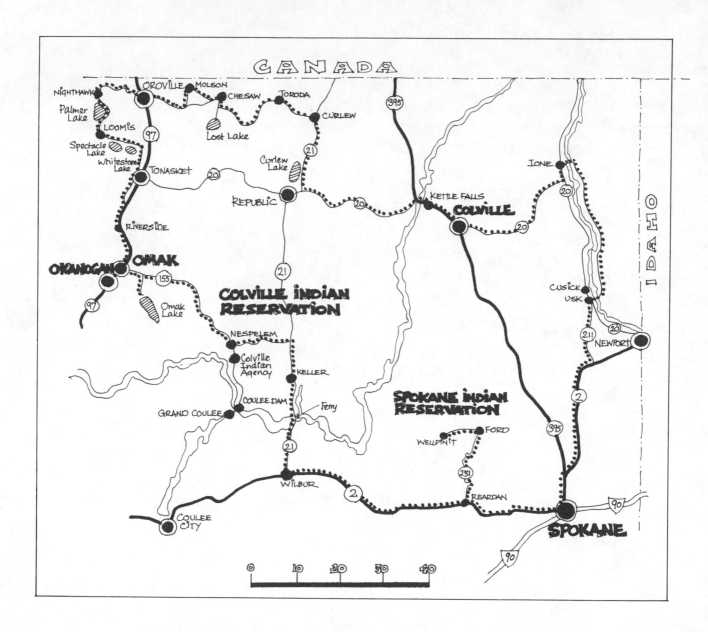

1. THE OKANOGAN HIGHLANDS
Remnants of a Gold Rush

We're off on a splendidly scenic journey of quiet mountains, missions, hidden lakes, and forgotten gold-mining towns. En route we'll talk with an elderly woman about life in a mining camp, meet a burly tavern owner in a ghost town, and learn about the irascible citizens of Molson, who couldn't agree on where their town should be located and so built three.

We'll also see evidence of a resurgence of tribal culture at the ceremonies of an authentic Indian powwow held deep in the wooded backcountry west of Spokane.

AT A HUDDLE of false-front buildings over the railroad tracks in Cusick the sign on the cafe read "Harve's and Pearl's Place. Pressure Fried Chicken in 10 mins." There was no one inside. Down the street the Carson Forge ("General Blacksmithing and Ironworks") was bolted up. City Hall, a three-room shack across from the store, was empty. A crow cawed in a drooping maple and a dog peered at me curiously through the tall grass at the side of the road. It was good to be in the backcountry again!

The journey north out of Spokane had seemed endless. Junk-food stands and muffler shops had clung like sticky candy to Route 395. At the Bigfoot Tavern (complete with smiling monster) Route 2 finally led off into a quieter landscape of pines and mountain vistas. The less-attractive traces of urbanity were left behind as the road headed plumb-line straight for the north. At Cusick I had reached the backcountry—the wide valley of the Pend Oreille river, the pine-covered hills, the vast cloudscape of the Selkirk Mountains. They call this region, appropriately, Panorama-land.

Take the road from Usk along the eastern side of the river to Ione and you'll have the valley to yourself. Note the marker halfway along, commemorating the expeditions of David Thompson, the famous British geographer who began his surveys along the 49th parallel westward from Lake Superior in 1796. Between 1807 and 1811 he established the first trading posts for the London-based North West Fur Company in this region, including Spokane House about 10 miles below the falls at the junction of the Spokane and Little Spokane rivers. Not long afterward John Jacob Astor built his Fort Spokane nearby as a base for his Pacific Fur Company, and the two traded amicably, side by side, for a few years until Astor sold out to the British company in 1813.

Just below Ione, Route 20 leaves the valley and climbs abruptly into the mountains. Secluded camping and picnic spots nestle along the jeweled necklace of the Pend Oreille lake chain. On the right there's a road leading up to the Dominion lookout. This brief detour provides a magnificent vista over our route to the west, deep into the Okanogan highlands.

Following the long descent into Colville, pause at the Steven's County Historical Museum for a glimpse of the rigorous pioneer past of this region. Before the frantic gold-rush era of the late 1800s this was trapping territory. Scattered forts and trading posts were the only signs of civilization. No one worried too much about national boundaries. This was just another pine-covered wilderness generously endowed with beavers, bears, and other valuable fur-covered creatures. The men who came here were not the empire builders of the East. They were not in search of fame and monuments. They were not driven, like later pioneers, by an insatiable urge for land ownership. They were quite content to hunt and trade with the Indians and generally enjoy an active and normally lucrative life. Even when Sir George Simpson, governor of the Hudson's Bay Company, directed that a fort be established at Kettle Falls in 1825, it was not built to destroy the local Indians (as was the second Fort Colville, erected in 1859 on the east side of the town) but as a center for the fur trade. Boat brigades often consisting of more than eighty men traveled from here down the Columbia River to company headquarters near the Pacific Ocean.

It was a peaceful era, unmarked by major disputes. Later the joint occupation of the Oregon Territory by the British and Americans was also generally amicable, although the czar of the Hudson's Bay Company, John McLoughlin, saw to it that his interests were in no way affected by such an arrangement. Russian intrusion had been limited to latitude 54° 40' north, and the whole situation seemed ideal until Polk's rousing cry of "Fifty-four-forty or fight!" in 1844. At that time Britain was entrenched in European wars and was reluctant to become involved in yet another skirmish with those "pesky Yankees." So, the 1846 compromise at the 49th parallel placed the Oregon Territory under American control, and the placid fur-trading era soon gave way to a period of frantic settlement.

Along with the pioneers came the missionaries. Some were pragmatic men more concerned with the Indian's ability to farm land efficiently than with his spiritual well-being. Others, entrusting such mundane concerns as food to the will of God, attempted a more direct assault on the Indian culture. St. Paul's Mission, a replica of which is located at the end of a wooded track off 395, near Kettle Falls, was founded in 1847 and seems to have generally maintained a happy balance of interests. But again problems were smoldering. The Indians, this time the Colville tribe, were being slowly legislated out of their lands. Pioneers smelled gold in the northern hills of the Okanogan highlands and had no intention of letting reservations and the like slow their pursuit of instant wealth.

While the gold rushes in Washington never attained the fury of the fifties in California, substantial deposits were found in the Okanogan highlands. The Washington gold rush began quietly in two places in 1855: near old Fort Colville on the east bank of the Columbia, and around Wenatchee. Both discoveries were relatively small, and there was a lull until later finds during the 1880s and '90s, when the traditional placer mining was soon overtaken by an enthusiasm for lode operations. A local newspaper emphasized that this was "not a poor man's mining country," and

St. Paul's Mission—Kettle Falls

thousands left, disillusioned and broken, having thoroughly raked and raped the Indians' land for a few ounces of gold dust.

The town of Republic was one of the many communities that boomed during the "opening up" of the Colville reservation in the 1890s. It's an impressive drive up out of the Roosevelt Lake national recreation area along the dammed Columbia River, and over the Kettle River mountain range. Republic sits on a steep hillside at the end of the long descent from the 5,575-foot Sherman Pass. A little of its Old World Western charm still remains from the boom days of the 1890s, but fires have taken their toll. Gas stations now break the unity of main street, and only a few bars still exist as a mediocre memorial to the twenty-eight saloons and two dance halls that once brought the miners rip-roaring down from the gulches clutching their buckskin bags of nuggets and pay dirt.

Just off main street there's a modest museum with regional displays and hundreds of sepia photographs of Republic in its prime. A wiry old woman was looking after the place the day I visited. She was disarmingly blunt about the town. "This isn't anything like it was when I was a girl. Why, we'd got the biggest hotel for miles around, th' Hotel Bailey. It was the first with two-level outhouses, one on top of the other. You should've seen those things. You'd to get across a catwalk to reach the top one and boy did that wind howl. But folks thought it was a real good idea! Course that was before all these indoor toilets and such-like."

I asked her about the miners who used the town as their base. "Well, all I know is, I was never let out at weekends 'cept to go to church an' the like. Nighttime all the respectable folks just stayed indoors. But you could hear the men all the way up the hill—singin' and shoutin' an' playin' around. Not much shootin', though. That's movie nonsense mostly. Nothin' like as much shootin' as you'd think. Heck, people died fast enough from natural causes in them days. We used to get real bad winters. I heard tell of four fellers they found dead outside the back door of a saloon in town. It was spring when they found 'em. They must have been drunk one night just before the snow and laid down for a sleep. They never got up again."

She paused for a moment, then added, "There was always somethin' interesting to see. I remember when they brought in camels once. Said they were good for transportin' things. They didn't last long, though. Th' horses got too spooked so they stopped usin' them." She chortled. "Heck, I usta get spooked too, 'specially when the Russies came" (a group of the Doukhobor sect from Canada) "and them Indians—the real ones" (Hindus). Finally she said, "But there was a lot of good solid folks too in these parts. Most made an honest living. They were the real pioneers, y'know. The others were always movin' on." A local historian, Howard L. Mooney, expressed the same thought: "Six-guns and Winchesters didn't make the West. It took the flow of covered wagons, a man with a dream and a wife with a nestful of kids—that did it!"

The drive north from Republic on Route 21 to Curlew passes along a valley filled with tailings left behind from gold-dredging operations. Many of the hills, once pine-covered, are now bald from over enthusiastic lumbering operations. Curlew Lake, halfway along, is a delightful spot for a swim or picnic.

10

There's not too much left at Curlew. In fact, according to the locals I met in the tavern there never really was that much (except during Prohibition, when Kelly Hall's garage was the center of a liquor-smuggling operation). It seems to have missed the gold-rush boom, and all that General Sherman could find to record about the area, in his 1883 trip through the Pacific Northwest, was a comment on its annoying insects.

But, of course, there is the 1903 Hotel Ansorge. This elegant relic still possesses its wooden sidewalk and its tin-and-stone facing, recently repainted a brilliant silver. The lobby has been converted into a notions store, complete with a print of Gilbert Stuart's unfinished portrait of George Washington on the wall above the barber chair, a window full of old bottles, two potted palms, and a sense of total timelessness.

At Curlew we turn left and begin our meanderings into the real gold-mining territory. It was this area, a narrow strip of the old Colville reservation immediately south of the Canadian border, that started all the problems with the local Indians' reservation rights. It's a confusing story and one subject to prejudiced interpretation, depending on whose side is being defended. However, it seems to be generally agreed today that the Indians were treated most dishonorably and that they have never been fairly compensated for the loss of their land.

The drive from Curlew follows the limpid Toroda Creek for a few miles and then swings off west just before the Canadian border to Chesaw. The road is paved for much of the way and is a splendid mountain route through the Colville and Okanogan national forests. There's one stretch, though, over a steep grade, that would be more appropriate for stagecoaches than autos.

Just before Chesaw is a turning to Lost Lake. It means 5 more miles of rough gravel road, but if you'd like a lake to call your own for an hour or two, this is the one.

Alternatively, take a dust-off at Dave Lyonais' tavern in Chesaw, a false-front affair and one of the few buildings still standing in this forgotten little town. Note the dollar bills pinned to the ceiling for "beer insurance." Each regular keeps some spare cash up there, in case he runs out. "You should come on here at rodeo time 'round Independence Day," Dave told me. "The place is swamped out—had more'n four thousand las' year. Was that some rodeo!" I looked across the dusty road, and indeed there was a rodeo compound, a weather-worn grandstand that looked as if it would crumble in a heavy dew! But Dave was already onto his next favorite subject—hippies. It appears that the hills around Chesaw are a popular squatting area for young welfare-supported people, and Dave, not one to mince words, vented on about their indolence. When pressed, though, he had to admit that the tavern benefited considerably from their trade, particularly on check day. "But I still don't think it's right," he grumbled. "I work more'n eighteen hours a day, seven days a week, my wife's just left me, my kid's always needin' somethin'. . . ." I couldn't help smiling during this tirade. He kept filling and refilling his beer glass, taking great pulls and thumping the bar top so hard with his fist that his beer belly wobbled like a jello dessert. Fortunately he saw the funny side too. "Aw, what the heck—I've got a good life. Wouldn't live no place else—and I got all the free beer I want! All I need is the wife back and everythin's just fine!"

Toroda Creek

A visitor here in the early days likened Chesaw's emergence to "a small cyclone rushing pell-mell across an erstwhile open space leaving behind it clumps of dirty tents and lean-to's." It's hard to believe, though, that in 1900 this was a bustling community of more than eleven hundred people, with six saloons, two hotels, and a renowned trade in millinery goods. But, as happened to most gold-mining towns in the region, its boom passed, one of the hotels burned in 1906, the Greenwood Saloon was sold as a church (a steeple was nailed on later!), and the miners moved off to new claims. Fires in the 1950s destroyed many of the remaining buildings, but somehow the place just would not disappear. The store and tavern were refurbished. Someone converted an old silo into a house and the rodeo area was fixed up. An elderly resident, Phyllis Smith, even came back after a brief departure. "I just missed the place. I missed the sunsets especially."

A few miles out of Chesaw on the Oroville road, there's a turnoff on the right to Molson, one of the most fascinating of the region's mining towns. The curving gravel road eventually makes the steep descent into the false-fronted remnants of a community that once boasted a population of more than two thousand. Actually there were really three communities here. The first town was built hurriedly at the turn of the century as the citizens set about making gold-mining fortunes for themselves. However, insufficient study had been made of land titles, and in 1904 a local farmer proved the town was built on part of his homestead. He also made it clear that he intended to take it over, the stores, the bank, the hotel—everything. Not to be outdone, the citizens founded New Molson half a mile down the road, and by 1906 it was even larger than the old town. For a while the local banker was unsure where to locate and so moved his establishment around on skids, one day in Old Molson, the next day in New Molson, until finally choosing the latter as a permanent base. When federal officials refused to create two post offices, a group of New Molsonians "requisitioned" the desks, fittings, and registers one lunchtime from Old Molson and relocated the post office in their own town.

The citizens were ambitious men, proud of their community. An illustrated brochure for Molson, put out in 1910, showed steamers on the "river" below the town and rows of docks filled with well-dressed merchants and manicured ladies. It was, of course, all fantasy. No steamer came anywhere near Molson. Even the *Dew Drop,* a sternwheeler that claimed it could ride in two feet of water, occasionally had problems reaching the upper Okanogan river, miles from Molson.

Reality was far less attractive. Feuding and brawling went on between the towns for years. These were tough times. An article in the *Molson Leader* of November 30, 1912, describes the fate of a defendant who had insulted the local judge in his courtroom: "On Tuesday the machinery in the Court of Judge J. Ward Bentley ground to a halt long enough to permit the judge to take the defendant outside and give him a licking."

In 1914 the citizens of the two towns finally cooperated to build an impressive three-story brick school at "Center Molson," midway between Old and New Molson. Today the school still stands, empty and broken, but little else remains of New Molson besides a restaurant in an antique

Remnants of Old Molson

store, a few houses, and Sidley Lake, a popular fishing area. Over at Old Molson, though, there's an authentic re-creation of the gold-mining era, complete with post office, shacks, assay office, law office, and store. Each building contains a wealth of objects appropriate to its original function. Hundreds of valuable antiques are displayed, and when I was there, no one was watching over them. There were just a few signs requesting "Please do not remove articles."

Along the road to Oroville the scenery becomes progressively more arid. The pine forests recede and the hills, sagebrush-covered, have a beige tinge. I found the descent into the Okanogan valley reminiscent of a Mediterranean scene. A bright, dry landscape with scattered white buildings contrasted with the dark-green orchards along the river. The sky was cloudless, a brilliant blue. I could hardly believe I was still in Washington.

The illusion continued as I climbed out of the valley on the Loomis Road. Dense groves of apple and pear trees lined the narrow mountain terraces, and sinews of irrigation channels fed the dry earth. One broad channel followed the road for miles into the hills.

I paused at Nighthawk, another remnant of a mining town. The store, a popular socializing center in the valley, was closed up, and the old footbridge that once crossed the river at this point had been replaced by a modern highway affair. On the west side of the river there are sizable remnants of mine buildings and tempting tailings for contemporary prospectors.

Without warning, a few miles down the road, Palmer Lake suddenly appears around a bend. Abruptly the harsh landscape is mellowed by more dark-green orchards and that placid stretch of water resting in a mountain-rimmed bowl. But it isn't always quiet and pastoral here. I remember one occasion when pickup trucks, old Chevys, and dusty campers lined both sides of the road and the orchards were full of bending, reaching, clutching figures. It was apple-picking time. In late September thousands of students, migrants, Indians, whole families complete with grandmothers pour into the Wenatchee/Okanogan/Oroville valleys attracted by the $7-a-box rates or the chance of fun times under the bowed branches. Many are soon disillusioned. Those boxes are big, and it can take the inexperienced picker more than three hours to fill one, three hours of bending and the promise of a nightful of backache. Backache and fun don't mix, so many novices vanish after a day or two, leaving the regulars behind, some of whom have followed the fruit and berry harvests across the country and are now nearing the end of their annual travels. If you'd fancy the experience for a few hours, stop and talk with the people in charge and start filling your box.

Loomis was once the home of Guy Waring, whose three-year journal of life in the region during the 1800s was later published as the popular *My Pioneer Past*. His descriptions of log-cabin building, Indian customs, ranching, local characters, and his own Thoreau-type experiences in this backcountry wilderness make captivating reading even today. Although he had previously spent much of his life in cities, his return to the East Coast led him to conclude, "It required only a very few months of renewed living in Boston to convince me that the simplicity of life on the frontier was more desirable, more wholesome, and finally more rewarding." I imagine most of the residents of the area would agree with Waring. I chatted with the woman who ran the local general store. "There's quite a few that moves away to see a bit of the world. But you'd be surprised how many come back and never leave again!"

To the south along Sinlahekin Creek there are more remnants of the old mining days around Conconully. Unfortunately, though, the track is too rough for most cars and campers, so we turn east from Loomis and follow the valley down past Spectacle and Whitestone lakes into the Okanogan valley again. Look for the "Phantom of Whitestone" sign near the market and notice its ghostly shape, seemingly hovering in space, against the light cliffs. It's usually most distinct on a sunny day when the shadows are pronounced.

Follow the road on the west side of the river to Route 97, a few miles north of Riverside. Then there's a stretch of highway driving into the twin cities of Okanogan and Omak, home of the famous Omak stampede held every August. On the fringe of Okanogan is the Historical Society's museum of early pioneer artifacts (11–5 daily during summer). It's worth a visit before we travel east on Route 155 into the remnants of the Colville Indian reservation.

After a long steady climb out of Omak, take the turn to St. Mary's Mission. Here in a quiet hidden valley above Omak Lake sits a tall-spired church surrounded by buildings of the Paschal Sherman Indian School, run by the Colville Confederated Tribes. I was lucky. I happened to meet the resident priest, Reverend Jake Morton, who enthusiastically described the mission's history from its founding in 1886 by the "Blackrobe" Father Etienne De Rouge to its present-day role as a boarding school for 170 Indian children. Then he leaped into his car and took me off to see a series of ancient but little-known Indian petroglyphs in a high valley overlooking Omak Lake. I whiled away the rest of the afternoon on the beach, and then remembered Jake had mentioned that the Spokane tribe to the east was holding its annual powwow at Wellpinit (usually the first weekend in September). He told me it was very much their own affair, not a tourist attraction. I decided I'd go to learn a little more about the Washington tribes, whose cultures have been so badly ravaged.

The drive east through the reservation brought me to the rather sad community of Nespelem, dusty and disheveled at a crossroads. The only sound was the spasmodic laughter from inside the War Bonnet Bar. Old automobiles, many without wheels and engines, sat in the streets, in gardens and vacant lots. Skinny dogs moved warily in the shadows and I saw no people. The place seemed to have no life of its own. Farther down 155 is the tribal headquarters, with its gleaming new buildings, one of which is designed as a modern-day long house. The tribal park nearby contains the Skolaskin Church, the first church in the reservation, built in 1874, and moved from its original Whitestone location. In marked contrast, a few miles to the south is the Grand Coulee Dam on the Columbia River, where self-guided tours provide an all-too-obvious reminder of the contemporary world outside the reservation.

The road east from Nespelem passes near the grave of "young" Chief Joseph (see Chapter 5, "The Wallowa Mountains") and climbs up onto wide meadowlands, where the grasses gleam silver and gold in the late summer. Then we enter the conifers, and meander through the mountains before descending to Route 21 and driving south to the free ferry across the Columbia. It's a lovely setting—the great grey hills, the river, and the sky. Only a few minutes previously I'd traveled through dense pine forests. Now I was sitting on the banks of this mother of rivers, looking out over a landscape virtually devoid of vegetation. The ferry crossing provided a total transition.

The climb out of the valley was steep, with incredible views back over the river. At the crest I experienced that sensation of entering a kind of dream world. It happened to me frequently in Washington and Oregon—in the Palouse, in the Hart Mountain desert, in the mists along the coast—usually when the shift from one kind of landscape to another is abrupt and absolute. After winding slowly up from the river, looking back over the pine-covered hills of the Colville reservation, I was not prepared for the sudden emergence onto a high plateau, with an expanse of golden wheatfields stretching as far as I could see and far beyond that. There were no buildings except the occasional farm way in the distance. Nothing but those endless flat wheatfields. Even on Route 2 as I headed east toward the Spokane reservation there was hardly a break in this wilderness of wheat. If I half-closed my eyes I had the sensation of moving across one of the world's bleakest deserts.

I reached Wellpinit after dark. At Reardon I had left the wheatfields and driven along narrow winding roads across the Spokane river to Ford. Here I turned west and traveled deep into the reservation. There was little traffic, and I wondered if I had mistaken the date of the Spokane's powwow. Then suddenly I was there, driving along a rough track on the edge of a pine forest. Everywhere were trucks and campers. I parked and strolled toward the din of drums. Stetsoned figures rode by on horseback. Other groups sat around cooking stoves, drinking and singing. Candles shone inside a hundred tepees, casting flickering shadows on their canvas sides. Ahead of me there were bright lights and crowds. Indians in majestic headdresses and costumes were gathered outside a large white building. Many had painted faces. All were speaking in native dialects. Inside the sound of drums was almost deafening. Hundreds of Indians from almost every tribe in the Northwest were clapping, pounding their feet, and watching the dancers in the middle of the floor as they swirled and bounded to the rhythm. There was no letup. The beat kept building and building. The dancing figures became a blur of feathers, skins, and beads. The drummers pounded harder and harder. The dancers leaped higher, wailing and beating the air with their arms. Their bodies seemed out of control yet in total control. Each man's movements were precise and measured. Bells jangled, rattles crackled, necklaces and arm bands flashed—all in time with the drums. Then with a final blow on taut skins, the drummers stopped and the dance ended. The audience, almost as one, let out a long gasp and wiped the perspiration from their eyes. The dancers, still erect, moved together off the floor.

Somewhere drums were still beating. I left the building and went to see if more dancing was in progress. There were few whites around, and I understood what Jake had meant when he called it a rather private gathering. Under a wide-raftered roof groups of Indians were sitting on the ground in circles, beating drums and singing sequences of hypnotic chants. I asked an elderly lady next to me what was going on and she replied, "Stick games." The rules are basically simple: a stick game is really a guessing game in which one side tries to determine in which hand their opponents hold the individual bone "sticks." But it's actually a highly intense process of chants and rituals aimed at confusing the other side, and it goes on literally for days. The Spokane powwow lasted for three days and the stick game continued throughout.

When I woke the following morning I could smell the breakfasts cooking on the campfires. Instead of having bacon, I strolled over to the snack bar for two portions of Indian fried bread and ate them with some dried salmon I had bought earlier from a young Indian girl. Across from where I sat, the stick game was still in progress. The drums had been going all night.

It was Sunday morning, and a church service was being held in the same building as the previous night's dancing. It was, as one of the white priests (the "Blackrobes") explained, "a mass to join together the Christian religion and Indian beliefs and songs." It was a moving ceremony. We walked together through the grounds of the encampment, led by Indian dancers. A Spokane chieftain explained the purpose of our procession. "We walk as one, to bring this ceremony to our brothers and sisters, to our families and to our grandparents whose eyes have seen things we shall never see, whose faces are a thousand years old. We walk to honor the trees and to honor the ground, for these are the old gathering grounds."

As the sacrament proceeded inside, the rain fell and the aroma of the pines wafted across the altar. Another Indian spoke of the need for the tribes to restore a state of self-respect and obedience of tribal laws. "We are a pitiful people today. We shall never regain ourselves until we return to the laws of our God." Then a young man and two elderly women wrapped in shawls stood together and in the silence of that building sang the harshly beautiful songs, secret songs of the long-house religion. The man had told us, "Look around you now and see. Tomorrow all this may be gone. Look at the person you are with. If you have lost someone, look at your brothers and sisters. You will see them there."

They sang their songs, ancient as the hills. The raw sounds echoed through the pine trees, curling up through the peaks and pinnacles of the mountains, soaring with the clouds. They sang of times long forgotten. They sang of tribes vanished and lands lost. They sang of cultures destroyed. But the songs were not angry songs. They were songs of truth, tinged with melancholy, songs of a past that will never be again, songs of hope for a new birth and a new pride among the tribes.

18

2. PORTLAND TO SEATTLE
A Land "Hallowed in Eternal Repose"

John Muir once wrote of mountains:

> Their marvelous beauty, woos the admiring wanderer on and on, higher and higher, charmed and enchanted. Benevolent, solemn, fateful, pervaded with divine light, every landscape glows like a countenance hallowed in eternal repose....

He was not, at the time, talking about the mountains of Washington, but his lines nevertheless are a fitting introduction to this journey through the most magnificent upland scenery in the Pacific Northwest. We shall not meet many people, nor pass through communities with extensive histories. Instead we shall enjoy the silence of the forests, the reflections of white peaks in blue waters, the panoramas of a primitive wilderness.

This is not the easiest way to travel from Portland to Seattle—just the best way.

NOTE: BECAUSE OF the maze of forest roads through the Gifford Pinchot National Forest, this route, particularly in the mountain sector between Swift Creek Dam and Randle, must be followed carefully. To eliminate the need for disjointed instructions in the text, the following is a brief synopsis:

> Take Route I–5 north from Portland.
> Turn right on Route 500 (Fourth Plain Road) east through Vancouver.
> At Route 503 turn left (north) to Battle Ground.
> At Battle Ground turn right and follow signs to Battle Ground Lake.
> Turn left (north) to Basket Flat Road.
> Turn right to Lucia Falls Road.
> Turn right through Yacolt to Route 503 at Amboy.
> Turn right through Chelatchie to Route 90 at Yale Lake.
> Turn right to Route N714 beyond the east end of Swift Reservoir.
> Turn right to Route N73.
> Turn left to Route 123.
> Turn left and continue across Route N819 to N88.
> Turn left to Route 90.
> Turn right to Route N84.

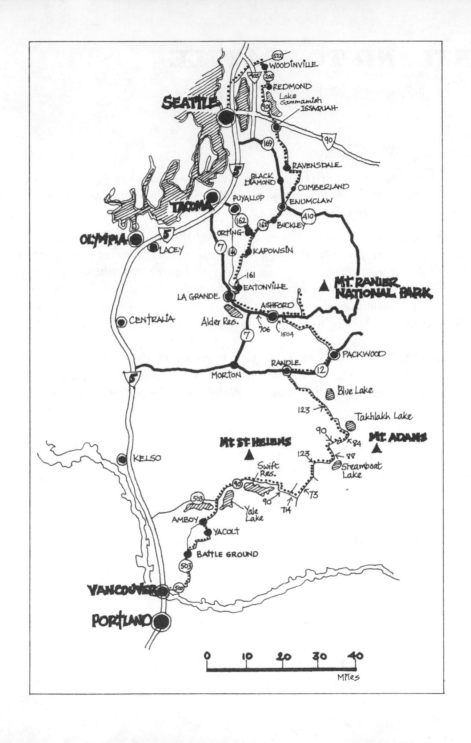

Turn left to Route 123.
Turn right and follow all the way to Randle.

From there the route is more straightforward!

I COULD SEE her way in the distance. It was a fall evening, and the flanks of Mt. St. Helens were bronzed by the sun. A cap of cloud perched on her peak. Around me leaves were starting to drop. The trees were golden.

I paused at Battle Ground Lake State Park. During the summer it can become a little crowded, but on that September evening there was no one around to disturb the silence in this pine-rimmed crater. It's a small lake, and there's a quiet path around its edge. The cities seem far away.

A mile or so north of the lake is the turn to Basket Flat Road, a narrow lane dipping and twisting its way to Lucia Falls. At this point there's a slight dilemma. The river here is a turbulent creature cascading over torn rocks, gouging out its bed, and lying in sinister black pools. It is also contained within privately owned land, and when I was there the fee to visit the Lucia Falls was $2. Even though this is an extremely impressive section of riverscape, I consider the charge outrageous.

Farther along I noticed a sign at the roadside for "The American Paint Horse" and paused outside an old Mexican-style residence surrounded by bushes. A young girl, red-cheeked and bubbly, came out and, after the initial pleasantries, launched into an eloquent description of paint horses and their characteristics. She owned four and competed at horse shows all over the West. I fell in love with one of them, a sandy-colored beauty with distinct white markings, called Hurricane Oddy. He had Scandinavian features—blond mane and blue eyes—and a nuzzling disposition. The girl also explained that the unusual house was her father's creation. "He designed it and then built it. Took about a year. He could have done it faster but the walls kept falling down!"

After Amboy the valley tightens. Odd-shaped peaks, obviously volcanic, loom ahead. Mt. St. Helens seems closer and more beautiful than ever. There are mountain rescue-team signs. The backcountry feel begins. We're entering Skamania County, one of the few counties in Washington that can boast a total lack of freeways, cloverleaves, one-way streets, and parking meters.

Yale Lake possesses an almost fjordlike profile. I paused at the boat-launching and picnic area and watched the shadows in the craggy valley, turning from gentle mauve to thick purple. The lake took on a strange translucent quality. It became very still. The fish stopped jumping, and no ripples disturbed its surface. The water gleamed a soft blue-silver in the darkening dusk, and even after the ridges and crests of the mountain had merged into the night, it continued to give off a phosphorescent glow, as if the light came from deep under its surface.

A couple of miles past the northern tip of the lake there's a turnoff into the volcanic region around Ape Cave. Ahead is Mt. St. Helens. Ancient lava flows are still encrusted on its flanks, brittle black blankets of cinder. Ape Cave is a relatively recent lava "tunnel," which carried fresh molten magma under the hard lava surface. When the flows ceased, the smooth-walled tunnel was left intact, and the subsequent collapse of a section of roof revealed its existence. Amateur spelunkers should wear warm clothes, sturdy shoes, and a hard hat and bring plenty of light in the way of flashlights and gas lanterns. This is the longest lava tube in the country, more than 2 miles, with an overall descent of 700 feet. It's dark and dangerous for the casual explorer, but if you have adequate preparation, it's an intriguing experience to walk down these smooth, curved halls.

Nearby, hidden in a mossy forest, are a few scattered lava casts, hollow remnants of trees felled in a lava flow more than 1,900 years ago. The best examples are quite a way from the road, along narrow paths that lead deeper and deeper into the half-light. When I first arrived, there was no one around and the forest seemed unusually quiet. I heard no birds, just occasional rustlings in the ferns and the ocean-like swish of the wind through the branches of the pines. I was all too aware of prior warnings about bears and remembered that I was supposed to play dead if one should take a particular interest in me. I was in such a state of nervous expectancy that when a deer hopped out from behind some bushes and bounded off into the forest white tail bobbing, I almost played real-dead on the spot.

In a state of confusion I must have taken a wrong turning and lost my bearings. This is rather easy to do in the forest, so be careful. Then I remembered the Sasquatch. It's funny how one's mind tends to delight in these little games, injecting the most nonsensical thoughts at the most inopportune moments. Like most others who have read these stories of confrontations with the Sasquatch around Mt. St. Helens, I dismissed such flimflammery as the antics of overexcited imaginations. Flying-saucer sightings, Loch Ness monsters, and the like have always made me far more curious about the witnesses themselves than their alleged experiences. Somehow, though, lost deep in this forest, with no one to share my cynical attitudes, I found that the Sasquatch tales suddenly seemed less ridiculous than I had previously thought. Only a few days back I had read a large U.S. Army Corps of Engineers study of Washington State in which the Sasquatch had been described as "an ape-like creature standing between 8 to 12 feet high, weighing in excess of 1000 lbs. and taking strides up to 6 feet. The Sasquatch is covered with long hair except on the face and hands and has a distinctly human-like form." The report went on to emphasize that "Sasquatch hair samples inspected by FBI laboratories resulted in the conclusion that no such hair exists on any human or previously known animal."

I can't believe I allowed myself to ruminate on these mythical monsters, but the louder I sang (and I sang very loud) the more my mind kept flinging out rather unnerving images. Then I heard it. I was in the middle of a particularly rousing chorus of "This Land Is Your Land" when I heard the sound of snapping branches followed by slow steady thuds. I peered ahead into the gloom and almost suffered my second seizure of the day. A lumbering shape, hunchbacked and black, was moving through the undergrowth at a determined pace toward me. What light there was filtering through the trees silhouetted this ungainly creature. Ferns and bushes swished and cracked as it careened

Mt. St. Helens

Steamboat Lake

past them. I leaped behind a tree and gripped its moss-covered bark. The sound became louder and louder. Then as I crouched, dry-mouthed and goggle-eyed, it reached me and turned abruptly.

"Hi," it said. I was standing now facing a tall cheery-faced young man dressed from head to toe in a loose black waterproof outfit and carrying a large pack on his back. "I wondered where you'd gone. I heard you singing back aways. After mushrooms are you?" I looked down at my left hand. It was clutching a great wad of green moss obviously torn from the tree in the final moment of suspense. Hanging off one end was a small orange fungus. "Be careful with some of those, they're poisonous, y'know." I was beginning to get my breath back and thanked him for the advice. He then explained that he'd just been down Ape Cave, hence all the floppy waterproof clothing and backpack. We chatted amicably for a while and he kindly directed me to the road. I walked back feeling rather stupid.

The road along Swift Reservoir is a pleasant relief after the gloom of the forest. It follows the lake's outline, often hundreds of feet above its surface. The views from roadside turnouts are a taste of things to come.

At the eastern end of the lake, Route 90 veers off to the right and we're back on gravel roads again. All the way to Randle it's now a confusing mixture of paved and unpaved sections (see the directions at the beginning of the chapter). In places the forest is thick, crowding in on the narrow road. In other parts clear cutting has opened up vast vistas of Mt. St. Helens and her Fuji-like profile. Other Cascade mountains are higher and more massive but none possesses the severe dignity, the even silhouette of her classic form.

At one point along N73 there's a view across a forested bowl of the three great peaks in this part of the Cascades—Rainier to the north, St. Helens to the west, and Adams to the east. Their summits are snow-covered, their flanks glaciated, their beauty unforgettable. One of the most enjoyable ways to pass an early fall afternoon is huckleberry picking in this area, pausing every once in a while to sit quietly with the mountains. Signs at the roadside usually indicate the better-known fields. Check with a ranger for others.

Look out for the lovely mountain lakes. On a rather arduous stretch of Route 123 (from the junction with Route N819 to Route N88) is tiny Steamboat Lake, hiding in a particularly dense section of fir forest. There's a quarter-mile stroll to its far end and then a superb view back of Steamboat Mountain, an odd-shaped pile of basalt crags and ledges. It's usually quiet here, as the road, while perfectly safe, seems a little too narrow for many drivers. (If you happen to be traveling with a trailer you may also find it advisable to avoid this stretch by turning right on Route N818 at its junction with Route 123, then left at N88 and continuing 5 miles or so to its meeting point with Route 123.)

The most truly classic Cascade lake on this transmountain drive is Takhlakh. Follow the signs a couple of miles north of the junction of N84 and 123. The gravel road twists its way up onto a plateau above the valley, and suddenly there's the lake in a bowl of virgin fir trees. To the southeast Mt. Adams towers like a craggy pyramid. Every detail of the mountain's profile—the chasms, the glaciers, the smooth snowfields, the crevasses, the sharp frost-shattered arrêtes—is reflected in the lake's surface. It's a place to pause, a place of peace. The first time I came here I was lucky. The campsite was almost empty and I sat for a long time at the reedy edge of the lake, listening to the pines, watching the fish jumping, and feeling the overwhelming presence of the mountain, gleaming silver, in front of me.

Although the drive itself over to Randle is an enticing series of visual experiences, far more can be gained by leaving the auto behind at intervals and exploring the backcountry on foot. Look out for trail signs to lakes and waterfalls. The trail length is usually marked, so select those that reflect your time and stamina. One of my favorites is the climb up to Blue Lake off Route 123. It starts about 15 miles north of the junction of N84 and 123, about halfway along 123 to Randle. There's a sign marking the trail head of this delightful 3-mile hike. Delightful, that is, unless you're here on a hot summer weekend when it tends to attract an excessive number of admirers. If you'd rather have the area to yourself, take the 10-mile Bishop Ridge trail, which starts a little farther toward Randle and climbs up to around 4,600 feet. The views are dazzling, both down into Blue Lake from the ridge and across toward the Cascade peaks themselves. The trail descends to the eastern edge of the lake and leaves you a choice of the easy 3-mile route to Route 123 or a rather dull, but certainly quiet, forested track to Cat Creek about 9 miles to the south.

Follow the road's meanderings down, down the long slope to Randle. In places the endless waves of forest ripple against abrupt rocky cliffs. Tongue Mountain, a great vertical shaft of shattered basalt, tears the clouds and forms a prominent landmark for much of the journey along the Cispus River. The first shacks and scattered barns came as a surprise to me after those miles of mountain driving. Then I was on a paved road and out into the pastoral Cowlitz valley, all greens and golds in the later afternoon sun. The first segment of the journey was complete and I was already missing those lakes and peaks.

From Randle take Route 12 east along the valley to Packwood. According to my map, Mt. Rainier was only a few miles to the north, but for the last 70 miles of the journey I had seen no sign of her. She had been cleverly hiding behind lower ranges. Then at Packwood she was there at the far end of a high fir-coated valley—all 14,410 feet of her—white and majestically aggressive. I turned north on Route 152 from the center of town, crossed the Cowlitz River, and was, to my relief, back on a gravel surface traveling upward through the forest. Unfortunately, Rainier vanished again. There were fleeting glimpses of glaciers and snowfields but she was elusive, determined not to show herself until the right moment. So I enjoyed the drive instead. The road was excellent and moved gracefully past the churning white waters of Skate Creek, up through the ferns and the moist, mossy forest and then down gradually into the Nisqually River valley at the base of the mountain.

At the Big Creek campsite turn right on Route 1504 to Route 706, one of the main links to the Rainier National Park. Turn right again and head toward the park entrance. Now, backroading doesn't normally include visits to national parks, but I had been told about one particular place on the western flank, just inside the park, where one could enjoy not only a splendid view of Rainier but also some of the finest panoramas in the state. So a mile past the gates I took the relatively little-used gravel road north to Gobblers Knob. First, though, a warning to the weary: in order to enjoy these experiences we have to take a 3-mile hike and climb more than 1,500 feet from road level—a tiring escapade. But the views from the summit are worth every aching muscle.

Encouragement comes quickly. After an initial steep climb up the narrow path, Rainier suddenly appears in all her magnificence from behind a screen of firs. And she is enormous, almost half as high again as St. Helens, scoured by millions of tons of crevassed ice, cracked and ripped by the elements, blistered from the fires within her still active volcanic heart. Yet she is gentle. On her lower slopes deer, mountain goats, rock rabbits, and marmots frolic in flower-covered alpine meadows. Embryonic rivers—the Puyallup, the Misqually, the Cowlitz, the Carbon, and the Mowich—drip and dribble from their glacial mothers, cascading over the ledges, down the shattered screes, over the icy boulders, through the forests and the ferns, joining with a hundred streams as they enter their individual valleys.

After that first glimpse of the mountain the trail continues upward through the forest. Chipmunks squeal warnings and deer graze warily among the roots of the firs. It's shaded and cool. There's a distinct smell of resin, the body odor of the forest. Underfoot the earth is springy. Mushrooms and fungi of every shape and hue peep between ferns or cluster along the rotting trunks of wind-felled firs. There's a steady stillness here. The only sound is possibly the pounding of your own heart and the panting of greedy lungs.

Pause at diminutive Lake George, turquoise-colored in a mountain bowl. Then continue up the second and more arduous series of climbs past marshy ponds and tiny mountain meadows. If you look up you'll see your destination, a wooden watchtower perched hundreds of feet above the path on a knob of bulbous basalt. Don't look up too often, it can get depressing. Just keep moving one leg in front of the other and eventually you'll make it. At the summit (5,510 feet) the wind is cool and blows with vigor. Spreadeagle and admire the view. To the east is Rainier herself—the whole mountain. From this height one feels a little more her equal. She's still impressive but seems more approachable than she did from Packwood. Then to the south are the ice-kissed peaks of the Goat Rocks Wilderness and the great cone of St. Helens, just as noble as ever. Mt. Adams is blocked by the rocky crest of nearby Mt. Belijica. Finally, to the west and north, on a clear day, there's Puget Sound, the Olympic Peninsula, and vague suggestions of Seattle and Tacoma, almost 80 crow-flying miles away.

As you sit gazing at the panorama you'll possibly be joined by a horde of cheeky grey jays with insatiable appetites. It's impossible to ignore these persistent creatures, so if you have any food you might as well share it with them.

At the base of the trail again the road continues to the north along the western flank of the mountain, passing various trail heads before ending abruptly below the Puyallup Glacier. Here is one of the takeoff points for the Wonderland Trail, that famous 90-mile round-the-mountain loop that can take up to two weeks to explore and passes by almost every notable feature on the mountain's

Mt. Rainier

flanks. If two weeks seems a little excessive, you can join the trail for shorter distances from trail-head points around the mountain.

If you have never explored the national park, get maps and leaflets from a ranger at any of the park offices and devise your own itinerary. Try to avoid summer excursions, though, particularly on weekends. It's almost as crowded as the beaches.

We now head west along a rather commercialized stretch of Route 706 to La Grande. (Unfortunately, there's no alternative, but we're soon on to backroads again.) Behind the store at La Grande there's a path leading down to one of the region's little-known delights—La Grande Canyon. Higher up, the Misqually is dammed and has lost much of its character, but here it flows through an immense natural gorge, more than 400 feet deep. Sections of the path are very dark. The sun rarely penetrates the thick firs at the bottom of this vertical-sided cleft.

Take the road (161) to Eatonville from La Grande. We're out of the mountains and the forests now. Eatonville, a prim little town, was once an important lumber-producing center but today contents itself with a less boisterous agricultural economy and service trade for tourists en route to the "Northwest Trek." This recently developed "safari" provides visitors with a convincing glimpse of all the major species of wild animals native to the Pacific Northwest and is an excellent family-oriented experience.

North from Eatonville the road passes alongside Ohop and Kapowsin Lakes and travels through gentle wooded country into the odd little town of Orting. Although the town is beginning to attract commuters who travel daily to work in the Puget Sound cities, many of its residents are still of German origin, related to some of the town's first citizens, who arrived here, believe it or not, from Hawaii. Apparently they had signed contracts in 1880 with a sugar company to leave Germany and work in Hawaii for seven years, after which they would be provided with free transport to any destination of their choice. For some reason, many of them picked Orting, and they arrived here in 1887, just in time to help harvest the town's bumper hops crop. Most remained, and today names like Hardtke, Engfer, and Knaark are familiar on local mailboxes.

I first arrived here just after the annual Red Hat Days festival, usually held in early October around the start of the hunting season. On the town "square," a vast rectangle of lawn bisected by a railroad line, hunting breakfasts were being served. The bars were full of burly men in padded waistcoats and tartan wool shirts. The conversation was all bear and elk. Old-timers expounded on traditional hunting methods while the younger men quickly downed their beers and moved off to their pickup trucks. Gun racks were full, pockets bulged with shells, and it was a crisp fall day just right for hunting. They roared out of town for the hills.

By afternoon the place was virtually empty. Only the cheese makers at Mazza's cheese factory seemed busy (mozzarella for pizza chains is their main product). The librarian dozed at her desk. The barman sat by himself watching a ball game. On the other side of the square no one moved past the old false-front buildings. The huge Oddfellows Hall stood, silent as a ghost. Hunting season had truly arrived!

As a brief detour take the drive down the valley on Route 162 from Orting to Puyallup. In spring this is an ocean of daffodils, followed later by tulips and Dutch iris. Old hops-drying kilns can still be seen in the valley, although hops are no longer grown in the area.

In Puyallup itself, pause at the elaborate Ezra Meeker homestead (321 East Pioneer Avenue; Sundays, 1–5). The diminutive "Hop King" arrived here in 1862 with a blanket for a coat and no shoes. Twenty years later he controlled nearly half the hop-growing acreage of the valley and owned most of the drying kilns. He commissioned the construction of his palatial villa in 1890 at the enormous cost at that time of $25,000 and went on to develop a legendary reputation as a banker, author, lecturer, and adventurer.

In a more contemporary setting, Bob Cook is developing his own regional reputation as manager and winemaker at the Puyallup Valley Winery (121 Twenty-third Street, S.E.; tasting and tours 10–6 Monday through Saturday, 12–6 Sunday). A few samples of his interesting dry-rhubarb, tart-cherry, gooseberry, and red-currant wines are a pleasant way to prepare for the final segment of the journey, from Orting to Issaquah.

Along bucolic South Prairie Road (162), almost in the shadow of Mt. Rainier, is the Puyallup Salmon Hatchery, a bizarre place to visit in the fall when the salmon return upstream by the thousands to spawn at the place of their birth. But it's also a sad place, for the salmon come here to die. Unlike the Atlantic salmon, the Pacific species spawn only once and then immediately enter the process of aging and disintegration that transforms them, with an almost Dorian Grey rapidity, from aggressive vigorous creatures into senile decrepit entities. Here at the hatchery the salmon are actually killed immediately prior to spawning and the fertilization takes place in controlled conditions to prevent the normal wastage of eggs. Visitors are allowed in the hatching shed. Almost 2 million salmon eggs are carefully processed through the fifty-day hatching period and the subsequent five-week "quiescent" stage, when each "fry" salmon is nourished by its own yolk sac still attached to its body.

Later the tiny inch-long fish are placed in the rearing ponds until they reach migratory age and size—usually three months for chinook salmon and up to a year for Coho. Then they are finally released and allowed to swim away downstream to the ocean, where they will grow to their normal size of 20 to 25 pounds before responding to their reproduction urges and returning to the place of their birth.

I stood by the stream below the hatchery and watched the huge creatures struggle their way upstream against the current and across the shallows. Many seemed worn out. Their journey may have brought them more than 2,000 miles, and while traveling up the fresh-water stream, they eat nothing and rely on stored supplies of fat and energy. Their color changes from silver to dark grey or mauve. Fungus begins to eat away at their bodies. They even change shape, developing odd lumps on their backs. Some had just rolled over and died a few yards from their destination. Others were attacking any fish that hampered their struggle to the final pond. I watched one, a noble chinook, attempting to cross a very shallow stretch of sand and pebbles. He was too large. He thrashed his body in every direction. His tail pounded the water and his jaws snapped. But all to no avail. He was stuck. He slowly stiffened and lay still. His eyes looked straight at mine. His tail flicked spasmodically. Then gradually he rolled over, exposing his white underside and rigid fins. For a while his body remained in the shallows before the current carried him slowly back downstream, under the overhanging branches and out of sight.

In a somewhat sober state of mind I drove north through Buckley to Enumclaw (410) and took the Cumberland road out of town, following signs to the Nolte State Park, where I paused to stroll by the lake and through the woods. Like many attractions in this region, summer weekends tend to bring crowds of local residents, but if you choose your time of arrival carefully, you'll have the place to yourself. The same goes for the Green River Gorge, a few miles to the north.

This beautiful wooded valley, filled with rapids, waterfalls, swimming holes, and riverside walkways can become rather hectic during peak season but is the ideal place for a stroll in the late spring or fall. Alternatively, if you would prefer a stretch of river all to yourself, follow the road a little farther north to the Green River Meadworks. Auto access up to the Hanson Dam is normally forbidden, but here are abundant stretches of quiet river to choose from.

Continue along the Cumberland road north to a T junction with the Kent-Kingley road, turn left toward Route 169, and then follow the signs for Issaquah. It's a lovely drive through the rolling foothills at the base of the Cascades. Seattle is only a few miles away to the west, yet there are no signs of urbanity until we reach Issaquah.

Here, if you wish, your journey ends at Interstate 90. However, for those who would enjoy one last diversion before entering Seattle there's an attractive drive from Issaquah, north on Route 901 alongside Lake Sammamish to Redmond and then on Route 202 to Woodinville and the Ste. Michelle Vineyards (daily, 10–4:30, tours followed by tastings).

Here is the Northwest's largest and most recent winery. A $6 million expansion program undertaken in 1976 created a French chateau-style complex, with formal gardens, trout ponds, shaded picnic areas, and a winemaking facility the size of three football fields. As you might assume, this creation is well known to regional residents, but those from out of state may be surprised to see that Washington possesses a winery of such a caliber. And it's not just the winery itself that is impressive. Ste. Michelle wines have been awarded top honors in festivals and tastings throughout the world, and a tour of the modern plant provides an impressive glimpse of winemaking techniques of the future. Here, time-honored processes developed over the centuries by winemakers of Europe have been combined with contemporary technological innovations to ensure the highest quality and an impressive quantity of wines, ranging from the classic Cabernet Sauvignon and Grenache Rosé to the sprightly whites—Johannisberger Riesling, Semillon Blanc, and Gewürztraminer.

What better way is there to end this long backcountry journey and greet the civilized world again than by a picnic of meats, cheeses, and wine under the old shade trees of the Ste. Michelle Winery. *Bon appétit.*

3. THE PALOUSE
A Journey Through the Inland Empire

Be ready for surprises on this journey. We loop through one of the most unusual landscapes in the Pacific Northwest, touch the fringe of a desert, and meet some independent-minded characters en route. This is not typical Washington country. We're far from the deep forests and the cove-etched coastline, but the endlessly rolling hills of the Palouse contain much of interest for the rambling backroader—towering waterfalls, deep canyons, buttes, and a strange lake said to be inhabited by a man-eating monster.

THE CHANGE is sudden. South from Spokane on 195, the climbing highway passes through deep pine forests. Then, with little warning, the trees end abruptly on the edge of a high plateau. Small rounded hills, brilliant gold in the sun, roll away to the south, endlessly. There are no buildings, no animals. Just the great blue arch of the sky above a strange empty land.

They call it the "inland empire," once a dry grassland wilderness similar in appearance to the Nebraska sandhills and now one of the richest wheat-growing regions in the world. The gold on the hills is not arid desert earth as it first appears. It's ripe wheat, stretching for thousands of square miles across this dunelike landscape. In a good year these rich loam soils produce more than fifty bushels of wheat an acre. The Midwest plains yield about half that amount.

The farmers know the value of their land. They're quiet men, not given to bragging and boasting except during occasional shindigs in their sober-faced Grange Clubs. They treat their land with loving respect. You can see it in the finely furrowed earth, deep brown and moist, in the gleaming eight-wheel tractors contour-plowing grades that would intimidate most lowland farmers. They are tough, durable men. Many of their fathers or grandfathers settled in the Palouse when it was raw, scorched land. Some came because there was nowhere else to go. All the best arable land had been taken in the West. One old man told me, "I just drove to where there wasn't anybody."

It's hard to tell where one farm ends and another begins. Cultivation seems almost "collective," where individual land holdings are less important than total commercial output. The farms themselves look similar, the equipment almost identical in size and design. The uniformity of the land itself, this endless sea of waving wheat, has imposed itself on those who live here. Evident signs of an independent spirit are rare. Where it exists it seems all the more exaggerated, even outrageous, when viewed against the pastoral homogeneity of the region. Take, for example, that 20-foot clock dominating the main street of Rosalia, off Route 195. There it stands on the sidewalk in all

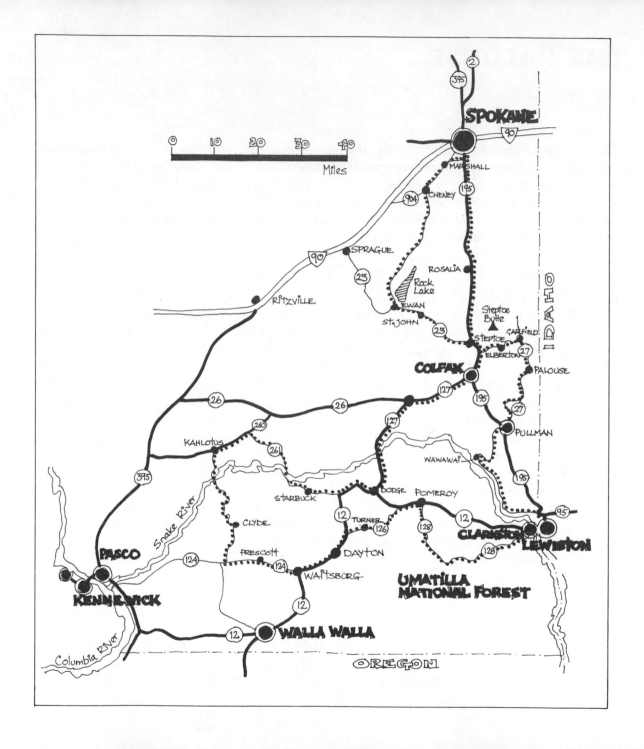

its green Corinthian glory, completely out of context and scale with the diminutive stores—a truly magnificent statement. The man responsible for its transfer from downtown Portland to this quiet farming community is Cliff Harthill. He lives in a house just off Main Street at the north end of the school. It's not hard to spot. There's another street clock, a 12-foot beauty from the old Union Station in Seattle, in his yard. Mr. Harthill loves clocks—in fact, he has amassed a large collection of antique and novelty timepieces and displays them here as the Harthill Clock Museum (most days, 9–noon and 1–5). He's regarded tolerantly by Rosalia's citizens. They've even got used to the great green edifice on their main street. And he's not the only independent-minded Palouse resident we'll meet on this journey.

While in Rosalia, look out for the signs to the Steptoe Battlefield Park and Monument and make the steep climb out of town to a pleasantly shaded park overlooking the rolling wheatfields. Here a tall granite shaft stands as a reminder of the "unenlightened dealings" between the distraught Indian tribes in this region and the United States government. The date was May 17, 1858. Lieutenant Colonel E. J. Steptoe led a raggle-taggle troupe of 158 poorly armed men into the Palouse to attempt an arbitration with the restless Spokane Indians. They were one of many tribes disillusioned by the government's efforts to force them onto reservations, which were then subjected to continued infiltration by settlers and prospecters. The young braves of the tribes were tired of the "forked-tongue" antics of the whites and collected around the Yakima chieftain, Kamiakin, in his attempt to repel further incursions. Steptoe's parleys with the Spokane and Coeur d'Alene chiefs were unsuccessful and so, disgruntled, he decided to return to base at Fort Walla Walla. However, tempers were hot, a gun was fired, and a skirmish ensued, later referred to as a massacre, in which seven of Steptoe's men were killed along with many more Indians and several important chiefs. Steptoe and his men had no more ammunition left, and at nightfall the Indians camped nearby, celebrating their expected victory. Fortunately for the beleaguered men, a group of friendly Nez Percé helped them escape across the Snake River, and the warring Indians found themselves with no one to fight in the morning.

Were it not for the slaughter, it could have been one of the more touching tales of a period sadly devoid of understanding and humor. However, some Rosalians regard the commemoration of the battle very seriously. There's a sign at the edge of town reminiscent of the Alamo: "Remember the Battle," and every year, the second weekend in June brings the "Battle Days" celebration, featuring parades, a play, muzzle-loader shoots, and the popular Longhorn barbecue. From Steptoe's point of view, the whole incident was rather unfortunate, and I'm sure he would have preferred it to be quietly forgotten!

A few miles farther south a lonely conical mound rears hundreds of feet out of the wheatfields. This is Steptoe Butte, one of those odd geological phenomena for which the Palouse is renowned. It provides travelers with a chance to view the region from an eagle's vantage point and gain a fresh perspective on its unique beauty. After precariously circling the cone a couple of times, the road ends on a tiny plateau at the top, high above the rolling wheatfields. I enjoy coming here in

Harthill Clock—Rosalia

the evening when the shadows are beginning to lengthen. They exaggerate the drumlin-like qualities of the landscape, and those miles upon miles of wheatfields take on a soft texture, rather like the golden fur of a teddy bear.

Sunsets are doubly dramatic from up here. A huge bronze ball burnishes the west slopes and crests of the hills, casting their rear-facing sides into deep mauve shadow. Long streamers of cloud glow with an inner fire, and their tiny tails twist and curl, flamelike, against a copper sky. And then, quite abruptly, the color leaves the land. The sun vanishes, almost audibly, and the moon, a delicate silver ghost, rises above the death-pale fields that seem drained of every particle of life and movement. The breeze stills. The wheat stands erect and silent. The sky darkens and the horizons close in for the night. It's a beautiful but somehow sobering experience. I don't think I've ever seen color of such intensity die so suddenly.

Nights tend to be quiet in the Palouse. I remember one evening as I was slipping down the hill into Colfax, snuggled in its cozy valley below the wheatfields, thinking I would pause at a tavern and chat with some of the local residents. Maybe I picked an off night, but I've never seen such deserted places since the California ghost towns—and I mean the real ghost towns whose only inhabitants are the spirits of the long-departed. The only excitement I had was while roaming some of the gravel roads a few miles west of Colfax. I noticed a flashing light in my rear mirror and, thinking someone needed help, pulled over to the side of the track. A short man, young, and with an enormous beer belly, strolled over to my window. He wore a stained Coors T-shirt and chewed an immense wad of something—tobacco, I think, by the pungent aroma that wafted into the camper. He proceeded to introduce himself as the local marshal and told me, in a valiant attempt at officialese, that I was the perpetrator of a traffic offense; to whit, I had passed through a town at 35 miles an hour when the speed limit was 25. I asked him which town he was talking about. He pointed back down the road to three houses. "That," he replied. "That's a town?" I gasped. "You bet it's a town, and it's got a speed restriction." I explained that I hadn't noticed the sign. "We ain't got it yet," he told me, adding defiantly, "but th' ordinance was declared more'n month ago." I explained that I was not familiar with the area but that I would certainly remember this community of three houses and its ordinance. He finally relented and smiled. "Well, I thought I'd jus' tell you case you didn't know. I only got this job last week and I like to meet people passing through. Feel like a beer?" So, I got my chance to chat with a local resident. I hadn't planned on a marshal but that's the beauty of this kind of spontaneous exploration.

If Colfax in the evening is a little dull, during the day there are a number of nearby attractions for the visitor. The 1884 Perkins House at Perkins Avenue and Last Street was the Victorian home of James A. Perkins, cofounder of the town, and is currently being restored as a replica of late-nineteenth-century life in the Palouse country. In the garden is an old log cabin, typical of some of the earlier pioneer homes. A few miles to the south is the second of the two Palouse buttes, Kamiak Butte, named after the famous Yakima chief who vigorously opposed white intrusion into the region. Mr. Perkins of Colfax thought it only fair, when he labeled this prominent, fir-topped landmark, to commemorate Steptoe's adversaries as well. There's a pleasant mile-long trail to the summit, and the view from the top is almost as memorable as that from Steptoe Butte.

Forty or so miles west of Colfax, along Route 127, is the Snake River, with its impressive series of four dams (from east to west, Lower Granite, Little Goose, Lower Monumental, and Ice Harbor) and many excellent recreational areas. The drive out here is through typical Palouse scenery, lonely rolling country with occasional herds of sheep and cattle in isolated valleys. Approaching the Snake gorge, the terrain becomes steeper, the hills more pronounced, with stretches of arid scrub country intruding like mold on a finely iced cake. Central Ferry, a collection of grain towers by the edge of the river, is one of many wheat-loading "ports" on the 150-mile river route from Lewiston, the head of navigation on the Snake, to the Tri-Cities region on the Columbia. Massive locks at each of the dams allow the long wheat barges to pass as they slide slowly downstream.

On the south side of the Snake, the land is harsher, drier. Grain elevators loom cathedral-like over the hills. Dusty towns, Dodge and Starbuck, lie prostrate under shade trees, just off the road. Starbuck has one store, one barber, one park with one picnic table, and, at the time I passed through, what looked like one resident. He responded to my wave and seemed pleased to see someone taking an interest in his tiny community.

Across the river again, past the marina at Lyons Ferry, all attempts at farming suddenly end. I had arrived on the fringe of the central Washington desert—and it felt like it. Exposed basalt strata protruded from the earth like the ribs of a starving coyote. Sagebrush appeared in its familiar clumps. The ground was grey, the air hot.

Look for a small sign on the right to Palouse Falls. It's a good gravel road downhill to a tree-shaded picnic area. I could see the top of the Palouse River cliffs, more lines of basalt strata, before I reached the railing overlooking the Canyon. I was familiar with photographs of the falls and so had expected something impressive, but never did I imagine anything quite so magnificent as the view ahead. I looked down into a natural rock bowl, hundreds of feet deep, and watched the churning white foam of the Palouse River tumble, a solid sheet, into the ocher-colored lake below. Try to come here in early spring, during the runoff, to see the most turbulent cascade. But even in summer, when the flow is reduced, it's hard not to be moved by this sight. To the south the basalt river gorge, with its Grand Canyon profile, meanders laboriously toward the Snake. For more intrepid explorers there's also a series of upper falls near Washtucna, to the north.

Back on 261 follow the signs to Kahlotus. According to my map there was supposed to be a lake just outside the town, but instead I found a sandy bunch-grass valley with nibblings of cultivation at the fringes. Apparently the lake had vanished. It also looked at first as if the town had vanished along with it, but the old grain elevator and the few dried-out buildings on the edge of the community hid a sturdy little heart. For the main street has been "redone" as a Western town, complete with false-front store, jail, old post office, the Kahlotus Ranch Supply Emporium, two

Palouse Falls

museums (one with a flower-filled bathtub outside), and Tom's Inn Digestion Tavern and adjoining store. Tom, another of our Palouse "independents," is Tom Keene, one of the enthusiasts behind this bootstrap project. He's usually in his tavern somewhere expounding on the town's history or folklore or discussing one of the hundreds of bric-a-brac objects that form his "Museum of Rust and Decay." This is the social center of the town. It also looks like the repository of every piece of junk in the region. Just examine the ceiling and walls of this crazy creation—skulls, lamps, harnesses, antlers, handcuffs, cartwheels, flags, boots, saddles, snakeskins, old bottles, plastic chickens, license plates, traps—pieces of junk hang by the hundreds above the pool table and bar. The locals huddle together with their "red beers," usually oblivious to the impact the place has on the visitors. On one occasion, though, the tavern had more than its quota of outsiders and the card-playing bunch of regulars were having a hard time concentrating. One old man looked around him, tipped his sweat-stained hat back on his head, and asked his buddies, in a loud drawl, "How long's Labor Day away now, then?"

One aspect of this remarkable renaissance that amazes most visitors is its creation and coordination by the students of Kahlotus High School, under a Title III federal grant. The project is convincingly done and it's a fun place to spend an hour in this otherwise desolate stretch of country.

A mile or so south of Kahlotus is the turnoff to the Lower Monumental Dam, down through a steep, dry gorge known appropriately as Devils Canyon. Even on a sunny day there's something a little unnerving about this long descent. The rock cliffs on both sides of the canyon always appear unusually dark, and the air seems to have an odd chill to it.

There's a view-it-yourself tour at the dam, with abundant explanations of dam construction, turbine operation, and the pioneer history of the region. Along one wall is a series of windows looking into the fish-run channels for which these dams are famous. Tape-recorded commentary provides an explanation of the types of fish floating by and their migration characteristics. I peeped into a tiny room near the viewing windows and saw an elderly lady perched on a stool watching the fish pass her own personal screen. As each one finned along she would press a button on a series of counting machines in front of her. She told me she was counting the different types of fish that moved upriver.

A chart on the wall showed the silhouetted profile of each species. She was totally engrossed in her work, so the interview was quite brief. I wondered aloud if counting fish was like counting sheep. (It struck me the major problem with this job would be keeping one's eyes open. I was already beginning to yawn.) She said she didn't know, she'd never counted sheep. End of conversation.

Lower Monumental Dam was the site of the Marme's Man discovery in 1968. Carbon-14 dating of the skeletal remains in a cave above the Snake suggest that he lived more than ten thousand years ago. Unfortunately, efforts to protect the excavation site from the rising waters of the new dam were unsuccessful, and the cave is now under water. Access across the dam to the south bank of the Snake is usually restricted to daylight hours. The climb away from the river is steep, and the views to the north and west become increasingly dramatic. At the summit, we're back in wheatfields again, although this time the vistas are broader and the hills less pronounced than those in the northern Palouse.

At the junction with Route 124, turn east (left) and drive through the comfortable market town of Waitsburg toward Dayton. En route is the attractive Lewis and Clark Trail State Park, which commemorates one of the explorers' many campsites on their journey to the Columbia River. The region abounds with Lewis and Clark links. To the east, the towns of Lewiston and Clarkston on the Washington–Idaho border are located close to another one of their campsites, where the Clearwater River joins the Snake. The two weary explorers thought they had at last found the long-sought Columbia and were dismally disappointed when they learned they had more than 400 miles to travel before reaching the coast. To the west, at the confluence of the Snake and Columbia near Tri-Cities, is Sacajawea Park, a popular riverside picnic area, named after the explorers' famous female Indian guide.

Dayton is the home of the "Jolly Green Giant" and center of extensive pea and asparagus cultivation. There are plant tours here during the "active" season (mid-April to mid-July, 8–5), and the local library displays an interesting collection of regional pioneer items in its museum. Also, for railroad buffs, there's one of the finest old depots still left in Washington, just off main street.

A few miles north of Dayton Route 126 branches off 12 and enters wilder country on the lower slopes of the Umatilla forest. This narrow road, graveled for a few miles in the central portion, switchbacks and hairpins its way through a landscape of high plateaus and deep valleys. If you'd like a change of pace and scenery, take it.

At Pomeroy, a pleasant community dominated by the splendid white Garfield County courthouse, there's another choice to be made. Route 12 provides a comfortable, scenic ride into Clarkston; 128 is an exciting ramble through primitive back country with a brief incursion into the Umatilla pine forest. Naturally, I recommend 128.

After the long climb out of Pomeroy we're suddenly in a land of distant mountain peaks, dark pine forests, and marvelous panoramas to the north over the Palouse country. It's a paved road for part of the way. Follow the signs carefully and avoid unmarked turnoffs that travel southward deeper into the forest. Keep those Palouse hills in sight wherever you can and there'll be no chance of getting lost.

High up on the crest of the plateau before the long slow descent into the Snake Valley, I found an unusual octagonal barn built out of solid logs. It was badly in need of repair and only the sheer bulk seemed to hold it together. Farther down the road I stopped at the Yochum family farm to make inquiries about its history. An attractive young woman who seemed pleased someone was taking an interest told me it was built by one of the Yochums in the 1930s as a dance hall! I expressed amazement that anyone should build a dance hall on that high exposed hill in the middle of nowhere. "Oh, you'd be surprised how many people live 'round here. You can't see them from the road but they're there, in the hollows," she told me. "Remember that there wasn't too much to do in these parts and people didn't mind driving twenty miles or more for a good dance on a Saturday night." She smiled. "You're not the first to ask about that place. Few weeks back we had a couple of old women from out of state come by and tell me it was an old Indian fort. Can you imagine. They wouldn't believe me when I told them we built it. Kept saying it was a fort! Then a year or two back we had a fellow who said he was doing a book on barns. He came to look at ours." She pointed to the unusual round barn across the road with a large domed roof. "He said it was the only one like it and took lots of photos. I thought he'd send us the book, but he didn't. Just an advertisement telling us where we could buy one. We never bothered. I thought it was a bit mean myself." I made a mental note to make sure the Yochum family get their copy of this book!

After a long descent, marked by superb views of the Snake valley, we enter the "banana belt" of Lewiston and Clarkston. The area is known for its mild winter climate, particularly conducive to fruit growing. Lewiston is one of the centers for river trips to the spectacular Hell's Canyon south on the Snake River. This basalt-and-granite marvel averages more than 6,600 feet in depth and at one point is the deepest canyon in the world. We explore it by road from the Oregon end on another journey (see Chapter 5, "The Wallowa Mountains").

A few miles into Idaho, east of Lewiston, is the Nez Percé National Historical Park visitors' center at Spalding (daily, 8–6). Only a small portion of the original million-acre Nez Percé reservation still exists, but this unusual area of isolated natural and historic sites reflects the resurgence of the local Indian culture and a new pride by the Nez Percé in their heritage. Different demonstrations of native dances and crafts, accompanied by slide and film shows, are provided daily at the visitors' center. The itinerize-it-yourself tour offers old mission churches, archaeological excavations, battlefields, and various Lewis and Clark sites, including the Long Camp on U.S. 12 near Kamiah, where the explorers spent a month with the Nez Percé on their return trip from the coast. This is not a strident exposition of the local Indian heritage. Rather, it provides an opportunity for quiet journeys into the beautiful countryside of western Idaho.

West from Lewiston we embark on one of the most dramatic segments of this journey, following the great grey canyon of the Snake back into the heart of the Palouse. To reach the river road, drive east on 12 through downtown Lewiston to 95, and as the highway begins to climb out of the town, turn left to Wilma.

The first time I made this drive, it was like having my own private canyon. All the way on the paved road to Wawawai, I saw no cars, no people, only an enormous wheat barge pushed by a stunted white tug that tooted in response to my wave. The sound echoed again and again in that majestic valley. There were a couple of boat-launching ramps, but no one was there. I had the impression that this road was one of the best-kept secrets of the region. On most maps it's shown as a rough unpaved track. Maybe that's why everyone traveling north to Pullman seems to use the infamous "spiral highway" out of Lewiston, a climb of almost 3,000 feet in 64 spiral curves. Well that's fine. That leaves the canyon to me—and you.

For much of the journey the broad cleft is more than 2,000 feet deep. Where the river bends against one side, the cliffs are steep and jagged. Rock falls are much in evidence. In contrast the other side is rounded and softer, the slope less severe. The pattern alternates with each twist and curve of the river. In many places the series of exposed basalt layers, sections of which are formed into octagonal basalt columns, resembles an enormous staircase. There's a sense of primeval wilderness here. No trees grow along the banks. Few birds fly over the dry slopes. The only movement is the occasional barge on its long journey through the locks to the Columbia River.

I was disappointed when the paved road ended abruptly at Wawawai and I was reluctant to leave the canyon. The climb back up to the Palouse plateau was a long hard slog, portions of it unpaved, and not one I would care to make too often. There's talk of paving it to provide a faster link from Pullman to the Canyon, but that would mean too many people, cars, and boats. The canyon would lose much of its awesome dignity. It needs silence for that. So, even though I didn't particularly enjoy the climb out of its recesses, I'll take it in preference to the alternative.

Pullman, named in honor of the railroad sleeping-car tycoon, is the home of Washington State University and a town full of activity and interest, most of it on the campus. A visitors' center here provides information on all the various attractions and events. These include the three museums, an art gallery, two planetariums, and the famous Ferdinand's Dairy Bar in Troy Hall, which serves excellent ice cream and the Cougar Gold and Cheddar cheeses—both produced in the agricultural department of the university.

As an alternative to campus cruising, a few miles to the north of town, deep in the Palouse hills, is the Rossebo family's unusual Three Forks Pioneer Village Museum (most Sundays 1–6, May through September, or call (509) 332–3889 for an appointment). There are no signs, so directions are essential: from Pullman, drive 1 mile north on SR #17(27) to Albion Road and turn left; drive 2 miles; turn right on a gravel road (at the Merry Mount Stables) and travel for 2.8 miles to the museum. I find this one of the most fascinating displays in the Palouse, and Roger Rossebo has all the characteristics of another rare regional "independent."

I first came on a weekday without an appointment and half expected to be turned away. Fortunately Roger had some spare time on his hands. He claimed he should really be out plowing but somehow couldn't get around to it. So he gave me a conducted tour of his family's collection of nineteenth- and twentieth-century antiques, displayed in a mini-village behind his house. The tour begins in Peter Hendrickson's log cabin, built around 1883. Inside there's a typical furnished parlor circa 1900 with an 1875 piano, once the pride of Uniontown Opera House, and an 1885 pump organ. The adjoining kitchen contains among its scores of artifacts a pitcher pump, an ancient dutch oven, apple peelers, cherry stoners, an ancient wooden washing machine, and a butter churn. Outside past the "Boot Hill" cemetery (with projecting boot) and the Chinese laundry, we enter the village square, with its settler's cabin and collection of farm and mining machinery. Around the square is the Western-style village, complete with schoolhouse, blacksmith's shop, dry-goods "shoppe," barbershop, general store, and even a spring house. Every building contains its own display of objects and bric-a-brac. There are literally thousands of items in the collection, many of them very rare. Roger was disarmingly modest about the whole creation. "Well, it's sort of a family hobby. We had a lot of

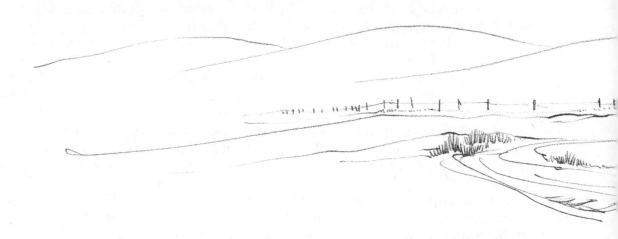

things lying around and thought we might as well arrange them in an interesting way. Somehow it just grew from that. People gave us a lot of things and we spend a lot of time antique hunting ourselves. It gets so it's hard to stop." He regarded his village with a slightly bemused expression as though he couldn't quite believe it was all real. "Someday I'll catch up with the farming." He chuckled. "Maybe."

The gravel road to the museum leads onto Route 27, past the entrance to Kamiak Butte, to the no-nonsense brick town of Palouse. If you're still in the mood for museums and find hundreds of antique bottles to your taste, you'll enjoy the display in the old school gymnasium on main street.

At Garfield, there's a pleasant back road to Route 195 near Steptoe. Then continue west on Route 23 toward Sprague. A mile or so outside Steptoe is a fine example of a twelve-sided barn with a domed roof, one of three left in the area. I chatted with the woman whose husband had recently bought the farm. She was concerned about the barn's future. "It's pretty old, y'know, built in 1916, and you can see it's beginning to lean. The architects from the university, we had some students up from Pullman, they came and said they'd like to help us preserve it, but we haven't heard any more since then. That was a few months back now. I hope someone knows what to do." So do I. Such fine structures need to be protected before we lose them.

In St. John, the tavern on main street was awash with beer and noise. At the card table, under the steady gaze of a dusty moosehead, four burly citizens bawled at one another over some

Barn—near Steptoe

infringement of the rules. The figures at the bar, deep in their own conversations, took no notice. The barman had seen it all before and was unimpressed even when one of the cardplayers smashed a beer glass on the floor to make a point. I talked with him as the hullabaloo continued. "It's the Germans. They're always at each other's throats."

Innocently, I asked why, and he told me a Rabelaisian tale about one group being "low" Germans and the other "high." The "low" group, so he explained, were descendants of German families who had once worked in Russia, under Catherine the Great, developing more effective farming methods for the peasants. They were virtual prisoners under the harsh regime, but most eventually managed to escape and find their way back to Germany. However, back home they were regarded as "Russians," a term of disparagement in Germany, and many moved on to the New World and a fresh start. Or so they thought. But they found the "high" German settlers of the Palouse just as status-conscious as those back in Europe, and the bitching continues—hence the broken glass and the bawling in that St. John tavern!

A few miles west of the town, at Ewan, something very strange occurs. The gently rolling wheatfields suddenly end in an arid landscape of buttes, canyons, and sagebrush. Just like that. There's no warning, no slow change in scenic character. We've arrived abruptly in the "scablands." This scoured region, devoid of fertile soil, was the result of the collapse of an ice wall in one of the warm interglacial periods. The wall formed a natural dam for Lake Missoula, a gigantic 3,000-

square-mile stretch of water covering much of northern Idaho and northwest Montana to a depth, in places, of 2,000 feet. With the glacial wall gone, an immense tidal wave swept southward, scouring the land and tearing deep into the underlying basalt rock. The uneven potholed surface left behind became a region of scattered ponds and lakes, the most impressive of which is Rock Lake. Many believe that the water fills an ancient volcanic fissure, which local Indians claimed to be the haunt of a ferocious serpentine monster. Certainly it's a fact that a number of people have been lost in the lake (sharp underwater lava pinnacles can easily tear out the bottom of small boats) and not one body has yet been recovered.

Fisherman are attracted here by the carp and trout. (Stand on the bridge over the stream at its southern end in the early morning and you'll be amazed at the size of some of these fish.) Yet there's an unusual stillness to the lake, almost eerie, when the sun goes down behind the raw basalt cliffs. It certainly is a much more convincing place for a monster than Loch Ness!

The road north to Cheney from Ewan travels across the scablands. On both sides, hidden from view, are dozens of smaller lakes and ponds. A few in the pine forests near Cheney have become popular weekend resorts. Others are gathering places for birds and animals, and the Turnbull National Wildlife Refuge provides a haven for more than two hundred species. The best time to visit is in October, when the ducks and geese gather by the thousands on their annual southbound migration. Also, for much of the year, there's a 5-mile self-conducted auto tour and hiking trails open to the public.

At Cheney, there are signs of the "real" world again. We have left the strange realm of the Palouse. On the journey to Marshall, Route 195, and Spokane, we return to the deep pine forests and sharp-edged hills of the north. Somehow, though, the sunsets here never look quite so brilliant as those from Steptoe Butte.

OREGON

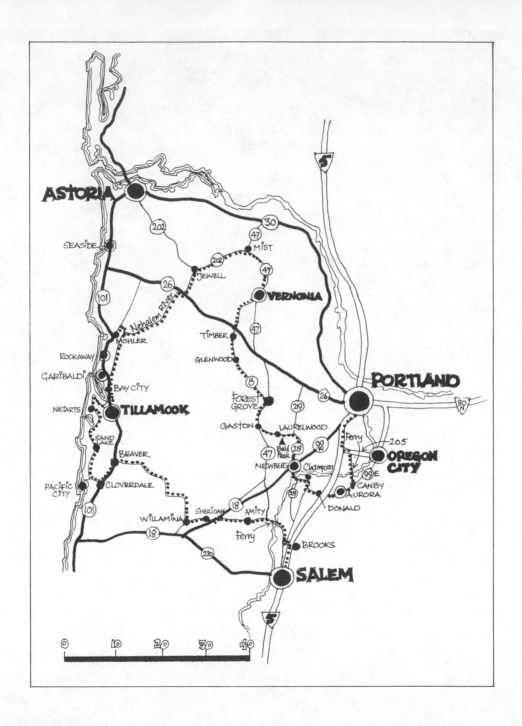

4. SALEM TO PORTLAND

Nibblings and Sippings Along the Coast

We cross over on a slow-moving ferry, leaving the freeways behind as we meander through the Willamette orchards, across the coastal range on narrow country lanes, to the dunes and capes of the northern Oregon coast. Then we embark upon an orgy of nibblings and sippings—cheeses, smoked meats, shrimp, crab, and wines—before following the turbulent Nehalem River into mountainous backcountry. We pause in the original "country store," watch Ham feed his hummingbirds, visit another couple of wineries, and end with a journey back into Oregon's early pioneer history.

THE SIGN READ "Antique Powerland Museum." I had just left I–5 at the Brooks exit, 8 miles north of Salem, and didn't expect to find something of interest so quickly. I drove down a long gravel track to a barnlike structure and heard a woman's voice: "Jerry, visitors." Jerry Ducatt, a wiry individual with a Vermonter's smile, emerged from the workshop and inquired if I'd like a tour. "Of what?" I asked. I still couldn't work out what kind of museum it was. "Well, we've got the tractors, the harvesters, and rolling machines. A week back we finished the 1903 seventy-five-horsepower Case and we've got one of the oldest steam-powered tractors in the country." I'm not much of a machine man, but by the time Jerry had given me his eloquent excursion around the place I'd discovered a whole new world.

"You should come here during the Great Oregon Steam Up (usually at the end of July). You'd be amazed how many people come to see these beauties." As he talked he stroked the gleaming piston of a 1900 Westinghouse tractor and checked the flywheel of a Rumely oil-pull engine. "This is one of the biggest collections in the country, y'know." I looked around at the scores of gleaming machines with their polished levers, chains, pipes, and pulleys and wondered how I could possibly have lived so long and never really appreciated these splendid creatures.

Wandering westward across the flat fields of Willamette Valley toward the Wheatland Ferry, I noticed contemporary versions of these machines, bright green and streamlined—in comparison, rather dull.

The valley boasts three free ferries across the river, and how much more pleasant they are than bridges. They give one a chance to pause and watch the countryside. The raftlike crafts never hurry. "If you're in a rush," they seem to say "more fool you." People leave their cars and stroll to the riverbank. The water moves sluggishly by, chittering over the shallows and through the reeds. All around are hops groves and orchards. I arrived after one of those short fall showers. The sun, low against the horizon, bronzed the bushes and the trees. Drops of rain flashed like diamonds on the

leaves, and the air was thick with the aroma of wet grass.

The ferry carried us slowly across the river and eased gently against the far bank. I moved off through the orchards. Barns rose rocklike from the moist earth. The road climbed abruptly through trees to the first terrace of the valley. Again more orchards and long views eastward. Prosperous farmhouses dotted the fields all the way to Amity, a fresh town distinguished by its green surrounded by churches and dainty civic buildings. A grain elevator towering above main street like a great grey cathedral was a reminder of the early days, when wheat was the predominant crop of the valley. It was only in the 1860s and '70s that settlers found that the high sagebrush plains of eastern Oregon and southern Washington (see Chapter 3, "The Palouse") were ideal for wheat and soon achieved the highest bushel yields per acre in the country. As a result, farming in the Willamette diversified, and today explorers of its myriad byways will discover, in addition to its famous hops fields, hundreds of acres of strawberries, peppermint, flax, bulbs, nuts, and peach and cherry orchards, and even vast expanses of lawn grass grown for seed.

Just outside Amity is an excuse for another brief pause, at the Amity Vineyards, run by Myron Redford and Janis Cheechia. Their first wine, a Nouveau Pinot Noir, was released in 1976. At the moment, capacity and range are limited, but plans for the future include a Semillon, a White Riesling, and a more traditional Pinot Noir. Although tours and tasting are not yet offered on a daily basis, call (503) 835–2362 if you'd like to visit. There's usually someone around to welcome you and answer questions.

Wheatland Ferry

After joining Route 18 near Sheridan, turn right and follow the signs to Eratic Rock, a glacial remnant of the ice age. There's an imposing view from here back over the valley and westward across the coastal range.

On the way south toward Sheridan note the small gallery on the right. Normally I don't pay much attention to commercial outlets on major highways, but this place is quite different. Lawrence Payne, a craggy-faced man with a quick smile, designed his gallery around an eighty-year-old country store and did most of the construction work himself. He's a relative newcomer to the area, and when I asked him about his previous life he referred vaguely to being involved in "Tuna boats, oilfield work—all kinds of things." But why the gallery? "Well, I just saw that building one day and thought it would make a good place to display pottery and paintings. You can do happy things with old buildings." Lawrence leaves the selection of exhibits to a jury of local and regional artists. "I don't like everything in there but I try not to interfere. They know what they're doing." They certainly seem to. The gallery contains a wonderfully varied collection of acrylics, pen-and-ink sketches, glasswork, sculpture, pottery, macramé, and other craft displays that change from month to month. Lawrence presides over his creation like a proud father. "Wouldn't mind doing another job like that," he said, pointing out some of the finer details of his conversion project. "Didn't work out too badly, did it?"

A little farther down the road is Scotty's Clock Shop, an old red schoolhouse whose walls now display a wonderful array of antique and "antiqued" timepieces. Even if you're not a clock freak, it's worth pausing to explore before continuing along 18 (business) to Sheridan, a lumber town near the Siuslaw and Tillamook national forests. Here farm trucks give way to towering log-carting Macks. The smell of resin rolls along main street, and burly characters in thick leather boots and plaid wool shirts down their "beer 'n' shots" in local taverns.

On the western edge of town, just past the lumberyard, note the sign for the Delphian Foundation School. High up in the pine-covered hills an austere brick edifice peers over the valley. Visitors are usually encouraged to come in groups, but curious single travelers are rarely turned away. The people in Sheridan don't quite know what to make of the place. The manager of a local gas station told me, "The kids up there are really polite but we don't see much of 'em. They seem to keep in the grounds most of the time."

The school was founded in 1973 by a group of Scientologists with the aim of applying the educational principles of the movement's founder, L. Ron Hubbard. Scientologists consider much of the nation's educational system to be in a shambles. Drugs, violence, and lack of interest in learning characterize many schools today, particularly in urban areas. So, inspired by the almost prophet-like Hubbard, the Delphian Foundation was established to teach young children and adolescents with new techniques that emphasized total comprehension, self-responsibility, and direct application of knowledge. The experiments here reflect many of the latest educational theories, and there's considerable interest in the institution. To some its linkage with Scientology, a movement that has occasionally been accused of using brainwashing and even blackmail techniques to ensure conformity among its members, is considered ominous. Others welcome any attempt to improve the abysmal state of education today. Even Buckminster Fuller has endorsed the Foundation's efforts as "extremely worthwhile and well thought out." So if the place interests you call (503) 843–3521 and see if you can arrange for a tour.

At Willamina we begin a beautiful backroad journey to Beaver on Route 101. Take Willamina Creek Road north about 7 miles and turn left on Coast Creek Road. (Watch for logging trucks. These notorious creatures often leave blanched and trembling auto occupants in their wake.) Coast Creek Road shortly joins Gilbert Creek Road. Turn right and follow this about 5 miles to Bible Creek Road. Turn left and then left again at the Rocky Bend campsite. A short stretch of unpaved road leads to a better surface, which winds its way alongside a tumbling creek to Route 101. And what a journey this is, full of long forest-shaded avenues, broad mountain vistas, glimpses of fern-filled dells, small meadows, and craggy cliffs gouged by violent torrents of water pouring seaward down the narrow valley. We enter a corner of Oregon rarely visited even by Oregonians. Don't rush this drive. Actually that's a rather redundant statement. You can't rush—so just enjoy it.

Follow Route 101 south a few miles to Cloverdale and then turn right across the old wooden bridge. The road meanders along the edge of an ancient inlet, now a pastoral dairying valley surrounded by dark-green hills. Then in the distance are the dunes and beyond them the ocean. Abruptly fields of cud-chewing cows and large lopsided barns give way to a ticky-tacky town of resort cottages, fishnet-strewn snack bars, and taverns with nautical names. The beaches are littered with visitors, the parking lots crowded. After those silent miles in the mountains I had no desire to compete for a square yard of beach and so started north along the Three-Cape Road.

This, without any doubt, is one of the most beautiful segments of the Oregon coast. It consists, as the name suggests, of three prominent capes separated by shallow dune-fringed bays and lagoons. Cape Kiwanda, just north of Pacific City, is famous for its steep, sharp-profiled dunes and the gigantic waves that smash against its sandstone bluffs. Photographers vie with one another to capture the most spectacular angles of exploding surf or crouch in groups on the beach as the dory fishermen launch their fragile-looking craft.

Farther to the north Cape Lookout offers quiet walks through a coastal rain forest. Evidence of its volcanic origins 20 million years ago is hidden beneath a dense covering of Sitka spruce, red cedar, and hemlock and a verdant undergrowth of box blueberry, wax myrtle, sword fern, and sadal. The trail along the crest of the cape is more than 2 miles long, but one doesn't have to travel the whole length to enjoy superb views of the coastline in both directions.

The third headland, Cape Meares, provides dramatic vistas for the traveler and also functions as a migratory bird refuge. Nearby is the Three Arches National Wildlife Refuge with its huddled mounds of barking sea lions. A short walk from the parking lot is the "octopus tree," a gigantic Sitka spruce whose central trunk has divided into numerous tentacle-like branches, some more than 5 feet in diameter. I first viewed the monster on a cold misty day. There was no one else around, and its writhing outlines filled the gloomy dell, leaving me with a distinctly unsettled feeling in the pit of my stomach.

This beautiful drive is surprisingly underdeveloped. Admittedly there is the occasional rash of Swiss-styled A-frame beach cottages, Cape Cod converteds, mini-Dutch barns, twentieth-century gothics, macho cabins, and monopitch modulars, but most of the journey is through virgin forest or alongside duck-flecked lagoons. Vista points provide panoramas of torn cliffs, rocky headlands, and great acres of white sand littered with driftwood. The only discordant notes are remnants of the 1933 Tillamook Burn, which destroyed 12 billion board feet on 300,000 acres of prime timberland. Subsequent reforestation efforts have brought about a revival of the local lumber industry.

The final part of the drive passes along the southern edge of Tillamook Bay, a broad stretch of water, home of the Great Blue Heron and a favorite haunt of fishermen.

Tillamook itself is a surprisingly cosmopolitan little town with an exceptional museum in the 1905 County Courthouse and an impressive array of shops and department stores. The museum (weekdays, 9–5, Sunday, 1–5) contains a major collection of Indian baskets, an extensive display of West Coast wildlife, and some interesting replicas of pioneer life, including Joe Champion's hollow-tree "castle." He was the first white man to settle in the county, in 1851, and as no one was around to help him build a cabin he cleaned out the interior of a local spruce tree and for a few months lived a cozy existence here. The Tillamook Indians were friendly, so friendly in fact that when settlers began

Garibaldi

rolling in larger numbers onto the coastal plain, they put up little resistance and even assisted in the establishment of the farms. The nearby Klickitat tribe were incensed by their lack of concern and threatened to invade the area and massacre the whites themselves. They even tried occasionally, but the Tillamooks drove them off using guns lent to them by the settlers.

All around the community are rich dairy meadows, backbone of Tillamook's flourishing cheese-making economy. The nearby plant provides visitors with a thorough explanation of the manufacturing process and beguiles them with samples in an abundantly stocked salesroom. Nearby on the road north to Garibaldi other lesser-known attractions include an oyster company, a meat-smoking and sausage-making store, and a shrimp plant.

Sam Hayes at the Olson Oyster Company in Bay City gave me a well-heeded warning to "watch your feet" as I walked across the slippery floors of his shucking room. Six women in long waterproof aprons wielding sharp little knives stood around a mesh cage filled with hundreds of barnacle-studded oysters. With a deft flick of the wrist they pried each shell open and removed the flesh. Outside I could see a small boat almost submerged by a grey mountain of fresh-caught oysters. A clanking conveyor belt carried them through a series of water jets up to the factory and released them into the cage. The flimsy building shuddered and clattered. In the quieter cleaning and packing room an elderly man stuffed the slippery creatures into bottles, filled them to the brim with brine, and fastened the lids. Basically a very simple process, but fascinating to watch.

Across the road at Art and Dick's C and W Home-Smoked Meats Store I gazed at the marvelous array of pepper-smoked bacon, salami, pepperoni, German-style franks, and smoked sausages displayed along the counter, before being shown the tiny smoking room in the back. Vine maple and alder are used to give the products their characteristic flavor. Although samples are not quite so readily available as they were at the cheese factory, if you look like a serious shopper you won't leave the small store without understanding what makes most of their meats so different from the mass-produced items normally found on supermarket shelves.

And so on into Garibaldi. The harbor and wharf here are reminiscent of a New England scene. Worn shrimp boats and trawlers huddle like poor orphans among the prosperous-looking recreational craft. Old wood buildings line the jetties, and crusty seamen move solemnly between the piles of crates and boxes. Smith's Shrimp Plant on the wharf, a sparklingly clean establishment, is quite a contrast to the ancient oyster factory we just left, but the process is similar—groups of apron-clad women picking, flicking, and preening the pink morsels as they move slowly down the conveyor belt after being scalded out of their skins. The women appear thoroughly engrossed in their work. Their eyes never leave that endless stream of naked shrimp as it moves relentlessly into the cans at the end of the line. They don't talk much. Their expressions are a combination of boredom and hypnotic neutrality. I was told they put in eight, sometimes ten hours a day, taking occasional breaks to rest their legs. It's a sobering sight. If you're curious about any part of the process, chat with Shirley Roberts, a bubbling individual who has the knack of answering difficult questions and serving a store-full of customers at the same time. We both had problems, however, understanding the sex lives of the shrimp, whose first two years apparently are spent as a member of the male sex and the second two years as a female—"something like that anyhow. I know they're bisexual," she added with a grin.

I chatted outside with Doug O'Rourke, a hefty fellow with a wide smile. He's normally to be found behind Joe's Deep Sea Fishing Charter office, filleting sea bass, perch, red snapper, and lingcod, a task he performs with effortless skill. "Oh yes, there's money in shrimp," he told me. "On a good trip, lasts about two days, they regularly bring back twenty-five, thirty-five thousand pounds." I did some calculating. The season lasts from April 1 to November 15, and a shrimp boatman makes at least two trips a week, and these little creatures, peeled and polished, sell for around $4 a pound in the supermarket . . . I couldn't believe my own figures. I asked Doug where all the local millionaires lived. "Oh, they're here all right. We got our share. They don't make too much fuss about it, though, otherwise everybody'd be doin' it, wouldn't they." He grinned. I was tempted to ask him why he'd chosen to spend his time filleting fish rather than joining in what seems to be a guaranteed get-rich-quick living. But I didn't.

Before leaving town stroll a few blocks north to Edmund's to see if any crab-meat packing is in progress. Then there's a choice of route. If you'd like to see more of this coast, continue north along 101 through Rockaway to Mohler. Alternatively, backtrack a short distance south of the town and take the Miami River turnoff. This follows a delightful winding valley through mountainous country to the Nehalem Bay Winery at Mohler (turn left at Route 53), an opportune place to pause awhile for samplings (daily, 10–5) before setting off into the real backcountry of the Tillamook forests. Located in an old cheese factory, the winery is known for its fruit wines made from peaches, pears, cranberries, blackberries, plums, and cherries. Pat McCoy, the owner and winemaker, and his wife Adrienne have converted the old boiler room of the factory into a charming Tudor-styled tasting center. By California standards it's a relatively small establishment with a capacity of 20,000 gallons, but great care and skill are exercised in the preparation of these unusual creations. If you've never tasted commercially produced fruit wines, this is a chance to make their acquaintance.

Now for the mountain road, the beginning of a meandering loop journey from the coast to Portland. First, assuming you chose the inland road from Garibaldi, return along Route 53 and turn right by the bridge, retracing your route a couple of miles to the Nehalem valley sign. Then turn left and follow the Nehalem River through pastoral valleys, deep forest, and steep gorges, all the way to Route 26. There are some short unpaved segments, but for the most part it's a narrow blacktop. The high sections offer views into the Nehalem canyon. White-water rapids churn around massive boulders. Secluded campsites provide riverside resting places and picnic areas. One almost feels to be passing through a private estate. Deer graze by the roadside and the sun shines through a delicate filigree of branches in a silver birch forest. There's hardly any traffic to disturb the peace of this unspoiled valley.

Log Bridge across Nehalem River

The road continues north toward Jewell after a brief dogleg on Route 26. We move through a more gentle landscape punctuated by large barns and open meadows among the pine forests. At Mist I found what must be the prototype of all "typical" country stores, a perfect Norman Rockwell setting. An elderly woman beamed at me brightly from behind a littered countertop. In the lopsided armchair by the cast-iron stove sat an ancient man smoking an equally ancient pipe. The smoke hung in a purple cloud above his head and rotated slowly around the stove pipe. The main part of the store was a murky, cavernous space with bowed shelves and wooden refrigerators. In a corner were piles of old paperback books, a swap shop of reading for the few remaining residents of the village. In an alcove lit by a flickering neon light was a soda fountain of sorts. A stout woman, her cheeks fire-colored from working over the hamburger grill, laughed uncontrollably as her only customer, a burly lumberman, whispered a risqué joke. He turned his head frequently to make sure no one else was listening. The old man in the chair feigned total lack of interest but leaned closer to catch the punch line. The lady at the counter looked a little sad at being left out. A dark mahogany clock ticked solemnly on the wall. The joke over, the lumberman munched his hamburger and the store fell silent again except for the creaking of the floorboards as I walked. The old man in the armchair rattled his newspaper and half turned toward me. My creaking obviously disturbed him, so I tiptoed up to the counter, paid my bill, murmured goodbye to the still-beaming woman, and moved quietly out of the door.

A few miles down the road I met Ham, the elderly superintendent of the Big Eddy Campground. He was sitting on the step of his sun-bleached trailer playing a guitar. "Can't get this dang thing in tune, just won't stay put." He tightened the top E string and it snapped. "Well, it was rusty anyway," he murmured. "I don't play the treble much, mainly the bass, so it shouldn't make much difference." He proceeded to strum a series of folk melodies and we sang along together. Neither of us could remember the words, but it was a warm day and even a badly tuned guitar sounded quite mellow. "Last time I played this proper was at our Bear Barbecue. We've had that for four years now, always around the start of September." I asked if they really roasted bears. "Course we do. Why d'you think we call it a Bear Barbecue? We cooked three this time—more'n three thousand pounds o' meat plus a good lot o' beef, four hundred pounds o' salmon, fifteen hundred ears o' corn. They came from all over, y'know—Montana, Arizona, Nevada—all over the place. Heck, it was so full here. People everywhere, playing guitars, singing, eating—it was quite a do." He strummed his guitar slowly, remembering the fun he had had. "They recorded me playin', y'know." I asked how bear tasted. "Prefer beef myself," he replied. Then after a long pause, "I suppose you'd like to see my hummingbirds." I had no idea what he was talking about. He went into the trailer and returned with a wad of rather worn color photographs. "Everybody likes to see my hummingbirds," he said as he handed them to me. A friend of his had taken a series of photographs showing Ham feeding and stroking a family of tiny, brightly colored hummingbirds. "They're usually back around March. 'Grandad' comes first just to make sure I'm still here, I suppose. He stays a few days then flies off again to bring the rest of the family. He really looks after them, y'know." Ham pointed to a photograph of a very red hummingbird, about 2 inches long. "That's him. If I forget to feed 'em, he's the one that comes down to where I'm workin' and flies around my shoulders and won't leave up till I come on back here and feed 'em—he follows me all the way."

Reluctantly I left this kind old man and drove south to the old lumber town of Vernonia. It still retains a sturdy character, even though the closing of the vast Oregon-American plant here in 1957 left the town without a stable economy for many years. The museum on the outskirts of town (daily, 1–5, closed Thursday) has an interesting display on the old lumber days in addition to a range of other exhibits depicting life in the area around the late 1800s.

The road from Vernonia via Timber to Forest Grove passes through quiet woodlands. As we move south the narrow valley gives way to broader swaths of meadows and arable land bounded by steep mountains, the last outposts of the coastal range.

Then suddenly, at Forest Grove, there's the pyramidal profile of Mount Hood, snow-capped and majestic, more than 100 miles to the east, looking as if you could almost touch it. The pure symmetrical outline of that mountain always has a hypnotic impact on me. Its sheer size and grace dwindle the rest of the landscape into insignificance. Buildings that would otherwise appear tall and impressive become children's toys. Everything seems subservient to its absolute dominance. Even long-time residents of Forest Grove never seem to tire of the mountain. "She's part of our lives," a farmer told me. "Days when she don't appear, when the cloud's low, you think there's something missin'. Just don't feel right without her. I know'd people leave here and the first thing they moan about is the mountain. You just don't get many mountains like that one."

Forest Grove has other attractions also in the form of the Tualatin and Charles Coury vineyards, both of which offer tours and tasting. The latter is open Wednesday through Sunday, 1–5. Visitors to the small tasting shed on Sunday can enjoy an additional bonus: a special cheese fondue served by Mrs. Coury along with the samples of the winery's famous Pinot Noir and Riesling. The Courys settled here in an abandoned hundred-year-old farmhouse in 1966 and began reviving the area's pre-Prohibition reputation as a wine-producing center that once contained eight wineries and more than 300 acres of vineyards. One of these establishments even won a St. Louis World's Fair silver medal for its Riesling in 1904. To reach the winery, turn left from 8 on Thacher/Kansas City Road just before Forest Grove, and then turn left again on David Hill Road.

For the second winery take the same road from 8, turn left on Clapshaw Hill Road, and fork right on Seavy Road. The Tualatin Vineyards occupy one of the most spectacular locations of any winery in the Pacific Northwest, and visitors can enjoy the vast panorama of the Willamette valley from a vantage point equipped with picnic tables. Unfortunately, though, the winery only offers weekend tours and tastings (noon–6).

From Forest Grove take Route 47 south and then follow the signs to Laurelwood, home of a large Seventh-Day Adventist academy. The climb up to the Bald Peak State Park is steep and narrow, but the vista from the summit is incredible. Now you can enjoy not only Mount Hood but the whole of the central Cascade range all the way from Mt. Jefferson in the south to Mt. St. Helens, Mt. Adams, and even Mt. Rainier way to the north. Far below is the Willamette Valley, with its delicate patchwork of fields and woodlands. The descent is arrow-straight. We turn south on Route 219 to Newberg, passing through prosperous orchard country dotted with elaborate contemporary mansions. Then we drop again from the high valley terrace into the valley heartland. As the road twists and winds its way down, spectacular views open up around every bend.

Just off main street, Newberg, is the delicately detailed Minthorn House, where Herbert Hoover lived as a boy with his Quaker uncle Dr. H. J. Minthorn (1–4 daily, closed Monday and Tuesday). A writer once described the town as possessing "an atmosphere of prim simplicity," reflecting its Quaker origins. The doctor's house is typical of late-nineteenth-century residences in the area. Unnecessary frills were avoided, and the building possesses an honest dignity, which is also reflected in its carefully laid-out garden. One senses that the town's citizens created a disciplined, upright society with little room for individual deviations.

On Route 219 south from Newberg, watch for signs to the Champoeg State Park. This popular recreation area commemorates the site of the first attempt by early American settlers in the region to break the benevolent but oppressive reign of the Hudson's Bay Company along the Pacific coast. Before the arrival of the settlers, these gentle valley meadows were the home of the Calapooya (or Kalapoulin) Indians. They named this large village "Champooick," meaning "field of roots," after the profusion of wild camass roots in the area. Then as the great fur-trading empire of the Hudson's Bay Company expanded, the Indian presence was virtually eliminated. Dr. John McLoughlin, chief factor of the company, welcomed settlers but required that they operate on an almost feudal basis with the company. American settlers were disturbed by this state of affairs and claimed that McLoughlin was trying to achieve British domination of an area under "joint occupation" by the United States and Great Britain. The missionaries were particularly vociferous, demanding that the federal government seize the "Oregon Territory" and establish home rule. On May 2, 1843, a "wolf meeting" was called, supposedly to discuss ways of eliminating the threat of predators in the Willamette Valley. However, it was soon clear to French and British settlers who attended that the Americans had other purposes in mind. The towering figure of Joe Meek, a trapper, rose up and shouted, "Who's for a divide?," and before the day was out, a local government of sorts had been formed independent of the Hudson's Bay Company. McLoughlin at first ignored the rebels and then later attempted to impose penalties. But the Americans persevered, and on August 14, 1848, President Polk finally persuaded Congress to grant the region a territorial government.

Even though by this time the provisional government was centered in Oregon City, Champoeg continued to prosper and became a center for steamboat activities on the river until 1861, when a disastrous flood eradicated all traces of the town. While the site continued to function as a shipping point, it was never rebuilt and in 1892 was finally abandoned.

The recently opened barn-style visitors' center provides an attractive and thorough explanation of local history, and two museums give an overview of life during the early years of the town. It's an excellent place to spend a few hours.

East of Champoeg, through a cluster of clapboards and false fronts known as Donald, is the community of Aurora, another focus of valley history. It was founded in 1856 by Dr. William Keil as a religious colony based upon concepts of mutual aid and benefit. "As a community," wrote Dr. Keil, "we are one family. No man owns anything individually but every man owns everything as a full partner and with an equal voice in its use and its increase and the profits accruing from it. From every man according to his capacity, to every man according to his needs—is the rule that runs through our law of love." Keil's group was the first of many idealistic communities that flourished in the Pacific Northwest. Most had rather brief lives, but Aurora existed for more than twenty years.

Dr. Keil had a remarkable gift for ensuring the survival and security of his followers—as, for example, when he led the first wagon train from his previous colony at Bethel, Missouri, across the hostile plains and mountain ranges to the Oregon territory. Scouts advised him to postpone his trip because the Indians were particularly hostile at that time. But Keil was determined to leave on schedule, and even the death of his son Willie immediately prior to his departure did not deter him. In fact he turned the sad occasion to brilliant advantage by embalming Willie's body in whiskey in a glass-sided coffin and placing the hearse at the head of the column of his twenty-seven westbound wagons. They met Indians by the hundreds on their journey, but not one of them dared attack the hymn-singing party led by a dead man. In the more dangerous areas, Indians even helped guide and protect the travelers, and they arrived in the Willamette valley without mishap.

Aurora prospered under Keil's gifted supervision. His famous hotel served gargantuan meals to astounded travelers. Trains made stops here, rather than at Portland, to feed their passengers. Declared one delighted epicure, "Aurora fried potatoes surpass all others, the home-baked bread is without peer . . . and Aurora pig sausage has a secret, if captured, that would make a fortune for an enterprising packer."

When Keil died in 1877, no one felt capable of assuming his leadership, and the colony disbanded shortly afterward, leaving behind it a stately ox barn, now the town's museum, and a few other original buildings, which can be visited as part of the Aurora tour (begins at the Ox Barn Wednesday through Sunday 1–5).

The final leg of this long, meandering journey to Portland takes us via the delightful Canby ferry north to Route 205 and on into the city. Remember the Wheatland ferry? Well, the Canby Ferry is even slower and an ideal place to rest for a few minutes before rejoining the hurly-burly.

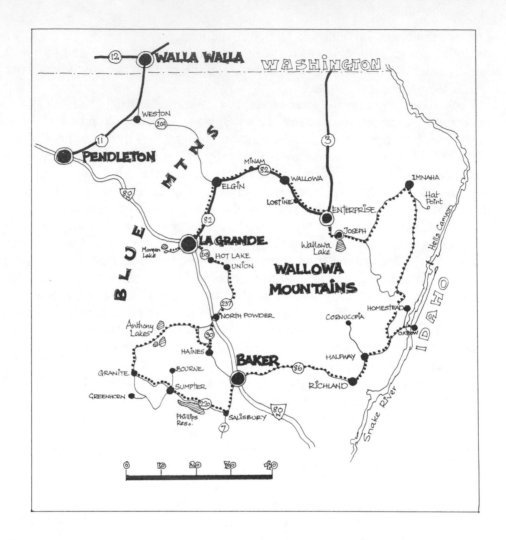

5. THE WALLOWA MOUNTAINS

Into the "Land of Winding Waters"

The Blue and Wallowa mountain region of northeast Oregon is beginning to attract a disproportionate number of tourists. Rangers even have to restrict the flow of hikers into the Eagle

Cap region in order to retain its "wilderness" appeal. Of course our route avoids the tourist traps and takes us instead to many of the lesser-known attractions—an old mineral spa, a huddle of gold-mining ghost towns slowly being revived by contemporary fortune hunters, the incredible Hells Canyon, far deeper than the Grand Canyon, hidden ranch valleys way down backroads, and one of the most beautiful lakes in the Pacific Northwest. We begin at La Grande, best approached on Route 80–N from Pendleton.

LA GRANDE is a neat bustling community, home of Eastern Oregon College and famous for its mid-June Indian Festival of the Arts, where craft works from scores of Western Indian tribes are displayed. It's also not the kind of place backroaders will want to hang around for too long, so let's get started on this journey into yesteryear by taking the I–80N south to the Route 203 exit and setting off across the flat fertile valley toward the remnants of an old mineral spa.

Steam rises wraithlike from the ponds at Hot Lake. The Indians named it Ia-Kesh-Pa (the Hot Place). A group of John Jacob Astor's traders en route to the coast in 1810 remarked, "The vapor from this pool was extremely noisome and tainted the air for a considerable distance. The place was frequented by elk . . . and their horns were strewed in every direction about the pool." Today deer can still be seen scampering across the flat valley floor, pausing to drink near the springs, which gush from the ground at a temperature of over 200 degrees. The sanatorium has an abandoned look, although Dave Pattee recently reopened it as a restaurant. "I'd like to get it going again as a resort but no one seems that interested. We'll see how the restaurant goes first. The chef makes a fantastic batter for onion rings. Well"—he laughed—"you've got to start somewhere!"

From all accounts the resort was once a splendidly sumptuous place where fashionable society came to spend long languorous days in the mineral baths and hot pools. The railroad delivered guests to the front door. The post office inside the hotel was one of the busiest in the region, and the richly decorated Roman baths echoed to the sound of decorous conversation. Believers drank gallons of medicinal fluids served in crystal glasses by toga-clad servants. Even when "taking the waters" became a less fashionable pastime, the resort flourished as a sanatorium and hospital for the treatment of tuberculosis, arthritis, and cancer. Then there were the inevitable series of disasters. Fires consumed the elaborate expansions, large hospitals along the coast diverted trade, and by the 1930s the resort had gained a notorious reputation as a whorehouse. After that it was all downhill, and today the still-impressive structure stands like a monument, empty and gaunt, wafted by the steam from the ponds. "You never know," Dave told me. "I hear tell there's a lot of people getting into the spa thing again. We'll just have to see."

The sleepy town of Union, a few miles farther down 203, had its heyday about the same time as the resort. Like many of the California valley towns to the south, it became prosperous as an agricultural center supplying nearby mountain mining areas during the late 1800s. Today its crisply detailed Victorian homes remain as evidence of an affluent past, and a walking-tour pamphlet is available at the museum on main street. Take time to stroll through the cemetery, with its ornately carved headstones and the delightful Victorian-Gothic toolshed. Enjoy the atmosphere of small-town life. On main street there's a store where fishing rods are custom-made to exacting specifications. Close by, Jim Rodda sits in his saddlery creating $450 "show saddle" masterpieces. ("A good saddle is the same as a good woman—you can tell the difference without even touching.") Jim learned the craft as a hobby in the early sixties and "one thing sort of led to another and here I am."

Look out for notices in the store windows. They say much about life in small rural communities. At the market there was a donation box specially set up for the Betts family, who had lost two children in a house fire the previous week. Nearby a rough hand-printed sign read "Wood collecting. We need volunteers to cut wood for our senior citizens for the winter." Even the Forestry Service seemed aware of the needs of older inhabitants, and a printed sheet stuck on a window described the locations of "easier wood-cutting areas especially set aside for people over 65 only."

Route 237 out of Union leaves the flat valley behind and climbs up through dry scrub-covered hills toward the Wallowa-Whitman National Forest. To the east the jagged peaks of Eagle Cap Wilderness rise above the dark-green forests of the lower ranges. The air is crisp and clean. The light has a mountain sharpness to it.

Just beyond North Powder take a short detour south on 30 to Haines, the "biggest little town in Oregon, a hustling, bustling, rustling little city with the greatest bunch of live wires ever gathered together in any one town this side of the Rockies." At least that's what some of its citizens seem to think. Perhaps it's an accurate description of the place during its Rodeo and Stampede (July 3, 4, and 5), but the day I was there the town seemed deserted, little whirlwinds of dust scooted down the short main street and off out into the flatlands, an old man sat in a rocking chair spitting tobacco juice at a tin can. He just sat, ruminated, spat, sniffed, and ruminated again. The ground around the can was stained almost black with misdirected shots. I never saw him hit the can once but that didn't seem to bother him.

The main attraction here is the Eastern Oregon Museum, four blocks up main street, in the old high school gymnasium (April 1 through October 31, 9–5 daily). And what a superb collection of artifacts this is, reflecting Haines' association with the Old Oregon Trail and its later importance as a railroad town. Inside the 1880s Union Pacific Depot are early railroading displays. Nearby is Caboose No. 5, built in 1926 and used for twenty years on the Sumpter Valley Railroad. The yard is littered with brewery wagons, old hay balers, hand-powered fire-hose carts, and threshing machines. But inside is where the real fun begins. It's one of the best "potpourri" museums in Oregon. In addition to room displays, the blacksmith's shop, and a magnificent recreation of the Bourne Bar, complete with its silent bartender, kegs, antlers, and spittoons, there are exhibits of pioneer furniture, buggies, branding irons, bootlegger's stills, dolls, dresses, organs, pianos, old phonographs, glassware, ancient musical instruments, wood stoves, and all the paraphernalia of armed conflict, from local

Indian uprisings to the Second World War. It's a place you can browse in for hours, followed by a visit to the nearby 70's Steak House Restaurant for a glimpse of its own museum-like interior, complete with a genuine chuck wagon used appropriately as the salad bar. Bill Byers, owner of this venerable institution, loves the tiny town. "Well, it may not look too much right now but it was a real live place not long back. Lots of wild goings on 'round these parts. Butch Cassidy used it as a hideaway and a few others like him. There's more than meets the eye in this old place." Okay, Bill, if you say so.

Returning north on 30, just outside Haines, you'll see Radium Hot Springs Park, with its campsite and natural hot mineral-water pool ("no unpleasant odor!" urges the brochure). If you've never experienced basking in such supposedly health-giving waters, pause here for an hour or so and then start the journey into Oregon's gold-mining country, following signs for the Anthony Lakes area, high in the peaks of the Umatilla National Forest. It's a long, long climb, with beautiful views of the Wallowas across the Powder River valley. The scrublands are quickly left behind. Pine forests shade the road, and cleared sections provide vistas over the great arc of the Blue Mountains to the north. Near the summit is a series of secluded lakes and camping areas beneath the 8,000-foot peaks.

On the descent the road deteriorates into a washboard gravel surface, snaking its way down through the forest past remnants of old gold-mining camps. A few worn shacks remain, peering through bushes. At China Gulch a tiny tent town known locally as Dog Patch has sprung up, and I passed a group of miners swilling beer. They told me that one of the old mines had been opened again. When I asked how it was doing, they looked at me suspiciously. "You a tourist or what?" I told them I was and they relaxed a little but still wouldn't answer my question except to say they're "doing okay" or "not complainin'—yet."

After a final arduous series of steep bends I arrived at the old mining town of Granite. A scattering of wind-worn clapboard buildings litters the steep hillside. I had hoped to meet Otis Ford, who in 1964 had become sole citizen and mayor of the forgotten town after the previous mayor hanged himself and "Cliff the Prospector" went looking for gold and never returned. Unfortunately, Otis was also gone. According to one of the new residents, "he wasn't feelin' too good so we persuaded him to go to the hospital. He never came back."

As in most other camps in the area, mining activities around Granite began in the '80s, and the town soon developed the traditional "shoot 'n' lust" characteristics normally associated with such male-dominated camps. But those days have long since gone. Except for a few dogs the place seemed deserted, and I was surprised to stroll into the rambling store, bar, and coffee shop all rolled into one and find an energetic bunch of locals arguing vehemently over a proposed new leash law. A CB chattered away in the background. Pauline McCracken, one of the newer residents, gave me a friendly greeting. "That's our lifeline," she told me, "we leave it on all the time. If somebody needs help an' we hear about it, we get everybody in here and see what we can do." "Is this everybody?" I asked pointing to the five other occupants of the store, talking over large cups of coffee. "Why no, we

Anthony Lake

got, what is it, twenty-three people here now, I think. That includes the mayor and our city marshal Bud Murrow if you can get him away from his girlfriend. Quite a few's moved in during the last year or two. Mining's started up again. Then there's city folks like me. I came a couple of years back, fat and overurbanized—and look at me now." She laughed and then asked if I wanted to have a look at her cabin. "You ever seen a bordello before? Well, I live in Rose Starkey's place. She was head madame 'round here in the 1880s and the original heart-of-gold whore. They say she died rescuing some kids in a fire down the street here."

Pauline was proud of her wood-burning cooking stove. "It takes some getting used to but it's really just trial and error. You make sure you start with dry kindling and then use green wood to keep the heat even. We couldn't manage without these things in the winter. I spent more'n a week cutting eight cords of logs. Should just about see us through. Hardly knew one end of an ax from the other when I first came. Now I reckon I'm a pretty good woodcutter."

Leaving Granite we pass miles of tailings left by the huge dredges that moved dinosaur-like across the flat lands during the 1935–54 period. This was the last major phase of mining operations in the area. At Sumpter one of those gargantuan creatures, more than 120 feet long and 52 feet wide, sits rusting in a gravelly pool on the edge of town. For a modest fee visitors can explore the innards of the monster and then visit Lloyd Dinger's small museum nearby with its odd display of mining and medicinal artifacts, including a set of false teeth said to be the only known remains of "Bittercoat

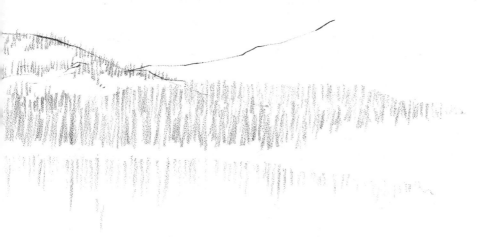

Ben" McCully. This unfortunate man found a rich placer pocket in the area but was ambushed and killed on his way back to the claim. Nobody, so the story goes, ever found the claim, and the gold still lies there waiting to be rediscovered. Of course, the story omits to mention that after Sumpter's first flurry of mining activity in 1882, hundreds of Chinese poured into the mountain valleys, scouring every inch of the terrain and reworking every abandoned claim. Usually what the Chinese didn't find wasn't worth looking for.

Unlike many of the Blue Mountain mining camps, Sumpter managed to survive long after the placer mines were exhausted. Deep lodes were discovered in the 1870s, and the subsequent completion of the railroad link with Baker in 1896 assured its prosperity. In 1902 the *Sumpter News* asked rhetorically: "Sumpter, golden Sumpter, what glorious future awaits thee?" At that time the population had reached the three-thousand mark and the output from the thirty-five local mines was more than $8 million. The Opera House flourished, along with more than twenty taverns and saloons and three hundred "rah-rah girls," according to one of the elderly residents ("Ah remember every single one of 'em"). Then, alas, the great fire of 1916 destroyed much of the town, and most of its inhabitants moved elsewhere. For years the place was left to a few old-timers, but in 1976 the Sumpter Valley Railroad was restored by a group of enthusiasts as a tourist attraction, using a rebuilt Heisler locomotive and two open excursion cars. Their ambitious plans include eventual linkage with Sumpter itself. Part of the route will run through the old dredge areas, which once were thought to be a wasteland after the devastation wreaked by the great machines but now provide such a bountiful haven for beavers, minks, eagles, hawks, geese, and elk that they are likely to be proclaimed an official wildlife refuge.

While Granite and Sumpter are the largest ghost towns in the region, two other communities, both accessible from Sumpter, are worthy of note. Greenhorn to the southwest is the home of Miles Potter, whose fascinating book on the mining country, *Oregon's Golden Years,* has made him a local celebrity.

Over on the other side of the Sumpter valley to the north of Sumpter are the remnants of Bourne, a town of fifteen hundred in the 1880s and one of the richest in the region. The Baring family of London owned the nearby North Pole Mine and considered themselves to be so superior to the raggle-taggle population of miners, card sharks, and saloon keepers that they insisted that the dining room of the town's hotel be cleared of all occupants before they would eat. Fortunately for the civic stability of the community their visits were infrequent, although to some extent their unsavory view of the inhabitants was justified. The town was famous for its elaborate investment swindles, and during one period the town newspaper company regularly published two editions, one for the locals, giving factual progress reports on mining activities, and the second for outsiders, full of glamorous fictitious accounts of new strikes and instant fortunes.

But today, of course, the tumult is gone. The miners were long ago interred in the earth they scratched and scrabbled over for those few furious decades. The buildings that remain are sad remnants of the once flourishing commerical strips, the taverns, and the razzmatazz hotels. At Sumpter an old wagon rots in a weed-filled garden; a log cabin with no roof leans wearily; a weather-bleached saddle lies in a heap on a lopsided porch. Most of the inhabitants are newcomers to the area, intrigued by its history yet not part of it. The older residents have either died or sold out for a tidy profit and moved to the valley. There are, of course, the usual complaints of "californication" by a resilient few who remember the way it used to be back in the golden days.

Route 220 east from Sumpter is paved (at last), and travels alongside the beautiful Phillips Reservoir to Salisbury. Old shacks, shaky footbridges, and small hidden valleys dotted with cows are evidence of the quiet pioneer-like life that still characterizes the region.

In abrupt contrast the ten-story Baker Hotel building rises rocket-like above the flat Powder River plain. For a brief period we leave behind the silence of the hills and enter the hurly-burly bustle of this mini-metropolis complete with junk-food restaurants, fancy motels, and neon extravaganzas. The gaudy exteriors, however, hardly disguise the somber greyness of the town. Many buildings are constructed of a gun-metal-toned volcanic stone, quarried locally, which has the unusual quality of "cuttin' like cake, hardenin' like steel," as one resident told me.

The town grew and prospered with the gold rush. (The First National Bank on main street has a small display of nuggets and gold dust.) Sheepherders from the dry slopes to the west and east mingled with the miners from the mountains, although outside Baker, such fraternizing was

Dredge at Sumpter

discouraged. Miners at Sumpter threatened that if the sheep men tried to invade the gold country they'd "fix 'em up until the angels could pan lead out of their souls." But Baker was neutral territory, and the two groups shared a mutual enjoyment here in their drinking and pursuit of "filles de joie."

The Oregon Trail passed close by Baker, and the museum in the Chamber of Commerce building on the edge of town presents an excellent overview of local and pioneer-related history. It's a good place to pause and consider the achievements of these early-day Americans who often spent more than six months making the 2,000-mile crossing from Independence, Missouri, to Oregon City, near Portland. It is estimated that more than twenty thousand died on these journeys during the 1840s and '50s—the peak period of trail travel. Few who reached their destination were the same people that had left Missouri months before. They had survived dust storms, Indian attacks, flash floods, parched deserts, avalanches, premature snows, and cholera epidemics. They had dragged their 4,000-pound wagons across creeks, through marshes, and along axle-deep dust tracks. They quickly learned that the harsh reality of the journey bore little resemblance to the fanciful literature distributed by promoters. The trail was littered with graves, and skeletons of oxen and mules. Treasured family furniture was often discarded in such abundance that a traveler once wrote: "I could have started a store and equipped it from a ten mile stretch." Yet the trail symbolized the spirit and the actuality of the West: charted by mountain men and trappers, endured by tens of thousands whose experiences made them strong for their new struggles ahead, followed by the Pony Express and later the Union Pacific railroad. It was truly the "river of the West," a river of people—terrified, elated, weary. One of them wrote in his diary as he approached Baker in 1842: "At a distance we could see what we supposed to be the Blue Mountains and they struck us with terror. Their lofty peaks seemed to be a resting place for the clouds. Below us was a large basin and at some distance we could discover a tree which we at once recognized as the 'lone tree' of which we had all heard. The tree is a large pine standing in the midst of an immense plain entirely alone and is respected by every traveler through this treeless country." The following year another group of travelers found that the tree had been felled and decried "the hideous wretch and vandal who destroyed it."

On the Richland Road (86) from Baker we pass through alternating areas of high scrublands and fertile valleys into a region of few people and wide horizons. To the north the grey-white peaks of the Eagle Cap Wilderness rise above the dark slopes of the Wallowa range. From a distance Halfway and its green valley seem almost like a Nepalese oasis. It's a sleepy town with large rambling stores, a few occasionally lively taverns, and a flavor of having been passed by. Ghost-town lovers should follow the signs to the old ramshackle community of Cornucopia, 12 miles up a rather erratic road. At its peak this was one of the richest gold mines in the country, and its 30 miles of underground tunnels resulted in a production of over $16 million before its closure in the 1940s. Recent increases in the value of gold have encouraged a revival of local mining, and No Trespassing signs abound. You need imagination to enjoy this kind of place. Little is left of the over four hundred homes and five hotels that once smothered the steep hillsides, and the few remaining residents are not particularly enthusiastic about outsiders.

From Halfway follow the road down into the Snake Valley at Oxbow Dam. Here in addition to free campsites is a tempting array of boating, hunting, and fishing trips all centered on eastern Oregon's greatest natural asset, Hells Canyon. This amazing geological phenomenon, in places more than 3,000 feet deeper than the Grand Canyon, should not be missed. Even if you don't have time to experience the canyon from a front seat on a rubber float boat as it careens through the white-water rapids, at least follow the narrow road along the east side of the Snake toward Hells Canyon dam. This is primitive landscape in all its stark nakedness, unchanged for millions of years, the home of elk, bighorn sheep and bear, the very essence of the earth. Unlike the serene colors and profiles of Grand Canyon, this gorge is a somber grey-green. Torn and shattered strata, piled layer on layer, struggle skyward. Deep gashes and cracks lacerate the uneven slopes. Pines struggle for a tenuous existence on the higher elevations; broken trunks, scoured by the churning river lie like bleached bones at the base of black precipices. Sounds echo again and again on the uneven wall, struggling to leave the canyon. Eagles spiral majestically, yet one wonders if even they must remain trapped within its grey confines. In places one can experience a distinct sensation of claustrophobia. There are no views out of the canyon, no vistas of mountains beyond. Everything is part of the canyon. Even the great Idaho mountains in the east, snow-capped and chilling, slope directly down into its depths. It seems to have no beginning and no end. The whole earth becomes the canyon.

A few miles back along the road to Halfway we begin the rather arduous but exciting journey through the Wallowa-Whitman National Forest to Imnaha. Be prepared for a few jolting miles in the central portion of the route. Drive slowly and enjoy the silence of the passes and the narrow homesteaded valleys. About halfway along watch for the sign to the Eugene Pallette Ranch, now deserted. During World War II Mr. Pallette, the famous character actor who played Friar Tuck in the 1930s version of Robin Hood, established a well-defended hideout here, complete with a 5-year food stock and accommodations for friends and family, in preparation for the German invasion of America he felt was imminent.

The clustered hamlet of Imnaha is a welcome relief after this superb but tiring drive. The last few miles following the river gorge are particularly scenic, and the small ranch houses set in the foothills away from the road leave many travelers envious of their occupants. Note the large boxes by the roadside, not intended for oversize mail but for grocery deliveries.

I had hoped to meet Lloyd Doss, the owner of the Imnaha store and a member of the famous Sons of the Pioneers country music group. Unfortunately, he'd left for a wedding, so I chatted with the locals over a few beers. They advised me to stay off the memorable Hat Point road that begins at Imnaha and climbs to a 6,982-foot vantage point overlooking Hell's Canyon. "It's a mighty rough road and the loggin' trucks don't pay you no mind." I took their advice, but if you bypassed the Oxbow Dam trip to the southern end of the canyon, then this is a splendid alternative, particularly recommended on weekends when the logging trucks stop running. (But start early. It's a long drive

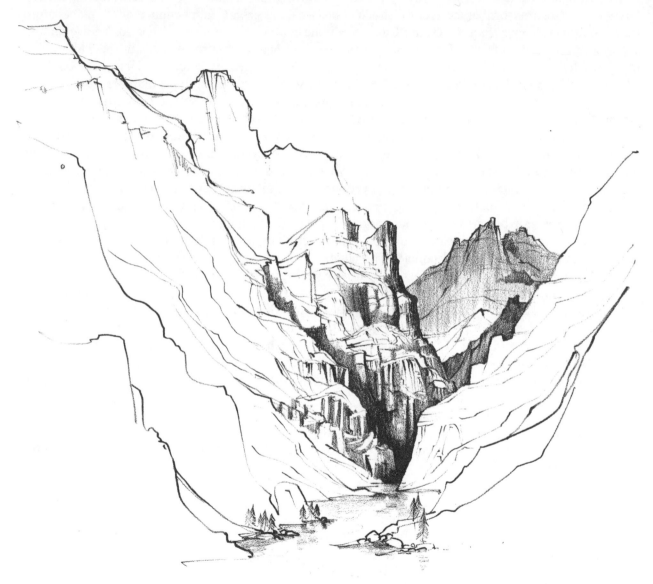

Hells Canyon

and ascents in the heat of the day should be avoided.) The view is staggering. Way in the east are Idaho's Seven Devils Mountains, and thousands of feet below a precarious perch on top of the lookout tower swirls the Snake. Even if you find the complete journey a bit excessive, there is a series of memorable vistas en route, of the Upper Imnaha Canyon and the Wallowas to the west.

Leaving Imnaha for Joseph, we climb slowly through some of the wildest mountainscape in Oregon. These mammoth creatures, their basalt ribs protruding, huddle together like ogres, and in places where the strata has tilted, they appear to be straining forward, almost leaning over the road. We finally escape into the high pine forests and then emerge on an upland plateau of waving wheatfields surrounded by the gentle profiles of the Wallowas. This region, during the summer particularly, seems to attract more than its fair share of travelers. Yet the main source of this attraction, Wallowa Lake, is one of the most beautiful bodies of water in the Pacific Northwest and an essential ingredient of any itinerary. Approached from the east it has a strangely elusive quality. Even in Joseph itself there is no evidence of it until you follow the signs through town, past the memorial to Chief Joseph, and suddenly, around a bend, the lake appears in a flash of brilliant blue. At the far end the pyramidal peaks give it a fjordlike appearance. The road follows the base of an even-profiled glacial moraine that forms the eastern edge of the lake. At the southern tip, a profusion of recreational activities await the enthusiastic visitor, including an aerial tramway to the top of Mt. Howard (8,200 feet), excursions into the Eagle Cap Wilderness, pack trips to hidden mountain lakes, fishing expeditions, or just lazy lolling by the lakeside.

This region, "the valley of the winding water," was once the ancestral home of a group of Nez Percé Indians. Although reservation treaties signed in 1855 recognized the valley as Indian territory, inevitably conflicts arose and treaties were ignored. When Old Chief Joseph died in 1871, his son Joseph, a more aggressive warrior, vowed never to leave his beloved homeland. His father had warned him as he was dying, "Always remember that your father never sold his country. You must stop your ears whenever you are asked to sign a treaty selling your home. A few years more and the white men will be all around you. This country holds your father's body. Never sell the bones of your father and your mother."

The arrival of federal troops in 1877 led to a long series of bloody skirmishes, as the Nez Percé under "young" Joseph reluctantly left their beloved valley and retreated toward Canadian sanctuary. Time and time again this valiant band defeated the reinforced white army, but within a few miles of the border they were finally subdued and eventually moved into what is today the Colville reservation, north of the Grand Coulee Dam (see Chapter 1, "The Okanogan Highlands").

The museum in Joseph gives a more thorough description of this era. Ironically the Indians tended to avoid Wallowa Lake itself, believing that it was inhabited by monstrous creatures, and preferred campsites close to the salmon streams. Even today there are those who warn against venturing into the center of the lake, where people are said to have vanished without trace.

Route 82 from Joseph to Elgin passes for much of the way along the borderline between the dark-green forested hills of the Wallowas and the dry upland wheat lands of the Wallowa valley. While hardly backroad travel it's one of the most scenic drives in this part of the state. Broad old barns reflect the scale and timelessness of this journey.

For those interested in exploring some of the lesser-known parts of the Wallowas, the road south from Lostine leads deep into a glacial gorge with plenty of opportunity for impromptu backpacking. The same goes for the Minam River Canyon south of Minam. This is exclusively hiking territory, and it's a long haul deep into the mountain forests; so, if you're a real backpacker you'll love it.

At the Elgin note the odd combination of City Hall and Theater at the northern end of main street, and then follow 82 southward down into the great mountain-ringed basin of La Grande. A visit to the Pierce Museum at the Eastern Oregon College here will provide a broader understanding of the region's Indian history. Alternatively, if you still have a bit of the exploring urge left and don't mind a 3-mile scramble up a rocky road, ask in La Grande for directions to Morgan Lake. This secluded beauty is unknown to most travelers and is a perfect place to end the journey whiling away a few hours under the pines.

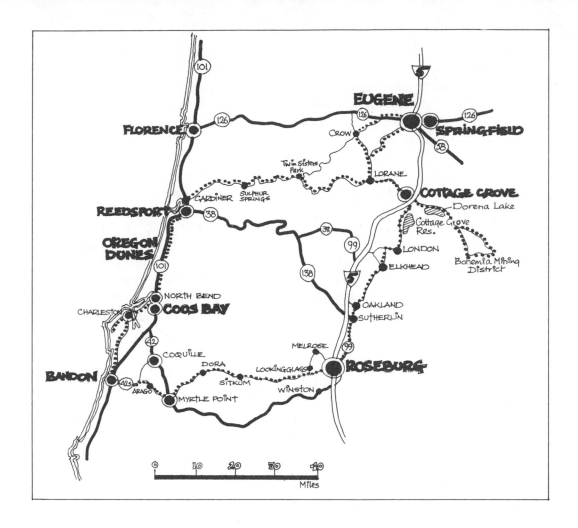

6. THE EUGENE–COOS BAY LOOP

An Out-of-Season Gourmand's Romp

This journey, best undertaken out of season around late September, is a gourmet's—or perhaps more accurately, a gourmand's—delight. We visit two cheese factories, generous with their samples, and three wineries (ditto), enjoy the barbecue at a cranberry festival, nibble smoked salmon right out of the smokehouse, devour the most delicious pies in an old lumber town cocooned in its past, and dance to German music at an Oregon Wine Festival. (Both festivals are usually held the last weekend in September. The wine festival is on Sunday only.) We also take time to explore sand dunes (quiet at this time of year), meander our way along little-known mountain roads, and explore an old mining area high in the Cascades.

"I BET I can tell you exactly where you were born." A small, stocky man with a bushy beard beamed at me infectiously. I was standing by the counter at the Reedsport Cheese Factory quietly devouring my fifth sample of cheese. A young lady kept handing them to me on a plate with an enthusiastic "Now, see what you think of this one," and I kept nibbling and pausing and nibbling and enjoying every mouthful. I could have gone on like this for quite a while and doubtless would have, were it not for the bearded man's interruption.

"I'm sorry"—I turned to him questioningly—"what did you say?" That was my mistake. He opened his mouth, a large one, and bellowed, "Hah, y'see, I knew I was right." And he was right! He told me, to within 10 miles, the exact place of my birth, and then, before I even had time to ask him how he'd known, he launched into a captivating monologue all about his experiences in that part of the world, how much he'd intended to go back there but the army had taken him away and he'd fought all over the place, somehow got himself an O.B.E. (Order of the British Empire) in Britain, shell fragments in every part of his body, a bout with the bottle, a hermit-like cabin on the Oregon coast, and a new wife in Roseburg. I think all I managed to get in were a few gasps of amazement and a couple of affirmative grunts. Apparently it was all the encouragement he needed.

And that's how my friendship with Henry began, in the Reedsport Cheese factory, in the middle of my sampling session. I never did sample the full range (although I doubt anything could beat their sharp white Cheddar). If you enjoy this journey, it's largely thanks to this generous-spirited man. It was he who suggested many of the little-known backroads, gave me an understanding of the area's history, and introduced me to a series of memorable characters. Henry, wherever you are and whatever crazy schemes you're involved in, thanks again.

Eugene to Gardiner along the Smith River is one of the most scenic backroad journeys across the coastal range. Just south of Crow, turn left on the Old Territorial Highway and follow it toward Lorane. A mile or so down on the right, at Battle Creek Road, there's a covered bridge, one of almost two dozen in Lane County. We meander on through a pastoral landscape of narrow green valleys and old farms. It's hard to believe we're less than twenty minutes' drive from the brash outskirts of Eugene.

Lorane sleeps at a crossroads. There's a dusty store with gas pumps, a typical old Lodge building, a church, and a few cottages. Very backroadsy.

Smith River Falls

Take the Siuslaw valley road west along the river. A few miles on there's a county park by Siuslaw Falls—a quiet place to pause awhile. The road at this point is unpaved, but a couple of miles farther west is a fork. Take the left spur across the bridge back onto paved surface and begin a challenging stretch of mountain driving through logging country, with high views in all directions. After a series of hair-greying twists and turns on the steep slopes, we arrive at the south fork of the Smith River. Turn right here and wander with the river, following infrequent signs to Eugene and the coast, as far as the Twin Sisters Park. The route keeps changing in character. We begin in a moist, almost Olympic valley. Moss-dripping trees arch over the road, sunlight shafts through the higher branches, spotlighting clusters of ferns and the churning stream below. Then the valley widens and the limpid quality of the vegetation gives way to a rocky landscape where the forest has been cleared and the underlying crags exposed. Farther on there's a delicate section of sparkling silver birch followed by dark passages through virgin pine.

At Twin Sisters Park we join the more direct mountain road from Crow and turn west toward the coast. It's a slow drive but now the river is broader and its meanderings less erratic. By the look of the towering rock cliffs this must have been a far larger body of water at one time, ripping and gouging its way to the sea. Now it's a quiet creature, broken by a flurry over the Smith River falls, then slowly maturing into a dark lakelike docility. There are broad rafts of logs moored to its banks a few miles from the coast, awaiting transportation to the sawmills at Gardiner, a tough town smelling of wood smoke and sea spray. Abruptly, we reach Route 101 and leave the quiet valley behind.

After a delightful pause for samples at the Reedsport Cheese Factory across the Umpqua River, visit the Oregon Dunes Information Center to prepare for the next excursion. Then drive over the last pine-covered hills to the beaches at Winchester Bay and Salmon Harbour, one of the most unusual sections of coastline in the Pacific Northwest. This 40-mile-long stretch of gently rolling, desert-like dunes between Florence and Coos Bay extends inland up to 2½ miles and is said to be still moving in that direction, more than 20 feet a year in some places. During the height of summer the dunes are inundated with dune buggies, picnickers, and hordes of young travelers in wide-tire VW buses. There's hardly a sandhill left without its smothering of footprints. Dunes and people do not mix well, and whoever conceived the dune buggy obviously failed to appreciate the subtle, silent beauty of this kind of landscape. Fortunately, there are plans to ban them entirely. Too many of the dune areas along the Pacific coast have been "Pismo Beached," and this region should be made an exception.

After Labor Day the repair work begins. The wind erases the footprints and the tire tracks, rounding out the dunes again, smoothing the sheer sides of their lee slopes, restoring their even color, scouring their crests. I came here in late September and for a day roamed the area, almost alone. I find this the only way to enjoy the dunes. Maybe my attitude is a little selfish, but they offer almost perfect solitude and silence at this time of year. The sight of other footprints can destroy the illusion of timelessness; the sound of an engine or other voices is an all-too-obvious reminder of the restless world beyond.

Like the desert, the dunes are whatever you wish them to be. If you learn to look and listen, they will tell you many things in their gentle metaphorical manner. I turned as I climbed the higher crests and watched the wind fill my footprints. Soon there was no sign that I had ever been there. I looked at the texture of the sand on the dune. It was gently rippled—a tiny, exact replica of the dunes themselves, a hologram of the whole. In places firm sand was eroded by the wind into miniature canyons, buttes, and stepped plains. The wind blew. A butte collapsed. Another started to form. Watching the rest of the dune I could see the spuming sand building on the lee slopes. The dune moved forward, grain by grain, slowly and endlessly. A landscape always changing, always the same.

It's hard to walk on the dunes. Just when you think you've found yourself a firm-packed section of sand to follow, it'll vanish abruptly and leave you floundering in ankle-deep grains. Try it barefoot. It's more comfortable and the liquid-like sensation of silica oozing between one's toes is delightful.

It's not all sand up here. There are steep-sloped oases of trees, secluded lakes, fingers of pine forest, and, always, those views of the Pacific, driftwood-fringed and surf-sloppy. The November–April period is the best time for beachcombing, especially if you're looking for Japanese glass fishing floats. These charming green spheres, varying in diameter from 3 inches to more than a foot, have now become so popular that if the Japanese ever start to use cork or polyurethane to keep their nets afloat, someone on the Oregon Tourist Board is going to have to arrange for a substitute supply to be surreptitiously launched a few miles off the coast just to keep the combers happy.

On Route 101 to Coos Bay, past one of the region's popular myrtlewood factories, there's an extremely unusual series of driftwood creations in a roadside field. Dominating the menagerie is a 20-foot-high figure waving an American flag with individual letters spelling LIBERTY erratically nailed to his body. Nearby are a dinosaur, the remnants of a 100-foot-long brontosaur, a whale with gaping driftwood-shaped jaws, a giraffe, and a pirate ship complete with masts and gun turrets—all wonderful creations but, alas, all in a poor state of repair. I chatted with a man standing at the roadside. He told me it was the work of a high school class, undertaken many years ago as a competition. "The brontosaurus won," he claimed. He pointed to the sad remnant. Only the head and a small section of tail remained. "My kid worked on that," he added proudly. "The local Jaycees used to take care of it, but nobody seems interested now."

Over the splendid McCullough Bridge, we arrive in North Bend, once home of Asa and Louis J. Simpson's vast lumber and shipping empire. Like the great cattle barons of the Oregon desert (see Chapter 8, "Burns to Bend"), these men reflected their era, a time of big schemes, big ambitions, and big money. There were others like them up and down the coast, each with his own empire. Their era was short-lived but it was certainly lived!

Pause at the Coos-Curry Museum on the northern edge of town. It's a pleasant potpourri place filled with old spinning wheels, pianos, sewing machines, Indian objects, flags, music boxes,

A Quiet Corner of Coos Bay

and an odd assortment of driftwood figures created by a Captain Harvey, who lives locally and seems to have a popular following. Outside, a Georgia Pacific Lumber Engine, No. 104, and a rusty spool donkey are reminders of the logging heritage of this town, home of one of the huge Weyerhaeuser lumber plants (tours are offered during the summer months).

In Coos Bay, one of the world's largest lumber ports, we reach the center of the region's timber industry, passing by a miniature Cascade range of golden wood-chip piles on the docks. Merchant ships tower over the road waiting to load the chips for their Japan-bound voyages. Tugboats hoot and churn their way to the sawmills pushing long log rafts. Steam and smoke billow over the town from scores of chimneys, mingling with the pungent aroma of fresh-cut lumber, burning sawdust, and pulp. East of the town along the Coos and Millicoma rivers, logs are assembled into rafts using "log broncs," tiny one-man boats that thrash and churn in the water like irascible mules. The rafts are then moved downstream by the tug, first to the log "lanes" and later onto the sawmills around Eastside. I paused to watch the tugs at work on the river. An old man stood nearby, also watching. "I used to be on one of those," he told me quietly. "I worked on 'em for years. Then mi' back gave and they retired me." He paused for a long time. "That was quite a life."

On the road from North Bend to Charleston look for a sign reading "Indian Museum." Up a gravel track beyond a housing development, there's a white wooden building painted with brightly colored totem figures. Inside I met Lucie Cox. She welcomed me to the museum and gave me a thorough description of the Indian artifacts in the small display area. Some of the arrowheads and implements had been unearthed at a nearby dig by an archaeologist from Britain. Lucie, whose "real" name is Angaleluk Patrovnioff, is a member of the Aleutian tribe, many of whom used to hunt with Russian trappers on their Pacific sealskin expeditions during the early nineteenth century. She is also one of the founder members of the museum situated on the tiny 6.1-acre reservation, and explained that it operates on CETA Title III Funds as a research, education, and craft center for local members of the Coos, Lower Umpqua, and Siuslaw tribes. It also seems to be evidence of a general resurgence of Indian self-awareness in the region. "But we have so much more to do," she told me. "It's incredible how ignorant people still are about the Indians. Last week a lady came in and asked me to demonstrate some Indian sorcery. She was deadly earnest. So I said okay, looked at her very seriously, and shouted, 'Poof! You're a frog.' "

South of the museum is the little community of Charleston, Oregon's second-largest commercial fishing center. Seven plants can and freeze millions of dollars' worth of salmon, tuna, shrimp, and crab annually. Chuck's Seafoods in the center of town usually has a representative selection of local wares. Look also for his smoked salmon leftovers. I bought a bagful of tails and fins here for next to nothing and, after a bit of judicious sorting, sat down to a lunch of some of the sweetest, juiciest meat I have ever tasted.

On the coast south of Charleston is a series of three state parks, popular during the summer but usually quiet off season. The first, Sunset Bay, brings the sea and beach almost right into your car. Surfers and skin divers come here for safe swimming on the coast in a sheltered cove edged by sandstone bluffs. Hikers take the 3½-mile trail along the ocean to Cape Arago, by far the best way to enjoy this stretch of coast.

South of Sunset Bay is the Shore Acres State Park, once home of Louis J. Simpson, the lumber and shipping tycoon. Overlooking the ragged cliffs, there's an observation shelter, where the whole story of the Simpson family is presented. All that remains today of Louis' two lavish mansions are the formal gardens complete with boxwood hedges and lily pond. Beyond the carefully manicured shrubberies one can hear the booming surf and the hoarse barking of sea lions out at Simpson's Reef.

A mile or so farther down, past a viewpoint over the reef, is Cape Arago, last in this chain of parks. Paths lead down to coves on either side of the rocky promontory. The more-sheltered South Cove is often used as an anchorage for vessels waiting to cross the sand bar into Coos Bay.

Return to Charleston and take the Seven Devils Drive south to Bandon. En route watch for the narrow road down to Whiskey Run Beach. It's a lovely spot for secluded shore strolls.

Bandon's normally quiet, rather quaint, main street was a bustle of activity. I had arrived just in time for the town's annual cranberry festival, and everyone seemed to be walking around with a great sense of purpose. Everyone, that is, except for a huddle of regulars at the two taverns, who seemed quite content to sip their salted beers and watch the activity from their Naugahyde perches.

The festival began more than thirty years ago and marks the approach of the cranberry harvest, a major event in Bandon's economy. Stretching along 101 for miles and in the marshy areas behind the pines are hundreds of acres of cranberry beds, fields of low vinelike plants crossed by ditches. The cranberry, although a hardy plant, requires careful nurturing in conditions not always the most pleasant to work in. The harvest means the end of gropings in the bogs, frost watches, and sprayings. After the frantic ten-day picking period, when often more than 10 million pounds are harvested, the growers, the pickers, the whole town can relax for a while. The festival is an omen of these good times to come.

At the barn in the town park, the judging of cranberry creations was about to begin. Spread out on a large table in the center of the room were scores of the most delectable-looking cranberry loaves, cranberry cakes, cranberry cookies, cranberry meringues, cranberry crunch, cranberry brownies, and just about every other kind of dish, from breakfast snacks to supper nibbles, that might conceivably contain cranberries. The three judges sat at a smaller table overlooking the array. "There's too many breads," murmured one elderly woman judge to no one in particular. "I prefer pies." The other elderly lady judge said nothing. She seemed a little embarrassed by the whole affair. The sudden glare of a flash bulb made her pop out of her seat like a champagne cork. "Well, let's get started then, I'm starving," bellowed the third judge, a robust man with a cheery red face. He seemed to regard the whole affair as a bit of a joke. "I'm not really that fond of cranberries, you know," he chortled to the judge who complained about the breads. She turned slowly, duchess-like, gave him a splendidly haughty "Oh really," and proceeded to ignore him completely. But he was one

85

of those characters who just will not be put down. He joked and wisecracked all the way through, on one occasion amusing himself so much he almost choked on a cookie crumb. Some of the ladies whose creations were being evaluated stood outside the room and seemed decidedly unhappy. "Is he drunk?" asked one. "He didn't even taste mine," moaned another. "He won't be here next year, that's for certain!" said a third firmly.

In the evening the whole town gathered in the high school gymnasium for the selection of the Cranberry Queen. Onto the regally decorated stage walked the five pretty contestants in long white gowns, accompanied by white-suited escorts. It was a slow process. The audience seemed more interested at first in the football scores of the school team than in finding a queen, but the emcee, a naturally funny man, soon had them in stitches with his one-liners and inside jokes about leading citizens of the community. During one lull he even slapped on a flat cap and gave a raucous rendition of "If I Were a Rich Man." The audience loved him. The candidate queens gave their speeches and demonstrated their dancing and piano-playing talents, and my favorite, the short chubby one, was finally chosen. Gushing and blushing she received her crown, and the evening ended as half the audience tumbled onto the stage to offer their congratulations. The emcee looked a little sorry it was all over.

The following morning, Saturday, the festival began in earnest. Promptly at 10 A.M. the parade poured down the hill, around the steep curve, and into main street past the cheering citizens of Bandon. Fragile-looking floats designed around the theme "Cranberries in Storybookland" wobbled along with the fire engines, police cars, old-time char-à-bancs, and a horde of young bicyclists who flashed by at regular intervals bombarding the crowds with cranberry candies. The high school band, all blues and whites, played Sousa at different tempos as it marched down the hill out of step. "It's only the second time they've played together, y'know," said one woman whose bespectacled son was being boa-constricted by a tuba. "Sounds like the first time to me!" murmured a nearby onlooker. Then the mayor trundled by in a tiny sports car followed by the second of the "Old Woman Who Lived in a Shoe" floats filled with schoolkids, who pelted the spectators with ripe cranberries. The queen and her princesses floated past, waving, followed by the local Corvette club roaring and spluttering, the Humbug Shrine Club in mobile bathtubs, and even the local knacker— "Your Used Cow Dealer"! When it was all over, the crowd paused for a moment and then began the scramble up the hill to the barbecue in the park, where 1,000 pounds of prime beef had been roasting in a deep pit since 4 A.M. The smell of the meat wafted through the trees and among the picnic tables. A line of three hundred waited, salivating, as they watched the huge roasts being cut into generous slabs and served with, of course, cranberry jelly, cranberry salad, and a cup of cranberry juice.

And so it rolled on throughout Saturday and Sunday. There was a crafts display in the barn, a football game, a track meet, square dances, a trap shoot, an old-time fiddlers' jam session, and even a soccer match. The poor queen with her slightly bedraggled princesses had to appear everywhere, smiling and waving and trying very hard to maintain a regal air. But everyone seemed to agree, when it all came to an end, that it was one of the best festivals they'd had. The royal court yawned happily in unison and retired to their separate homes to sleep.

Even if you miss the Bandon Cranberry Festival, it's a lovely spot to pause awhile off season. On the north side of the Coquille River is the recently restored lighthouse at the tip of Bullands Beach State Park, and south of the town along the coast is an attractive loop drive past a series of parks and wayside viewpoints. Beach roaming, again preferably off season, is a dramatic experience here.

Before you leave Bandon you are almost obliged to visit the Bandon Cheese Factory, a clean bright establishment facing Route 101. While you munch on cheese and crackers, there's a view over the cheese-making vats and an excellent slide and tape description of the "cheddaring" process. More than 2 million pounds are produced here a year. Bob Howard, the master cheese maker, watches over every part of the process with an eagle eye. "It may look simple enough," he told me, "but it doesn't take much to spoil cheese. There's only one way to make it and that's dead right." The most popular variety, sharp, is aged for more than a year, the others for between three and six months. The cheesery also produces its own butter and a range of flavored cheeses.

From Bandon we head east along Route 42S toward Roseburg and the Oregon Wine Festival. This popular event is now in its tenth year, and I had no intention of missing it. The road follows the pastoral Coquille valley. Where it suddenly springs to the north, take the unsigned turning right along a partially paved road through the hamlet of Arago to Route 42. We're really in backcountry now. Note the unique round building at Myrtle Point just behind Main Street, erected in 1910 as a Russian Orthodox church and patterned, so a sign claims, after the Mormon Tabernacle in Salt Lake City.

Immediately before the bridge, turn right on the narrow road to Dora and Sitkum, following the meanderings of the Coquille River. This superb drive, the old Coos Bay Wagon Road, passes through small meadowed valleys surrounded by pine-covered hills. During the week the occasional logging trucks can make driving hard work, but the weekends are usually quiet. Near Dora I paused to chat with the owner of a large mansion surrounded by verandas and set back from the road. Most of the other homes along this little-known backcountry road are diminutive affairs, half hidden in bushes. But this place is different. A charming elderly lady, Mrs. Abernethy, told me it had been designed and built by her husband in 1910 as a roadside hostelry for carriages crossing the mountains. Mr. Abernethy apparently owned his own sawmill, which explains the excellent quality of both wood and workmanship. Unfortunately for him the automobile emerged as a popular conveyance precisely at that time. He never completed the upper level of the hostelry, and the couple lived on the lower floor.

A section of this road, the steepest part, is unpaved. It's also frustratingly narrow, particularly in those places where the stream cascades over rocks or tumbles in perfect waterfalls. There's nowhere to stop and take photographs. After a couple of such experiences I found a relatively straight stretch and stopped on the road itself. There was no traffic anyway.

Following a long descent with flickers of views across the mountains ahead, there's a turnoff right to Tenmile. Take this for a short distance and look for a sign to the Bjelland Vineyards. Here's an opportunity to sample a series of grape and fruit wines at one of Oregon's thirteen wineries. (Tasting hours daily except Tuesday; June through September, 8–5; other months, 11–5.) Production is usually so limited at many of these wineries that they are still virtually unknown out of state, and regular customers often refer to a favored establishment as "my winery." The lively bearded vintner, Paul Bjelland, claims, however, that "bigness tends to be inevitable. We're trying to remain small but the demand for Oregon wines is increasing fantastically and we're all getting rushed along with the tide." Both Paul and his wife are teachers. Mary is still active but Paul now gives all his energy to the winery and the adjoining vineyards. "We've got about fifteen acres of grapes at the moment," he told me, "ten for us and five for the deer!" Paul is also an avid organizer and for the last nine years has supervised the Oregon Wine Festival in Roseburg, usually held on the last weekend of September. After sampling a few of the Bjelland wines, including the prize-winning wild blackberry, we moved on to the festival.

Return up the road to County Road 5 and follow the signs to Lookingglass. There's one more optional detour here, north to Richard Sommer's Hillcrest winery near Melrose (ask for directions in the town) for another tasting session, along with a descriptive tour of the winemaking process. (Hours: 10–5 daily.) Mr. Sommer, "father of the Oregon fine wine industry," is particularly proud of his medium-dry white Riesling (accounting for more than 70 percent of his production), although he is also known for his other red and white wines, including Gewürztraminer, Cabernet Sauvignon, and a recent Pinot Noir. His tours are informative. Like the cheese maker in Bandon he describes the process in a disarmingly simple way. But again, it's attention to the finest details that distinguishes the best wines from their pallid inferiors.

Now we descend into Roseburg, nestled among its ring of hills, and head straight to the fairgrounds for the wine festival. Paul Bjelland has done a splendid job. Inside the large hall hundreds of happy pink-cheeked visitors move past the individual winery stands where the samplings are in progress. In addition to the two we've just visited, most of the other Oregon wineries are represented—Oak Knoll, Ponzi, Coury, Tualatin, Knudsen-Erath, Eyrie, Nehalem Bay, and Honeywood, famous for its fruit wines. A few of the major California wineries are also here, along with the Ste. Michelle Vineyards from Washington State. As if the wines weren't enough, large platters of cheese selections from the Tillamook, Bandon, and Reedsport cheese factories are laid out as palate cleansers.

Henry is also here, his glowing face peering at everybody in the crowd, seeking old friends— and potential new ones. Henry is a teetotaler, a strict one, but he loves to see others enjoying the wine and keeps approaching with a whispered "now I'm told their Gewürztraminer is exceptional." Or, "Did you know their Zinfandel won the 1976 award at . . ." He introduces me to Bill York, a stocky

Britisher who is head zoologist at the World Wildlife Safari at Winston just outside Roseburg. We get into a long discussion about the economics of game reserves in Africa, and Henry beams. "I see myself as an instigator," he told me later, "bringing people together and seeing what happens." He even wanted to arrange a meeting for me with the belly dancer who had just completed her rather lithe exhibition, to the delight of the crowd. I told him that was an unnecessary "instigation" and escaped back to the tasting tables.

The key to successful tasting at this kind of festival is to take it very slowly, try to "sequence" the wines from white through rosé to red so that the palate retains its sensitivity, nibble on cheese, crackers, or bread between each tasting, and perhaps most important, keep a record of your reactions to each of the wines.

A truly international flavor was obviously intended at the festival. Shortly after the belly dancer the Krautwurst Konzert Band lumbered, lederhosen and all, onto the stage to begin their rendition of German drinking songs. The wine was obviously having a warming effect, and couples began prancing across the floor in time to the tuba's steady bass. Henry, for some inexplicable reason, was not with them. Then the next thing I knew I was being whisked off to see the curator of the Douglas County Museum, located nearby on the fairgrounds. "You must meet him," said Henry. "He knows this area inside out. You'll find him fascinating." Unfortunately, the curator was not around, but the museum was open and we wandered through its contemporary galleries, admiring a series of excellent displays on the local lumber industry, mid-nineteenth-century room settings, the history of Roseburg, and a special exhibit on the Stenhouse archaeological dig, the one we heard about at the Indian museum near Charleston. "Would you like to meet him?" asked Henry. "Who?" I replied. "The archaeologist fellow, Stenhouse." Henry, the master "instigator," was off again.

If by any unfortunate chance you missed the Roseburg festival, you can at least compensate by a visit to the third winery on our itinerary, the Jonicole Vineyards. It's a short distance west of the junction of 42 with Interstate 5, along Winery Lane. Although a relatively new addition to Oregon's growing list of wineries, the place is expanding, and tastings are offered usually on weekends from 12 to 5 or by appointment.

Route 99 turns north from Roseburg just beyond the lane to the winery and is a rather decadent little highway until Wilbur, where it improves considerably. Pause at Oakland. In fact do more than pause. Stop, park, and come and enjoy this perfect specimen of a small late-nineteenth-century town. What makes it so charming is the lack (to date) of those self-conscious additions that immediately label a place "historic." The town has a life of its own. It doesn't rely completely on tourists for its trade and livelihood.

Oakland was founded in 1851 about one mile south of its present location. When the Oregon and California railroad was built through the area in 1872, most of the "old" town was moved on skids, building by building, to a more convenient location. It was hardly worth the effort. In the 1890s two fires destroyed every wooden structure on main street and the whole place had to be rebuilt, this time in brick and stone. It was one of those towns that just would not give up. Even its economy has been as erratic and varied as a steer-busting ride. Before 1900 it was famous for its hops and prunes, then during the 1920s it became known as "The Turkey Capital of the World" before a brief interlude as a logging center after World War II. Today most of the money comes from nearby cattle and sheep ranching, although there's a growing antiques and bric-a-brac trade in the town.

The main street has changed little since the 1890s. A couple of the buildings still boast their original cast-iron trimmings and richly decorated brass door handles. There's a small museum here on the south side of main street (daily except Monday, 1:30–4:30) usually tended by Verge Chenoweth, author of a book on Oakland, and past owner of the town's hardware store. He's one of those happy people always ready to trade a yarn or explain the intricacies of the local history.

Across the street is Tolly's Deli, "where sodas flow and friendships grow," run by Terry and Carol Toleffson as an adjunct to their antique store. This chintzy establishment is best known for its splendid homemade pies and cakes. Even as I was window browsing on main street a car drew up and its driver leaned out and asked me, "Where's that place with the cakes?" I had just downed a slice of German chocolate and was obviously the right person to ask, as I had forgotten to remove all its traces from my cheeks.

Across the street from Tolly's is Art and Donna Homewood's "Double Door" store, with an excellent range of paintings mainly by Oregon artists. Art, whose family were once gardeners to royalty in England, still keeps his thumb green with scores of African violets, which he tends like children.

Around the corner at the bottom end, Bill Clemens and Lotus Kingery are normally busy restoring or replicating old wagons and carriages at their Beaver State Carriage Works. Many of the parts, including the delicate wood-spoke wheels, are bought from the Amish colonies in Pennsylvania. Bill is usually the one who handles the bulky activities, bending and grinding the metal flanges, bowing and bolting the wooden frames. Lotus has her own workshop, where she concentrates on the upholstery work. When the two are brought together—the bouncy bodies of the carriages and the gleaming black leather seats with red trimming—it's a proud moment for the two of them and often the result of months of work.

While we're on the subject of work, down at the Oakland Feed Seed and Western Shop, Nell Garrison is the bemused owner of a score or more overworked hats, nailed to the rafters. Many of them have little cryptic notes pinned to them. "It shrunk." "Was he in it when the truck hit?" "It just died." Nell explains, "I take 'em in trade. Don't know why. Just got to be a local custom."

It's time for a change from all the eating and the talking. This next beautiful drive will lead us to a quiet lake ideal for fishing, boating, or plain lazing. Take County Road 22 around the corner from Nell's store and follow the signs for Elkhead/Elkhead Road. Route 22 becomes 50, and in the center of Elkhead it changes to 7. Keep your eyes open. Elkhead consists of a house and a half. A short distance down the road take the unpaved road to the right, to another almost nonexistent

Carriage Works—Oakland

Cottage Grove Museum

hamlet, London, and then through lovely pine woods to Cottage Grove Reservoir. If you've followed this journey in its entirety and managed to attend even one of the festivals, you deserve a long rest by the shores of this pleasant lake.

The main attraction at Cottage Grove is, of course, Railroad Town U.S.A., just off Interstate 5, a popular collection of old railroad engines and cars, each with its own exhibits and displays. In addition an old locomotive, the Goose, provides a two-hour, 35-mile journey, to the fringe of the Bohemia mining country deep in the Cascades. Schedules keep changing, but during the peak season, July 1 through Labor Day, the train leaves at 2 P.M. every day. In the off-season period—May, June, and October—it departs at the same time but on weekends only.

A lesser-known attraction in Cottage Grove is the Historical Museum, housed in a former octagonal Roman Catholic Church over the bridge at Birch Avenue and H Street (June and September, 1–4 P.M., second weekend of each month; July and August, Wednesday through Sunday, 1–5 P.M.). In addition to the now-familiar array of domestic artifacts and old photographs, there are exhibits of the famous Bohemia Mining District, including a miniature working model of a stamp mill, ore samples, mining tools, and assaying equipment.

A pleasant detour up into the mining district past Dorena Lake gives a glimpse into the region's heritage. After James "Bohemia" Johnson made the initial discovery of ore in 1863, the area became one of the richest sites in the Cascades. Bohemia City was founded, and the prospectors flooded in from all parts of the Pacific Northwest. Today with the exception of the old stage stop and rebuilt post office, little remains of those frantic days.

Fortunately, however, I met Ray (E.) Nelson, who knows the area better than anyone alive and wrote his *Facts and Yarns of the Bohemia* after years of research on the area—research that included the reopening of the Vesuvius Mine. He was a little cagey about his success as a contemporary goldminer and even more concerned that I didn't confuse him with his cousin, another Ray Nelson, author of a popular book on moonshining! But he gave me some useful background on the area and persuaded me to take the loop drive into the hills. He's attempting to have signs erected and roads improved to make it more attractive to the passing traveler.

The journey is almost complete. If you're anxious to return quickly to the comforts of the city, take Interstate 5 from Cottage Grove. Alternatively, if a final stretch of backroading appeals, drive west to Lorane and then north to Eugene through more quiet valleys and pine-crested hills. Henry recommends the latter!

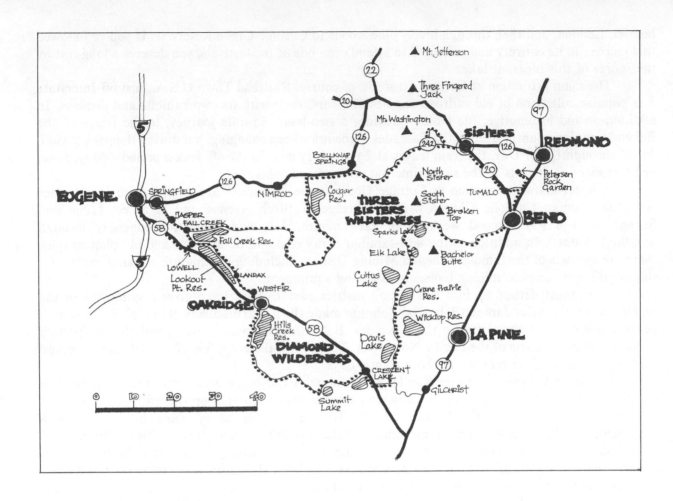

7. THE EUGENE CASCADES
High Peaks and Ponderosas

We journey through real Oregon country, deep into the heart of the Cascade range, where black lava lands wriggle below icy volcanic peaks and deep ponderosa forests invite quiet rambles by hidden waterfalls and lakes. This is a peaceful journey. We meet few people except for Joe and his horse wandering through the high country, and Harvey Hegardt, guardian of a fairy kingdom of rock creations. We end up, however, in the middle of Eugene at one of the state's finest pioneer museums, after enjoying unusual snacks at the city's Fifth Street Market.

THE SIGN by the footbridge read "Cross at your own risk." There was a cottage on the other side of the stream, smoke curling from its chimney. Someone must obviously use the bridge and regularly. So I started across without hesitation and everything was going splendidly until I approached the middle. I'm not what you would call lightweight, and the bridge was one of those free-swinging rope-and-plank affairs. I think the secret is to walk slowly and exactly down the mathematical middle, holding tight to the ropes on either side. That, or run like hell and get to the other side before the laws of physics jettison you parabolically into the water. I was certainly moving slowly but must have placed one of my feet a centimeter or so off dead center. The bridge immediately swayed to the left leaving my body at a rather alarming angle to the perpendicular. Bracing myself, I immediately tried to remedy the situation by leaning to the left. It was the correct thing to do, but I must have overcompensated a little too much, as the bridge swung to the right leaving me again dangling directly above the stream. I repeated the procedure to the right and watched dismayed as the bridge swung back to its left-leaning bias. This process went on for quite a while until the back-and-forth swaying motion of the bridge developed a momentum and volition of its own and I stood crouched like a parrot on a perch in the middle. There was only one thing to do. Retreat. Unfortunately I couldn't turn around, and walking backwards on a foot-wide plank that keeps disappearing is an art I have yet to master. So I ended up spreadeagled on the plank, hands still gripping the support ropes, feet dangling down toward the stream. In this uncomfortable position I inched my way back and, almost in disbelief, finally stepped onto terra firma. I left the bridge still swaying and gave a final glance at the cottage in admiration of its residents, who presumably made that crossing daily. As I looked I'm sure I saw one of the curtains move. Is it possible that someone had been watching my dismal efforts? Well, after all, I had been warned by that sign. I have never ventured on a rope bridge since then, but I've had fun watching others!

All this happened a little way off the Jasper–Lowell road, within a short distance of the crowded Route 126 on the eastern edge of Springfield. Once you turn south off that ghastly strip of recapped-tire stores, junk-food outlets, and gas stations, you soon find yourself meandering along pastoral backroads, tree-shaded and flower-clustered. At the crossroads hamlet of Unity I sketched a covered bridge, one of almost two dozen in Lane County. Why this area should possess such a remarkable number is a mystery to me, and to most other residents, apparently. The majority are quite recent structures dating from the 1930s. The area around Cottage Grove is particularly well endowed and boasts a 1920 specimen on Lang Road, east of the town. Also, farther east, off Route

126 at Vida, is perhaps the most photographed of all, the Goodpasture Bridge, and along the same highway west of McKenzie Bridge is the popular Belknap Bridge. Myself, I like the Unity Bridge. It has a utilitarian appearance and seems to have escaped the prettying process that characterizes many of the others.

Just after Fall Creek take the road alongside Fall Creek Reservoir. For the first few miles it's well paved. Then after entering the Willamette National Forest, it reverts to a good gravel surface. This is where our adventure really begins.

The climb is steep and persistent. At the edge of the track there are glimpses, between thick beds of ferns, of abrupt drops to a turbulent, boulder-filled stream. Trees, their branches dripping with long tendrils of hairlike moss, droop over the gorge. We move upward all the time, past still pools, white rapids, and waterfalls, where the stream cascades down rounded rocks dappled with spots of sunlight.

As the alpine curves of the track become more marked, the humid sweetness of the lower slopes gives way to tight, straight clusters of pines. It's cooler up here too. The wind moves through the trees with a sound like distant surf. The sun sends shafts through a dark-green ceiling of high branches. Two deer standing warily at the side of the track turn together and bound into the darkness. The road continues to climb. Suddenly there are breaks in the trees; fire and lumber cutting have removed whole swaths of forest. Far, far below lies the green-glowing Willamette valley. Ahead are tantalizing glimpses of the Cascade range. Follow the infrequent signs to Route 126. At one confusing junction it's said to be in two different directions. Take Forestry Road 170 and stay on it. Getting lost in these hills is not a very enjoyable experience, especially if the mists descend, which they do with alarming rapidity.

I have traveled here in one of those mists. Visibility is reduced to near-zero. There's no warning of sharp curves or dropoffs. Worse still, the cold, clammy air kills sounds, and it's hard to tell if other vehicles are approaching. (Although it's rare to find much traffic up here, you'll invariably have that experience when you least expect it, just as you're cutting a corner or traveling in the middle of the track to avoid bumps!)

I met Joe up here in one of those mists. I didn't catch his last name. He and his horse materialized abruptly out of the forest and stood by the side of the road to let me pass. They made a strange sight, he with his great red beard and the horse laden with camping gear, prospecting pans, and an old shotgun. I stopped to talk with him. He was a young man with a weathered, wrinkled face. His stained suede jacket was torn at the seams and his denims were frayed. Around his neck he wore a grubby red scarf and a large bronze medallion. He'd been traveling with his horse for three months.

He told me he worked at a bank in Eugene. "Well, y'get tired of the same old game, so once in a while I take off into the hills and wander around a bit." I asked him if he ever wrote about his experiences. "Heck no, I'm no writer. Even gave up sending letters two months ago. No point. Never get any back." He said he thought he'd keep on going for a few more weeks and then return to the

Covered Bridge—Unity

bank and make some more money for his next trip. I asked him what he did on his journeys. "Not much. I pick up old bottles and sell them, talk to the shepherds—not too many Basques left now, just drunks—find a bit of gold here and there. That kind of stuff." I wondered if there was any hidden purpose to his trip. "Purpose. Heck no. Just finding peace. That's about it. Just finding peace." He stroked the horse's cheek and smiled, and they ambled off together into the mist. They must have entered the forest. When I set off there was no sign of them.

The long descent is as exciting as the ascent. The track crosses the western foothills of the Three Sisters. To the north are the craggy profiles of the Cascade ridges. Below, a long way down, is the thin sliver of Cougar Reservoir, turquoise blue against the deep green of the pines. When you finally reach its shores, pause and rest before the next part of the journey, up to McKenzie Pass.

After a few miles east on 126, the road divides. Take Route 242 headed for the Pass but note the warning about trailers. The road is narrow, steeply curved, and not suitable for extra-long vehicles.

Shortly after the initial climb, look for a sign to Proxy Falls on the right-hand side. To reach the upper falls, it's a half-mile stroll through an old lava field covered in wild rhododendron bushes. Here silver cascades tumble hundreds of feet to a deep ocher-colored pool. The rock face has a green coat of mossy fur. Large trees lie uprooted across the falls; some must have tumbled years ago, because new trees are already sprouting from their rotting trunks. Roots, like bulbous boa

constrictors, clutch and crack the round boulders. Curiously, there appears to be no way in which the water leaves the pool. There's a stream bed, but it's dry and I can't find any indication of an underground exit. I stroll, bemused, to the lower falls. Of the two this is my favorite. The water here tumbles through four distinct phases. At the top it comes churning like cream out of the forest, then sheets down a sheer rock face before breaking into thousands of silver filaments and mistily floating into the pool at its base. The pool is deep and still, but the water pours from it in an angry torrent, crashing against rocks and snatching the earth from the roots of dying trees before disappearing out of sight down a gorge. A lovely place to pause a while.

As we continue to climb up toward McKenzie Pass, the road becomes more and more contorted. The Douglas firs of the lower slopes, majestic trees of towering dignity, give way to short pines, anemic in size and color. Then, abruptly, we're traveling across a burnt-black plateau of writhing lava rock, part of the great Belknap eruptions. The road skirts the southern edge of the flow, following an old Indian trail. And beyond, at last, are the great snow-capped peaks themselves. The sudden sense of space is overwhelming after the close confines of the lower pine slopes. The sharp outlines of Mt. Washington and Mt. Jefferson flash like polished steel blades. To the south the Three Sisters rise regally from the forest, and old Broken Top, a collapsed volcano, rips the scudding clouds with its jagged crown. Stroll out across the lava field and enjoy one of the finest Cascade panoramas in the Pacific Northwest. Up here, time has no meaning. A minute often seems like an hour. An hour sometimes like a minute. It's just you and the mountains and the sky and that wonderful roaring silence.

Look across at the lava flow. It seems to be moving. Half close your eyes and you'd swear that seething mass was slowly rolling toward you. On one side is the pine forest. On the other side is a vast pockmarked blanket of purple-black cinder rock, sharp and brittle, full of cracks and crevasses. It's treacherous unless you stick to the narrow trails that wander a little way into the morass and then end abruptly as if there's no point in going any farther. Skeletons of pines, bleached white and twisted into nightmare shapes, poke up at the sky. If one didn't know better it would be easy to assume that the lava had killed them, that they had died furious contorted deaths as the molten rock engulfed their roots, burnt off their leaves and branches, and blazed out every molecule of moisture in their hearts. But the lava flows occurred some three thousand to ten thousand years ago. Traces of everything that died in those fire-and-brimstone holocausts have long since vanished. But all else remains just as it was—a petrified landscape, unchanging and unrelenting.

Those interested in the more technical details of the flows should follow the signed tracks into the wilderness, from the Dee Wright observatory. This circular tower almost seems an integral part of the lava flow itself, and there are individual view windows of the great Cascade peaks to the north and south. Photographs of these ancient volcanic giants across the barren lava lands are fine studies in texture and contrast. Comparisons with moonscape are apt—in fact, lunar astronauts trained here a few years ago.

The lava fields end as abruptly as they began. Soon we move down through gentle groves of Ponderosa pine with pink-tinged bark and delicate green outlines. A few miles down from the pass there's a pointer on the left side of the road to Four Mile Butte. If you'd enjoy more real backroad driving, follow the forestry signs and spiral up a conical hill to an overlook offering imposing panoramas of the Cascade peaks, the virgin pine lands, and beyond, to the east, the Oregon desert itself. Nearby there's an ancient lava tunnel, Skylight Cave, and a second viewpoint, Five Mile Butte, with an even more dramatic vista. You can return directly to 242 along the same track or take a more meandering route through the ponderosas (signed to Route 20 at first, and later to 242.).

At Sisters, 242 and 20 converge just past Patterson's Arabian Stallion stables. (Yes, those are llamas you see in the field by the road. They're bred as mountain pack animals and used by the more serious climbing expeditions.) Normally I'm not keen on pseudo-western towns, but Sisters has a captivating quality. Maybe it's because there's just enough genuine ranch-days architecture to give the place authenticity. Or maybe it's the Sisters Craft Works in a small clapboard shack on main street, where boxes of obsidian, agate, and thunder eggs are displayed near the sidewalk. No one was in the store and a sign read "Please deposit money for rocks under door." Or maybe it was George Linn, a broad, beaming man with a silver goatee—a western version of a Southern Colonel. He's normally with his wife, Ava, at his White Buffalo Indian Museum and gift shop on the western edge of town. He's obviously taken a lot of care with his museum, although there are welcome touches of humor too among the displays of beadwork, clothing, and replicas of a potlatch house and a hogan. In one corner he has the only known bigfoot hide on display! The creature was also referred to by the Indians as "Tsonoguah," the cannibal woman whose main diet was naughty boys and girls. In the other corner there's the wooden figure of Chief Tommy Thompson with his worldly advice on longevity: "Eat lots of salmon and don't drive autos." George, who also happens to be the editor of *Cascades East* travel magazine, is a modest man—"Heck, I'm just an old Okie making a home out here"—but proud of his unusual creation, in this unusual town.

Just outside Tumalo, off Route 20, is the impressive Tumalo Falls. Pause here awhile, and then head off through Tumalo to Route 97, following the signs for Petersen's Rock Gardens. This remarkable example of folk art is worth the necessary detour.

Rasmus Petersen (1883–1952), a Danish immigrant farmer, created over a period of seventeen years a bewitching display of miniature buildings, fountains, castles, ponds, bridges, and statuary, set in a garden full of exotic bushes and shade trees. Not only did he build every part of the display himself, but his materials consisted almost exclusively of rocks found within a 90-mile radius of his farm—predominantly agates, lava rock, thunder eggs, obsidian, petrified wood, fossil rocks, sandstones, and basalt.

I talked with Harvey Hegardt, who was Petersen's friend and neighbor and is now caretaker-curator of the whole exhibit. He's usually to be found in the museum among the rock collection. "Rasmus designed his first building in 1935. He was fifty-two then. They're all originals, y'know. He didn't copy anything." Harvey emphasized the last remark after I had mentioned that one of the rock-encrusted buildings resembled Philadelphia's town hall. "No, he dreamed up everything himself. He just had a talent for it, I guess. He'd draw an outline on the ground with a stick and if he liked it, he'd build it. All the plans were in his mind." Rasmus spent the winters casting carefully measured concrete shapes in his basement, and then, in the spring, he'd assemble the pieces in the garden. By 1940 the garden was becoming a popular attraction in the area, so Rasmus gave up farming altogether and devoted himself to his fairy-tale land beneath the shade trees. "I've known him since I was a boy," Harvey told me. "I used to go with him rock hunting in the hills, but I never helped him build anything. Nobody did. He did it all himself." The garden has the conviction of a Tolkienesque creation without the darker undertones. It's a happy little land for pixies and gnomes and the gentle spirit creatures of nature. Visitors always leave with a twinkle in their eyes. "That's what Rasmus liked," Harvey told me. "He loved to see 'em smiling."

The neon razzmatazz of Bend's highway strip also has an unreal but less appealing quality. Surprisingly the town, safely ensconced behind this garish facade, is a pleasant place full of parks, nestling against the slow-moving Deschutes River. There's a small museum here at Greenwood and Harriman Streets (Tuesday through Saturday, 1–5) and, if you'd enjoy one more panorama of the nine Cascade peaks from Mount Hood to Bachelor Butte, there's a drive up Pilot Butte at the eastern edge of the town.

We leave Bend, following signs for the Cascades Lakes Highway (Century Drive), and begin a long climb into the foothills around Bachelor Butte (9,060 feet). The first 60 miles of the journey follow an excellent paved road past a couple of modern ski resorts and a necklace of quiet ponds and lakes, rimmed by pine forests. Traffic and mosquitoes can occasionally be irritating during the summer. Early fall is perhaps the best time to explore this area, especially if you intend to try a bit of wilderness hiking. Abundant trail heads close to the highway provide access into the Three Sisters Wilderness. First explored by pioneer-trapper Peter Skene Ogden in 1825, these hemlock and lodgepole-pine-covered foothills, broken by towering lava flows, offer a wide range of activities to suit all tastes—pack-and-saddle trips, half-day family hikes, week-long journeys on portions of the Pacific Crest Trail, and for the true enthusiasts, climbs up South Sister or the more difficult North Sister. Don't forget, though, to check trail conditions at the nearest ranger station or the Deschutes National Forest office in Bend and obtain a wilderness permit. This is difficult land and should be treated with respect, especially if you plan a trip to the high slopes. It also happens to be some of the finest mountain country in Oregon, with icy, clear streams, hidden lakes, deep lava crevasses, pine-ringed meadows, and, once you leave the half-day hikers behind, a land of great silences.

South along the Cascades Lakes Highway, there's an osprey sanctuary at Crane Prairie Reservoir. These majestic fish eaters, often mistaken for bald eagles, nest during the spring and summer in bleached timber snags at the northwestern end of the lake. I first visited here on a chill day in mid-September, walked the required quarter-mile (more like half) through the forest to a clearing overlooking the nesting area—and saw absolutely nothing! Not one bird, not even a sparrow, moved as I stood shivering in the biting wind. I noticed someone in the forest and thought I'd ask him if the birds had just flown off for an hour or so and might be back for lunch. An elderly, wizened man was grubbing in the soft pine-needle earth and mumbling to himself. He was totally absorbed in his work, and looked rather startled as I stopped a few feet from him. He told me the birds had gone south. "They've got sense. It's going to be a bad winter. Y'can forget fall. There won't be any." The rather dour little man resumed his grubbing. I asked him what he was doing. "Cones," he replied. There was a pause. He looked up. "Cones, pine cones. Y'know." He pointed to a gallon paint can half full of tiny pine cones. "I sell 'em. They're worth money." That was news to me, although since then I've noticed quite a few "cones for cash" signs in store windows. I asked him how he located them. "Squirrels. I find where they hide 'em and then I pull 'em out. Here, watch." He proceeded to dig under a rotting branch with his fingers and soon discovered a hoard of eight cones obviously buried by some diligent squirrel for times of need. "But what about the squirrels?" I asked. He gave me an odd look. "I mean, don't they need those for food? If you take their cones, what are they going to eat?" He continued to regard me curiously, then made a throaty sound somewhere between a gurgle and a hiss, and proceeded to grub around again in search of more hidden larders. "Maybe if you left a few here and tried somewhere else . . ." I ventured, but I think I'd lost his attention. He was mumbling to himself again. On the way back to my camper I couldn't help feeling sorry for those poor squirrels. I had some nuts in a jar inside the door and poured out a small pile at the base of an old ponderosa pine. I hope salted cashews are part of a squirrel's diet.

Follow signs for Route 58. In a few miles there's a brief stretch of gravel as we pass Davis Lake, a secluded body of water well known to fishermen for its trout, kokanee, and whitefish. Ahead are two more fine Cascade mountains, Diamond Peak and Mount Yoran.

At Route 58 we turn north (right) and then west (left) a few miles farther on to Crescent Lake. Here begins a particularly rigorous section of the drive. It's best to pause first at the store and check the condition of the Summit Lake "primitive road." As you're already reading and, I hope, using this book, you must have a backroads mentality and won't mind a bit of bumping and rocking to find places unknown to many travelers. If so, look for the sign to Summit Lake, turn right, and off we go.

The first few miles along the edge of Crescent Lake are delightful. With the exception of a scattering of weekend homes at the lower end, it's virtually unspoilt, and the little turquoise-blue pool at the western end is aptly named "Tranquil Cove." Nearby the road crosses the Pacific Crest Trail, which provides hiking to the eastern part of the Diamond Peak Wilderness. Then begins a narrow, winding climb of about 8 miles along an earth track. Take it slowly. (The "stop" signs refer to snowmobile trails, not the road.)

Summit Lake is one of my favorite Cascade Lakes. It's a couple of miles in length and maybe half a mile wide. A long line of low pine hills surrounds it, and at the far end, the craggy peak of Cowhorn Mountain is reflected in its placid waters. There's a small campsite here appealing more to fishermen and hikers than casual tourists. The Diamond Peak Wilderness lies directly to the north. Named after John Diamond, who scoured the Cascade crest in 1852 seeking a passable wagon route across the mountains, it is a magnificent region for solitary exploration and climbing. If even Summit Lake gets too crowded for you, there are literally dozens of smaller glacial lakes to be discovered up here.

Follow the steep descent toward Oakridge, along the line of an old pioneer trail, through more spectacular mountain scenery. Access roads lead up to the western section of the wilderness area, but again, obtain details and trail maps from a ranger station or the National Forest office in Bend.

Hill Creek Reservoir is a charming interlude before we reach Oakridge. Then it's the crowded highway until the Westfir turnoff and the last leg of our Cascades journey. Look for the Edward Hines Lumber Company bridge in Westfir, the tallest in Oregon and the only one with a separate covered walkway.

A gravel road through Landax travels northwest along the edge of Lookout Point Reservoir. Take it and enjoy the quiet drive to Lowell. Here, either join our original route through Fall Creek to Springfield or cross Lowell's attractive covered bridge back to 53 and on into Eugene.

Normally I avoid the big cities, but in the case of Eugene, I make an exception. The "jogging capital of the world" not only possesses a fine university campus with many exhibits open to the public but also a landscaped pedestrian mall in the downtown area and a very unusual Fifth Street Public Market at Fifth and High. This light, "woody" structure contains dozens of craft stalls displaying a high standard of ceramics, macramé, tie-dye clothes, leather goods, woolen creations, photographs, original sketches, and jewelry. It's a refreshing place to visit, and there's usually a lot of activity—craftspeople painting, weaving, stuffing toys, creating necklaces, and enthusiastically discussing their work with interested visitors.

Eugene's museums are exceptional. The cultures of more than a hundred Indian tribes are sensitively capsulized at the Butler Museum of American Indian Art at 1155 First Avenue (Tuesday through Sunday, 10–5), and for a glimpse of early settler life in the area, visit the Lane County Pioneer Museum on the fairgrounds at Thirteenth Street and Monroe. This spacious building contains room displays, weaving and quilt-making exhibits, a blacksmith's forge, a covered wagon, a dentist's office (today's high-speed drills are a welcome sight after a glimpse of this grisly array). On the side of an old pioneer wagon a list of suggested supplies for an 1880s "plains crossing" includes, "400 lb of bacon, $40; 2 bushels of beans, $3; 200 lb of sugar, $25; 50 lb of rice, $5; and 4 gold pans, $3."

At the time of my visit the museum had just assembled a fine old-time fiddling exhibition, complete with photographs of the weather-worn mountain men who developed the art. Their ancient fiddles were also on display, one made out of an old square can with the label still intact—"Tea Garden Drips Best Quality Syrup"—along with tape recordings of the raw, bouncing music. Below the photographs were extracts of interviews with the fiddlers. Here's John Hoerster of Wimer explaining the subtle way of "toning" a new fiddle: "When it was new it'd sound kind of squeaky. So I found out by pouring hot water in it—take a tea kettle full of water, slosh it around then dump it out—it'd play nice, deep, beautiful tones." The same man explains how fiddle design was really quite a flexible process. "See this whittled-out place? We was playing on the stage in a theatre in Portland and my bow kept catching—made me mad and I dropped my bow, grabbed my jacknife out, carved that out, grabbed my bow and went on fiddling. They got to laughing so much it disrupted the whole outfit!"

The museum made me think of that young man I met high up on the western slopes of the Cascades. He'd given up a good job to go and roam the mountains and live with nature. The museum reflected many of these same elements. The pioneers who struggled and scrambled over those mountains more than a hundred years ago learned much about the land, about living close to the earth and understanding its moods and rhythms—much that we have since forgotten. This museum is a good place to learn to remember. Alternatively, if you've got a few spare weeks and a good packhorse. . . .

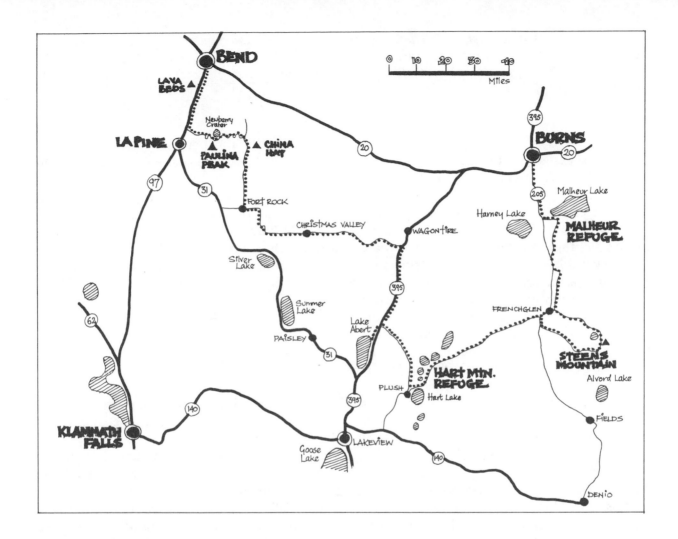

8. BURNS TO BEND

The Hard Way

Route 20 along the northern fringe of the east Oregon desert is the easy way between the two towns. Easy and dull. Instead, why not give yourself a few adventures in these high range lands, a vast area of endless sagebrush plains, lost forests, wild antelope and bighorn sheep, sand dunes, and strange volcanic remnants. It's a big land, full of stories of big men—the great cattle ranchers like Pete French, Bill Hanley, John Devine. It's also a quiet land, a land of peace, a land that cleans and refreshes the spirit.

"WOULD YOU PLEASE sign my register?" A small lady with a meticulously assembled bun of white hair sat erectly at the museum desk. She pointed to a thick leatherbound book lying open near the wall. "It's fifty cents to come in."

I slipped the coins into the dill-pickle jar with a hole in the top. The lady nodded, like a sparrow pecking. I smiled but she had turned back to her book. It was very quiet in the museum.

Burns itself is a quiet town. A few touches of the Old West days remain, the days of the great ranches and the cattle barons whose names are etched into the bedrock of the desert—Pete French, Bill Hanley, John Devine, Tom Overfelt, and John Todd. But most of the buildings are gone or have dwindled into stuccoed anonymity. There used to be a hitching rail along parts of Broadway. That's gone too. So are many of the raucous taverns, popular watering holes for the company-hungry ranchers and their vaquero hands. The historical society has put together a short self-conducted walking tour of what remains. Not far from the museum, at B Street and Buena Vista Avenue, is the Holland House. This modest mansion was once headquarters of the great Miller and Lux Pacific Livestock Company, which in 1900 was the largest conglomerate of ranchlands in the world, totaling millions of acres—bigger than Belgium!

But the museum is without doubt the highlight of the town. It's one of those potpourri places where almost every aspect of community life has its own proud exhibit. There are collections of old dresses, guns, quilts, Indian flints and beadwork, old hats, saddles, spinning wheels, a printing press, and an odd collection of glass jars covered in cigar rings. I spent a long time inspecting the "pioneer kitchen" display at the far end of the museum. The lady with the white bun warmed to me a little. She stood demurely, hands clasped in front of her pink dress, her head slightly to one side. "Do you like this room?" she asked. I found the collection of old candlemakers, waffle irons, muffin tins, and coffee pots fascinating, and told her so. "Yes, well, I did it, you know," she stated proudly. She seemed about to take my arm and lead me past all her favorite displays. Instead she modestly asked if I had seen the ball of yarn. I hadn't, and so followed her to a boulder-sized creation against the far wall. A little note explained, "Mrs. Henry Stewart began to wind this ball in February 1947. On December 26, 1966 it weighed 265 lb. and was 40 inches in diameter." I asked if this was some kind of local pastime, rolling balls of yarn. She gave me a curious look and her reply suggested that any housewife who had failed to roll her ball of yarn was hardly living up to her duties. We passed on to the next exhibit. This was the Hanley room, a replica of the dining room at William Hanley's ranch. The "Sage of Harney County" or "philosopher of the plains" owned 26,000 acres of high desert ranchland near Burns and was one of the most revered citizens in the county. Along with many other larger-than-life ranchers he projected a kind of self-effacing modesty that belied his enormous power and influence. "Heck," he is often quoted as saying, "I'm just a kid hazing a bunch of horses through the sagebrush."

Such men had one characteristic in common: they loved the Oregon desert. They loved its vast openness, its silence, its moods. This is Hanley's description of his first glimpse of the area around Burns after a long arduous trek overland from his father's farm in Idaho: "At last I saw the great Harney Valley that I had been headed for so long. It seemed a resting place for space and all that flies or roams seemed to have found it. I was afire with feeling for its bigness."

"As Bill Hanley says" was a well-known antecedent to witty and pungent statements in newspapers and barroom conversations. He was a man of his time, a man who deeply felt and understood his environment: "On the road again this morning. Off in the big light for the ranches. It's harmony, where the mountains meet the valley floor. Old fellow [God] didn't hold out much on you when he wrote that book. It's all there if you can read it. Feelin' fine."

I left Burns with Hanley's words in my mind . . . "off in the big light." South on 205 toward the Malheur Refuge the sagebrush plains begin to ease themselves out languorously toward a hazy horizon. The fir-dotted hills of the Ochoco National Forest are soon left behind. Up a steep craglike escarpment, and down the other side onto a billiard-table landscape. Already I could feel that wonderful exhilaration of nothingness, that sense of endless space going on forever. In the far distance were low mountain ridges and beyond them more and more desert. All the way through Nevada, all down the eastern edge of California, down, down, deep into Mexico, as far as the sweltering jungles of the Yucatán. Desert all the way, crossed by a few sinuous tracks and highways—no cities, no suburbs, no smog, no traffic jams. Nobody and nothing. Just the wind in the sagebrush, the great heat of the day, the chill at night, and the occasional eagle scouring the land for a morsel to fill its empty belly.

If you have a tendency to blink excessively you may miss the entrance to the famous Malheur National Wildlife Refuge. The sign is as understated as the area itself. A paved road leads out across the plain toward the refuge headquarters, a tiny huddle of buildings in a willow oasis by the edge of Malheur Lake. It says "lake" on most maps and is normally shown in a brilliant blue color but in fact it's a very spasmodic feature, appearing briefly during wet seasons, then vanishing for months. A few marshy sections and fields of bright-orange grasses usually mark its existence.

There's an exhibit here displaying some of the more than 260 species of birds found on the refuge. (To see the wide range of species, come in the March-to-mid-May period or in the fall.) Regarding visitors in silent scorn are a number of stuffed hawks and eagles. The owls, particularly the great horned owl, seem a little more quizzical, and the ducks, geese, herons, and egrets—even the great long-billed pelican—sit or perch with serene dignity in their white display cases. I looked at the visitors' book just inside the door. There were names from every state of the union, numerous

Scandinavians, Italians, Australians, Canadians, and Japanese, but hardly any Oregonians. At the information desk I asked a charming warden why so few natives found the refuge interesting. She had been equally perplexed but had concluded that it was just "too close to home." Then I asked for details on the desert road from Frenchglen to Plush. It starts a few miles to the south at the tip of the refuge and traverses, so I had been told, some of the bleakest high desert in eastern Oregon. I was very anxious to travel it. Ironically, no one seemed to know anything about it. One persistent warden even tried to persuade me the map was inaccurate and no such road existed. "Why not take . . .," he began, but I was adamant. In fact, I was now even more determined to cross that stretch of desert no one seemed to know. The three staff members apologized for not being able to give more details. They were all Oregonians! Maybe it was too close to home.

There's a self-guided auto-tour pamphlet available at the headquarters. It provides useful background and insights into the 42-mile-long journey south through the refuge, which was established by President Theodore Roosevelt in 1908. The preliminary advice is worth taking:

> Go slowly. Stop, turn off your engine and get out of your car; free yourself from that machine. Listen to the refuge sounds . . . the birds, water, wind, leaves, rustling grasses, insects; REALLY LISTEN! Watch the horizon, look for movements near water, smell the sage. "Feel" the weather. It's time to become a part of your world.

For most of the way the track is comfortable. In two spots, though, it seemed my delicate fillings would be lost as I washboarded from side to side, but then my shocks had been in need of replacement for weeks. Remember, however, that this is no pseudo–safari trail. The animals have not been trained to pose elegantly for camera-happy tourists. This is a wild land. The place is full of antelopes, mule deer, porcupines, raccoons, coyotes, and beavers, but they're cautious creatures and soon head for the sagebrush if their privacy is disturbed. The birds, particularly the cranes, can be tantalizing. On one occasion I set up the camera for what was to be a classic study. Then without warning the cranes started flapping and dancing around and finally took off just as I pressed the button. As a result I became the proud possessor of a magnificent picture of an empty pond with just a suggestion of wingtips and feet in the top right-hand corner.

A marsh hawk caused me equal exasperation. I trailed it slowly along the edge of a ditch. It would perch on a branch or a fence post, prune itself, and watch me out of the corner of its eye as I nearly crawled along the track. It would even seem to brace itself proudly for a portrait and then, as soon as I focused the camera, it would leap into flight and skim low over the reeds to the next resting point 20 or 30 yards farther on. I thought it might eventually tire of the game or at least have the courtesy to allow me one successful shot. Not a chance.

Except for a brief point at Buena Vista station, where the refuge road joins Route 205, it's a quiet track along the Blitzen River, past marshes, ponds, and recent lava flows. Hidden in the reeds at marker 11 is the grave of Nettie McLaughlin, one of the early pioneer wives in this arduous land, who died, exhausted, at the age of thirty-five. Way out in the distance, at the southern rim of the desert, is Steens Mountain, a fascinating environment we'll explore later.

Pause briefly at Buena Vista and climb the overlook. Here you can perch among the rocky crags and watch the birdlife in the marshes hundreds of feet below. Listen for the odd sound of the sandhill cranes, the throaty cry of the great blue heron, and the unmistakable parade-ground cacophony of the trumpeter swans. On a warm afternoon, time passes slowly up here.

The refuge road again joins 205 at Frenchglen, a dusty huddle of buildings at a junction. The town was named for the King of the Cattle Ranchers, Peter French, and his backer, his father-in-law, Dr. Hugh Glenn. French's story is typical of those of others like him who settled in this region. He left California and reached Oregon in 1872 with his cattle and immediately began building an empire of over 130,000 acres. Bill Hanley described him as "a little man, all power and control . . . an immaculate dresser." One of his hands said of him that "he's not afraid of nobody, of nothing . . . never saw such eyes—brilliant, wrap right around your head . . . smartest man in the country . . . couldn't nobody look in Pete's eyes for long." He gained an early reputation as a fearless Indian fighter from skirmishes with the Paiutes. Many of the smaller ranchers built fortlike houses for defensive purposes, but not French. He had lumber hauled 150 miles by mule train from the Blue Mountains and erected his huge "White House," control center of the vast "P" ranch. John Devine, one of French's competitors, was determined not to be outdone and built his own version of a White House on his Alvord ranch, at the other side of Steens Mountain. For a while it was neck and neck between the two empire-makers. Then Devine, a flamboyant extrovert who loved gambling on horses, overreached himself financially and had to sell out to the burgeoning Miller and Lux organization. When Dr. Hugh Glenn, French's partner, was murdered by his ex-bookkeeper, French gained control of the whole corporation and was finally established as the largest landowner in the region.

This was the great era of the cattle-ranch aristocracy. The barons would gather at each other's palatial mansions or meet during the drives, at Wagontire. Life began to take on the spirit and pace of the old days in Mexican California. Colorful vaqueros were brought from the south to manage the cattle. Horse races and marksmanship competitions filled the days of the ranchers. Hundreds of thousands of dollars were gambled away on the desert race tracks and over the ornately carved card tables shipped "around the Horn" from France.

Then, quite suddenly, things began to go wrong. In 1879 there was a devastating drought that bankrupted many of the small ranch owners, followed by long freezing winters in 1880 and 1884 that decimated the herds. During the same period, sheep farmers and homesteaders began moving into the range lands. The barons were threatened and resisted brutally. Homesteaders vanished without trace. Range wars broke out with the sheep farmers. There was talk of railroads and new towns. Bill Hanley likened the tensions to a cattle stampede: "Everyone got under the atmosphere of uneasiness.

Steens Mountain

Something had to happen—something did happen—feuds blazed out into gunfire—the gun days were in. No man at breakfast knew but what he might be stretched out in six feet of earth by dinnertime."

Finally in 1897 a disgruntled homesteader, Edward L. Oliver, shot and killed French as he was out inspecting fences. The trial was a confusing affair, and Oliver was finally acquitted by a jury that understood all too well the desperation of the lonely homesteader against the power of the barons. After that it was merely a matter of time before many of the great ranches were fragmented and their creators relegated to the history books.

The 180,000-acre Malheur refuge contains much of French's "P" ranch, and the road leading from the refuge to Frenchglen passes a few scattered remnants of buildings. Over to the east near Diamond is his famous round barn, now repaired, with the original interior still intact. To many residents of the area, French's spirit still seems very much alive. As one old man told me at Frenchglen, between long silences and spits of tobacco juice, "Fella like that don't die. He'll be 'round here forever, I reckon. Y'can't kill a man's spirit—not a man like Peter French."

Malena Konek, who runs the Frenchglen Hotel, seems to agree. "Most of our guests come here to get a feel for the old ranching days. Many of them know much more about Peter French, John Devine, and all the others than any of the locals. They were fascinating characters." Whether you're interested in the area's history or not, the hotel is an excellent place to spend a day or two. There's no TV, no extraneous distractions—just wide, soft beds and huge platters of home-cooked food served family-style in the dining room overlooking the refuge. It's also a convenient base for exploring Steens Mountain—which we now proceed to do.

I first heard about Steens Mountain a few years ago when I was living in California. At one of those poolside gatherings all too familiar to residents in the southern part of the state, I listened enraptured as a Hemingway-type character, grey beard and ice-blue eyes, told us tales of a lone mountain deep in the heart of the Oregon wilderness where one could swim in lakes surrounded by whispering aspens, watch bobcats and mountain lions stalking their prey through alpine flowers, and stand in the midst of a roaring thunderstorm while, thousands of feet below, the parched desert baked in 100-degree heat. I was enthralled but didn't really believe him, until I arrived at Frenchglen and set out on the 60-mile loop to the 9,600-foot summit of that incredible geological phenomenon. To my delight, it was just as he had described.

The western slope from the desert is a steady climb through four distinct vegetation belts—sagebrush (up to 5,500 feet); juniper (up to 6,500 feet); aspen (up to 8,000 feet) and finally the delicate alpine belt, dotted with tiny lakes and thousands of wildflowers. This is an enchanted landscape of green glaciated valleys, cool breezes, and tingling air. But watch for those storms. They come quickly and can be violent. East Rim, with its majestic panoramas over the Alvord desert, is notoriously lightning-prone.

Take your time on this journey. To rush is to waste what the mountain offers—a sense of perspective, a view across a world that seems endless, and an understanding of the subtle balance of landscape, climate, and all the living things on its slopes. Find a secluded place at the Kiger Gorge or Little Blitzen overlook and watch the signs of life in these high valleys. It's like peering into a lost world—like going back through time to an age before man, when the earth belonged to the animals. Watch for the bighorn sheep, antelope, mule deer, and even mountain lions. Timid chukar partridges scutter from rocky hideout to thick brush; coyotes fox-trot daintily alongside a narrow stream bed, then crouch suddenly as a likely meal looms up. Golden eagles spiral down the currents from their rocky aeries thousands of feet above the desert floor.

For those who fall in love with this strange and beautiful mountain there are primitive camping places, but remember to bring warm clothing. In the evenings the temperature drops faster than the sun. For those who prefer the comfort of desert lodgings, the loop drive from Frenchglen can easily be accomplished in a day without rushing. Enjoy. There are few parts of this country where one can find solitude in such extraordinary surroundings.

Back in Frenchglen (it's advisable to return here and fill up with gas and water) we begin a rather arduous part of the journey—the route to Plush and the Hart Mountain Antelope Refuge. If you found the Steens Mountain road hazardous, it may be best to continue south along the 205 to Denio, take the 140 west to the 395, and rejoin this route north of Lake Albert. Even this way has its gravel sections, but for the most part it's a smoother drive than the cross-desert route. If you're unsure what to do, read on a little and then see how you feel.

Check first on road conditions with one of the Stott family. They run the post office at Frenchglen. Son Doug also owns the nearby shack that is encrusted with elkhorns, cartwheels, horseshoes, bells, skulls, branding irons, and old cooking pots. Inside it's even more chaotic, but he won't sell any of it. However, if you're interested in one of his hand-tied fishing flies, that's a different matter. He's an avid enthusiast and dispenser of valuable information on the vagaries of angling.

Between June and November the 65 miles of track are normally passable unless there's been an unusually heavy rainstorm. Most of it is comfortable gravel-and-earth road driving, but there's one stretch, about 15 miles in, that needs careful negotiation. It's about 7 miles long, so just go slow, and watch for tire-tearing rocks. Again, fill up with gas, water, and anything else you might need at Frenchglen. There's a long journey ahead, all the way to Christmas Valley.

The road begins behind the hotel and climbs abruptly to almost 5,000 feet before leveling out on the great Harney plateau. The turnoff to Plush is clearly marked about 7 miles south of Frenchglen. Take it, grit your teeth, and go!

This is true high desert, flat, dry, and endless. I once heard an exasperated traveler remark, "But there's nothing here!" Well, that's the desert. Some people loathe its endless nothingness. To me, that "nothingness" makes the desert an intensely personal landscape. It's a place where the spirit of the land and one's own spirit are easily linked. One can almost become the desert—feel the dryness of the earth, the heat razing the brittle scrub covering, the night ice cracking rocks and the sound echoing endlessly across that still land. The desert will reflect your mood. It can be friendly or threatening, monotonously boring or full of interest, dull or sparkling. The desert is whatever you wish it to be. The desert is, quite simply, you.

For mile after mile the track crosses the flat sagebrush. Nothing moves out here. There's no sign of any other vehicle ahead or behind. You have the world to yourself. Again, don't hurry. Allow three hours for the drive to Plush. Stop the car occasionally, stroll away from the track, and just listen to the land. The panorama is immense. I have stood and watched five simultaneous climatic occurrences: on the mountain peaks of the Hart Mountain Antelope Refuge snow was falling, to the north a dry desert thunderstorm boomed and flashed, to the south a rainstorm dragged long tentacles of cloud through the sagebrush like a great grey jellyfish, at the side a dust storm was raging, spiraling sand hundreds of feet into the air, and behind me Steens Mountain was basking in bright sunshine beneath azure-blue skies. All this I could see just by standing in one place and turning full circle. One can have similar experiences when flying in a small plane, but it was the first time I had seen such a range of weather from the ground.

Shortly after negotiating the bad stretch (there are plans to "improve" the road, but no one seems very enthusiastic about the project), we enter the Hart Mountain National Antelope Refuge, established in 1936 by the other President Roosevelt. At the headquarters there's usually someone who can tell you how likely you are to get a glimpse of pronghorn antelope, bighorn sheep, or mule deer from the road. Also, notice the odd array of pickled snakes, toads, and lizards, all local species, behind the warden's desk.

Now comes the part of the journey I enjoy most. Geologically Hart Mountain is a massive fault-block ridge, and a few miles west of the headquarters the rolling desert ends abruptly in a terrifying ridge escarpment on its western edge. The track plunges over the crest and contorts its way down the broken cliffs. Below, far below, stretches a strange landscape of dunes, lakes, and white flats. It could be the surface of an alien planet. After the miles of high barren plateau, this change of scene seems unreal, a dream world full of beiges and blues. Put the car in low gear and drift slowly down into the valley. One almost expects to find lumbering creatures of prehistoric dimensions and appearance roaming alongside the necklace of lakes and ponds. Those black winged forms could just as easily be pterodactyls as eagles. Those huddled shapes by the lake's edge could be brontosaurs. As reality slowly replaces the dream, they in fact turn out to be cows or, if one is unusually lucky, antelopes pausing to refresh themselves.

The track follows the base of the towering basalt cliffs, past Hart Lake and into the parched hamlet of Plush. There's a single store, a church, and, surprisingly, a tiny landscaped park at the southern end of main street. Years ago when this was sheep country and Basque shepherds roamed the hills, the cottage across from the store was Mrs. Basta's restaurant, a place famous for its family-style multi-course dinners. Today, little remains of that era. The sheep have "gone west" to the

Cascades and coastal ranges, and we shall have to wait until California before enjoying one of those gargantuan Basque dinners (see Chapter 10, "The Mount Shasta Loop").

The 35 miles of gravel road north from Plush to Route 395 at Hogback Summit is a considerable improvement on the Hart Mountain route and leads again into the high sagebrush desert. I love this drive. From the Coyote Hills to the south, the land slopes gently down toward Wilson Butte. It's a silent, peaceful road. Doe-eyed cows take the place of wildlife.

At 395 make a short detour south to turquoise-green Lake Abert and the Abert Rim. Discovered by John Frémont and his party in 1843, the 19-mile long, 2,000-foot-high fault is one of the largest in the world. The profile is similar to the great cliffs at the edge of the Hart Mountain Refuge, but its proximity to that solitary surface of beautiful blue water makes it singularly impressive. There are even small secluded beaches at the edge of the lake for the weary.

Return along 395 to the turnoff to Christmas Valley, approximately 35 miles north of Lake Abert. Here we begin another long stretch of desert driving on a good gravel road across relatively flat terrain to Christmas Valley. About two-thirds of the way along, a track leads off north to Fossil Lake, site of some extraordinary fossil discoveries a few years back, and the odd "Lost Forest." This tiny remnant of the once pine-covered shores of an ancient lake can be seen from the dunes around Fossil Lake. It's an unusual anachronism in this bleached, dry wilderness. As is Christmas Valley itself. This scattered community, sitting in the middle of a scrub plain, was—and, for all I know, may one day be again—Oregon's answer to Palm Springs. There aren't too many homes here yet, but the town boasts all the accouterments of a desert resort—golf course, lake, clubhouse, Western-style stores, and even a gift shop. It was a cold day when I first came here. A biting wind blew from the west, sending tumbleweed cartwheeling across the desert and stinging sand into my eyes. Inside was a huge fire in an enormous fireplace. Groups of elderly residents, smartly dressed and manicured, sat chatting quietly. Muzak played softly in the background. Ice slowly melted in cocktail glasses. Outside two geese by the lake tried hard to pretend it was summer but obviously wished they had flown south weeks ago. Nothing really seemed to be happening. Maybe nothing much does happen in this odd little place. I walked outside into the howling wind and felt in contact with the world again.

North of the town a gravel track leads to "Crack-in-the-Ground." Here on the fringe of an extensive lava flow is a claustrophobic canyon varying in width from 10 to 20 feet with a depth of 70 feet in places. It looks like the beginning of some catastrophic geological occurrence that hasn't yet occurred. It's worth the 8-mile trip, though, especially if you own a good camera.

Twenty or so miles west of Christmas Valley is the dramatic Fort Rock State Monument, a prominent feature in this part of the desert. The ring of "tuff" rock is the remnant of a 500-foot-high wall of volcanic debris that collected around an active vent about 12,000 years ago. At that time most of this part of the desert was covered by lakes. Wave action helped create the vertical wall of the "fort," and wave erosion is very evident on the high northern wall. Inside the amphitheater, sections of the volcanic walls still look molten, and rockbound air bubbles, some large enough to form

Fort Rock

man-sized caves, resemble the results of a ferocious bombardment. The "fort" is well named and was used by early settlers during Indian raids. The Indians themselves also used the rock for shelter, as evidenced by the discovery in 1938 of a virtual storeload of sagebrush sandals in a secluded part of the amphitheater. Subsequent carbon dating suggests that they were more than nine thousand years old.

Part of the land for the monument was given to the state by another one of the region's "desert sages," Reuben A. Long, who died recently after a tumultuous lifetime as horsebreeder, cattle rancher, trapper, surveyor, pool-hall owner, and moviemaker (to mention just a few of this unusual man's accomplishments). He was truly a legend in his own time, and his quotations, full of worldly wisdom, were household sayings for years before he died. There's a plaque at the base of Fort Rock listing a few of his more famous ones.

A few miles to the west of Fort Rock is "Hole in the Ground," an almost perfectly circular depression in the desert, a mile across and over 300 feet deep. While romantics conjecture that this is a splendid example of a meteorite crater, most scientists consider it to be the result of the area's virile volcanic activity and similar in origin to the "Big Hole" located nearby on the south side of Route 31.

At Fort Rock a choice must be made. We're going on to Newberry Crater and, as usual, there's a hard way and an easy way. The easy way via Routes 31 and 97 is rather dull. Much of the road is arrow-straight through dense groves of pine trees, and the town of La Pine provides an all too immediate transition to the garish world of the highway. However, if you've had enough backroads for one journey or need gas urgently, that's your route. We'll meet you at Paulina Lake road off 97 a few miles north of La Pine.

Meanwhile, we continue north past Fort Rock to South Ice Cave on the southern flank of Newberry Crater. This interesting creation, the result of a natural "tunnel" through a large lava flow, is one of many similar features in the volcanic region surrounding the crater. The bones of extinct animals have been found here, but exploration should be undertaken carefully, as the floor is often solid ice and the place is invariably wet. Arnold Cave, 20 miles to the north, is also an impressive ice collector. Before refrigerators, it provided a reliable supply of high-quality ice for the citizens of nearby Bend.

Beyond South Ice Cave, near China Hat Mountain, an adequate gravel-and-earth road climbs the east flank of Newberry Crater up through the pines to East Lake and Paulina Lake, two of the most superbly situated lakes in Oregon. Be warned, though, the crater is not altogether undiscovered territory, and campsites or secluded picnic spots may be rather hard to find during the summer months. But it's still worth the journey, especially if the weather is clear.

Take the challenging 4-mile drive up Paulina Peak, and you'll be rewarded with incredible vistas in all directions. The "peak" is actually a modest remnant of Mount Newberry, a 10,000-foot volcanic cone that towered higher than many of the Cascade peaks. But the mountain was flawed. Cracks and fissures developed in its lower slopes and siphoned off the fresh lava from its core. The surrounding landscape of more than two hundred cones and buttes resulted from these geological weaknesses. Lava no longer reached the mountain peak itself, and it became a brittle, worn-out shell. Around ten thousand years ago the top of the mountain collapsed, leaving a caldera almost 5 miles wide. The impact regenerated lava flows within the concave bowl. Streams of black volcanic glass, obsidian, scores of feet thick, poured into the caldera. A series of smaller volcanic cones began to build up again, and venting hot springs created the two lakes that still exist today. The whole story is almost self-explanatory when you stand on the edge of the peak looking into the heart of the mountain.

Again, allow time to enjoy some of the unique features of this area. Stroll on the slopes of the obsidian flow, watch the hot geysers by East Lake, boat on one of the lakes, or rest near vigorous Paulina Creek Falls. If it's Saturday night and you enjoy the occasional splurge, try a prime-rib dinner at the delightful Paulina Lake Lodge. If nothing else, celebrate the fact that you successfully negotiated almost 150 miles of desert track without mishap. If there were mishaps, celebrate your arrival here all the same and rehearse tall tales for the neighbors at home. If you are truly desperate for an excuse, remember that the Forest Service has noted that "future volcanic activity is possible in the region," and celebrate the crater's docility.

There's one last place to explore before reaching the brash commercial strips of Bend. Just off 97, a few miles south of the town, is the Lava Lands Visitors' Center. This popular attraction, immediately below a high black cone of volcanic cinder known as Lava Butte, presents an excellent diorama display of the region's geological and pioneer history. If you've never experienced an actual earthquake, try the simulated version here. Also there are interesting side trips to the Lava Cast Forest and the baronial halls of the Lava River Cave, where one can explore a mile-long tunnel with hand-held kerosene lamps.

I met Joe Mead at the visitors' center. He was conducting tours along the various interpretative trails around the base of the butte. His commentary was encyclopedic and he answered every question with great precision and depth. I noticed he was accompanied by a large black dog, but it wasn't until I was back in the center, watching Joe point out routes on a specially notated map, that I realized the young man was totally blind. We chatted for a while. It had taken one brief year from the onset of blindness for him to master all the intricate details of the Lava Lands geology and memorize every twist and turn of the interpretative trails. "I always wanted to work with the Forest Service and I decided that blindness wasn't going to stop me. So, here I am!"

Earlier on I talked about the big men of this region—the great cattle barons whose endurance, foresight, and sheer determination made this desolate land work for them. Their spirits are reflected in the scale and power of the desert. But the era of big men didn't end with the barons. There are still such men today in the region, and Joe Mead is one of them.

CALIFORNIA

9. THE REDDING–EUREKA LOOP
Into the Heart of Lumber Country

We journey from the hot dry fields of the Central Valley high through the coastal ranges to the Oregon-like beaches around Trinidad, and then back again, through the old northern gold-mining region. We travel along some of the most dramatic backroads in the state. We visit old mining camps, lumber towns, a perfectly preserved Victorian village, Eureka's old town, and a Chinese joss Temple. We pass along surf-sprayed beaches, then twist and wind through the redwoods high into the Klamath and Salmon river wilderness. We meet an old miner, Indians, a store owner whose grandfather was a blacksmith on the Old Oregon Trail, and a lovely girl at a mountain retreat. It's a backroad journey full of variety and excitement, peppered with a few driving thrills!

"SURE IT LOOKS quiet now. There's nothin' left. Even the flume's gone and that was quite a creation, y'know—more'n thousand feet long. Chinese built it. We had hundreds of 'em in the gold days." The old man, a long-time resident of the mining community of Igo, waved a rusty pair of gardening shears as he talked. He was standing in the middle of a rhododendron bush, wearing a sweat-stained shirt and an ancient pith helmet. "They were quite a bunch," he continued. "They knew if they got outa line there'd be all hell to pay 'cause no one liked 'em. Shootin' a Chinese was like shootin' a jackrabbit. No one thought much about it. I dunno why, maybe 'cause they kept to themselves too much and talked funny. Who knows. One thing I learned, though, was to mind your own business. The more you stuck your nose into other people's business, the more likely you were to get it blasted off. We lost a lot of fellas that way. Too damn curious for their own good."

I was in the center of the village, which consisted of a few cottages, a store, and a post office. I had left Redding, traveling west on Route 299, turned south on Lower Springs Road, and, after a left and a right turn, found myself on Route A16 passing through an old gold-mining area. Prior to the frantic days of the 1870s the place was known as Piety Hill because of the extreme religious convictions of its inhabitants. Then in 1869 the Hardscrabble Mining Company decided it needed to dredge the townsite, so Piety Hill vanished overnight, to be replaced by the community of Igo. (There are numerous tales about the origins of its name and that of its brother community, Ono. No one seems to agree which one is true, and they're all equally outlandish.) In typical gold-country fashion, the Chinese tended to move in as the Americans pulled out. They were content to rework the placer diggings and tailings but as a result often discovered new sources of ore, much to the chagrin of previous prospectors. When this happened, trouble began. "Oh yessir," my pith-helmeted informant

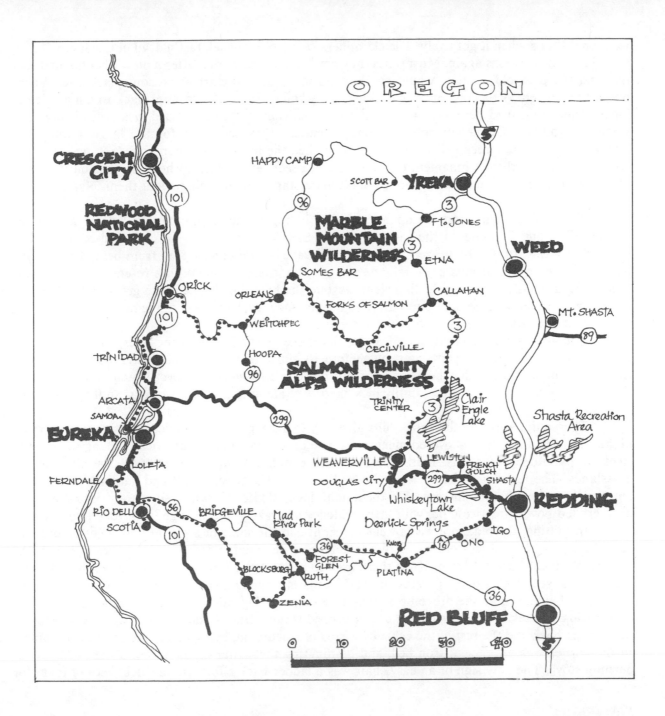

went on, "that's when it got lively. The old miners would scurry back fast'n devil outa heaven and try to claim their workings again. Most times they got 'em back too, often after a bit of shootin' and such like and the poor old Chinese would just have to move on and start again someplace else. Wasn't much fun for 'em, I reckon. But they kept goin', y'know. Some of 'em went back to China rich as kings. Them that died here were later sent back too. They had to be buried in a special way; then when the folks in China got enough money together, they sent over for the body. Family was important for them, I reckon." He paused and studied the bush he was clipping. "Strange ain't it. I seen thousands of them Chinamen. I seen 'em here, I seen 'em in Texas when I worked on the rigs, I seen 'em all over the place. But y'know, I don't understand a damn thing about them. Not one damn thing."

This is fine rolling country up here, similar in appearance to the mother-lode region around Nevada City and Sonoma on the east side of the San Joaquin Valley. Oak-covered hills undulate endlessly southward. Cattle graze in tiny secluded valleys. Old cabins peep from behind manzanita bushes. Some groups of hills are totally devoid of trees, their gentle outlines resembling green sand dunes. Occasionally there are fleeting views beyond the hills. Far below is the great valley itself—a broad swath of hazy beiges and blues. Beyond are the snow-capped peaks of the northern Sierras and to the west the eroded crests of the coastal range.

The air is sweet-smelling here. Breezes rustle the drying leaves on the trees, and the bleached grasses wave like flowing white hair, old before its time. In the scorching afternoons of summer there's welcome shade under the oaks. Squirrels move in darting rushes, ever watchful, ever hungry. Deer, usually in family groups, daintily pick their way along faintly worn tracks, sniffing, listening, nibbling.

Then quite abruptly the gentle hills give way to a steeper, more eroded landscape as we move higher into the dark, scrub-covered mountains. The narrow road twists erratically along the edge of steep drops into dry canyons. Brittle bushes, with bunches of sharp leaves, take the place of the grasslands. The last few miles to Route 36 at Platina test a driver's skill and patience as the road zigzags around every fold and crease in the mountainous slopes. The views southward into a series of deep eroded bowls are awesome, with little evidence of grazing and no sign of anyone living here.

In Platina, the old store was a welcome sight and the smile of a girl in a long cotton dress as refreshing as a glass of ice-cold water. We talked about the mining days in this eastern corner of the Trinity National Forest. "Up at Knob there used to be a lot of mining. You should talk to old Perry McGhee, he still does a bit of prospecting and knows more than anybody else 'round here about the old days." I followed as she drove up a track to an ancient log cabin perched on a piece of flatland overlooking a creek. Perry wasn't home, so I peeped through the window. There was a workshop of sorts in the back and the rest of the cabin consisted of a bedroom, living room, and kitchen combined. In the corner was an ancient iron bed, and dominating the center of the room, a big black wood-burning stove. The only sign of an easy chair was a ladder-back affair with a thick piece of foam for a cushion. On the wall hung two yellowed Coca-Cola posters featuring large-bosomed girls with puckered lips. Everything was coated in a thin, even covering of dust, as if the place had been unused for a long time. It was like looking at some early photograph, all greys and slightly diffused.

"He must be away again," the girl explained, still smiling brightly. "Why not come and see our place?" I agreed and followed her again, up more bumpy track to a large cinder-block building on top of a hill with wide views of forested valleys and ridges. To call the place a commune would be misleading. A group of evangelistic Seventh-Day Adventists had established this "Green Mountain Retreat" both as a school for young children and as a place for people to come for counseling and friendship. In the main room, six children sat in a circle as a girl in her early twenties read to them. A fire blazed vigorously in a baronial-sized stone fireplace. Windows looked out over the lawn and across to the wooded hills beyond. In the kitchen a group of women prepared a tempting lunch of thick split-pea soup and buttermilk pancakes. All around were large jars filled with beans, pastas, and grains. There was no sign of meat—not even a little ham in the split-pea soup. Everyone looked very happy—"radiant" might be a more appropriate word. The room was filled with smiles and laughter.

The children followed me around as I was shown all the various work areas, the engineering shop, the print shop, and the offices where the group's published literature was packaged and distributed. I read some of the pamphlets. They referred to the more familiar problems of modern-day life—drugs, alcohol, pornography, and rising crime—as signs of a decaying society. Their solutions included a return to a simpler life, a reaffirmation of such basic values as cooperation, sharing, and compassion through mutual love. I looked again at those clear open faces. A few weeks before one of the girls had been a hooker in San Francisco and another a hopeless alcoholic; a third had run away from home, confused and lost. And here they all were, working together, helping one another, sharing their lives, gaining strength to live independently in the world again.

I left the little enclave on the hillside and wandered down to the ranger station at Harrison Gulch on Route 53. Here I was shown a display of old photographs depicting activities in the Midas Mine around Knob in the 1890s. The rangers will provide details on routes into the hills around the mine to such places as the Hall City Cave and the still-operative Deer Lick Springs, where hardy travelers who brave the rather bumpy 13-mile road can bathe in mineral waters long renowned for their curative properties.

At Knob a charming elderly lady regaled me with tales of the old mining days when the precariously steep main street, which now provides access to a few cabins, was lined with hotels and saloons. She pointed out the tall stone chimney used as a vent for the ore furnaces. "It's hard to believe, but they took out almost $5 million of gold from the creek between 1894 and 1914," she told me and then nodded knowingly. "There's plenty more left there, I'm sure of it. I've still got claims here and I'm keeping them, too." She pointed to a dry stream bed. "That's the old Sunday Gulch. The fellows who worked for the big mining operations 'round here—and they were big, some of 'em

Zenia Store

had tunnels more'n fifteen hundred feet in—well, they would pocket bits of ore whenever they could and sneak 'em out. To make it look legal they'd go working their own claims on Sundays—the day off, y'know—and they'd pan out all this gold like they'd just found it in the creek. Worked well for a bit, then word got around that Sunday Gulch was a rich pannin' place because they'd been seedin' all that gold in it and it got pretty hectic here for a while, I can tell you."

This small area at the eastern fringe of the National Forest seems full of interesting people, and one comes across the most unexpected places. Just past the Harrison Gulch cemetery, for example, up a rough forest road, I found a trailer in the process of being converted into the Mt. Brook Holiness Church. A lopsided sign hung from a branch: "Non-Denominational Services 11 a.m. Sunday. All Welcome. Sermon by Rev. Williamson." A young woman with a knee-high boy told me about the church. She pointed to the huddle of trailers and cabins in the vicinity. "We're all family," she said. "Dad's the preacher. He's out cuttin' wood right now. He puts on a lovely service. It's not what you might call 'structured,' he just lets it go naturally. I suppose you'd call him pentecostal—there's some speakin' in tongues an' suchlike but it's not crazy like some of the places. It all comes natural to him. You'd like it, I think. Most folks around here do." She gazed at the trailers, the piles of logs, old cars, a rusty bicycle, and then back at the tiny church with its white wooden cross nailed above the door. "I'm a city girl myself. Hardly ever been to the country till a year back when we moved here. Now I wouldn't want to be anywhere else." We smiled and she wished me a cheerful "God be with you" as I drove away.

For backroad explorers, the most dramatic route linking Route 36 with Ruth Reservoir to the west is along the old mountain road south of Wildwood. It's unpaved for most of the way and rather rough in the central portion near Horsehead Ridge, but it provides courageous users with a series of unparalleled vistas of the coastal ranges and a sense of real mountain backcountry. However, I should emphasize that it's a hard, slow drive and rather wearing on a normal car. Consult first with the rangers at the Harrison Gulch Station, and if you have any misgivings, take the scenic and far easier drive to the reservoir via Forest Glen. At the Mad River turnoff there's another choice to be made. If you're enjoying the 36 route you may wish to continue following this through Bridgeville to Route 101. Alternatively, if you missed the more direct cross-mountain route from Wildwood, you may now be ready to explore some of the finest backcountry the coastal range has to offer. In which case follow the Mad River Valley south beneath the towering South Fork Mountain ridge to Ruth Reservoir and then take the Zenia–Alderpoint road on the reservoir's west side. An abrupt zigzagging climb up through the pine forests precedes the long descent into quiet Hettenshaw Valley, with its cozy ranches rimmed by mountain ranges. At the far side is a prominent rock standing high above the valley floor. Head straight for this, then turn left at its base and travel south through a wonderland of deep woods, ferny dells, and occasional glimpses of receding mountain ranges—broad brush strokes of mauves and purples on a sky-blue canvas.

Pause at the Zenia store and look out over the deep-green valleys beyond. On most maps the coastal ranges seem a rather insignificant barrier between the central valley and the Pacific Ocean. From this vantage point, however, they can be seen for what they truly are—a gloriously carved continuum of space, majestic yet intimate, intimidating yet beckoning.

Blanche and Henry Rumley see the view every day from their store here on the hilltop. They arrived in 1943 from the southern part of the state, noticed the place was for sale, and decided to buy it on the spot. Since then they've hardly moved from their aerie. "Why should we go anywhere else? We can see all we need to see from here," Henry told me with a sweep of his arm. Inside the store Blanche was behind the post-office counter reading a magazine. Shelves of books filled one wall. "That's our local library," said Henry. "Anybody wants a book just comes up here." Of course, "coming up" to the store can be quite an arduous business for local residents, many of whom live hidden in the forests or on ranches, miles away down rough dirt roads. So invariably a visit here is a social occasion, time for a chat around the stove and a few beers before the long haul back. While I was there a rather disgruntled local hunter strode in complaining about the absence of bears in the mountains. Outside in his truck, four impatient dogs yapped and howled as he and Henry traded bear stories for the better part of an hour. Blanche had fallen asleep behind the post-office counter. Somewhere a clock ticked slowly.

Leaving the store we descend through woods and meadows to Dobbyn Creek, following the signs toward Alderpoint until the Blocksburg turnoff. Here we travel north, winding along the erratic course of a turbulent stream and then slowly climb up into a delightful hillside village of steep-roofed houses clustered around a white-steepled church and a rather bowed schoolhouse. Georgette Ripple, the postmistress, smiled sadly when we talked about the history of Blocksburg. "Most of it's gone, the old buildings have burned down over the years. In the late 1800s, though, it was quite a lively place. There were three hotels then. All we have left now is Boot Hill." She pointed across the road at the cemetery. "That was for people killed in barroom brawls and suchlike. There's quite a few up there, so I guess the place was pretty active at one time. Now it's quiet most of the year, 'cept, of course, when we put on one of our Home-Made Ice Cream Day Celebrations. That really brings 'em in from all over. Last year we had more than twenty-five hundred folks come here!"

North from Blocksburg we continue to follow the valley, twisting our way precipitously above the churning stream. The scenery loses some of its softness. The mountains become more craggy and the forests thicker.

At Bridgeville we join Route 36 again. Below the bridge the Van Duzen river crashes through a jumble of massive boulders and cascades. Far below I can see a bunch of kids splashing in a still pool, a tiny backwater undisturbed by the river's turbulent tumble to the sea.

Traveling east the scraggy forest abruptly ends at the edge of a deep grove of redwoods and the Grizzly Creek State Park. These are the real coastal redwoods, thick-barked and towering more than 200 feet above the forest floor, soft as a mattress from centuries of pine-needle deposits. The famous Redwood National Park along the coast north of Eureka provides a much more extensive

Timber Architecture—Scotia

example of these magnificent 2,000-year-old creatures, but this small park is usually quieter and, as a result, is a better place to appreciate their dignity and beauty. Take the short nature trail and lose yourself in the silence of these groves. Remember that these are living creatures, many of which were saplings when the Roman Empire was in its infancy. Their thick insulating bark has prevented their destruction in forest fires, and many bear the scars of past conflagrations. They seem virtually indestructible, although the illusion is short-lived once we move outside the park. Before the logging days of the mid-1800s they stretched all the way to the coast, covering the mountain ranges, growing more than 300 feet high along the banks of the rivers. Then came the axes, peaveys, pokes, saws, ox teams, and floating cookhouses—all the paraphernalia of an industry that, within a few decades, had decimated these magnificent forests, leaving behind a wasteland of stumps and eroded mountains. Subsequent replanting at least restored the vegetation cover, but the scrawny pines that inundate much of the area today seem weedlike, mere striplings, compared with the creatures that once inhabited these slopes. The park is a sad reminder of the way we once thoughtlessly raped our environment—a tiny token of regret. Even as we drive slowly westward, the road is littered with soft fibrous segments of redwood bark, blown off the broken trunks on a logger's truck. The rape still continues, although the industry has matured considerably since those early days when "selective felling," "replanting," and "forest management" would have been meaningless terms to the great lumber barons busy making their annual fortunes from these coastal ranges.

A visit to the Louisiana-Pacific Redwood sawmill at Scotia on Route 101 shows how mechanized the whole system of lumber cutting and processing has become. Tight regulations controlling the activities of lumber companies encourage minimal waste of timber. The conical burners, towering above the cutting shops and storage yards, are sparingly used today. Timber is too valuable now to permit indiscriminate burning of "waste." There is, in fact, very little superfluous wood left when the process of sorting, barking, cutting, grading, and finishing is completed. Allow an hour or two for a visit to the plant (free passes can be obtained from the office on Main Street). Then take a closer look at this perfect example of a company town, with its neat rows of identical houses painted in carefully selected pastel shades, its own palatial inn, credit union, blood-pressure clinic, and social clubs. Note the two masterpieces of bold lumber architecture, the theater (Winema) and the old bank building, now used as the company museum. These incredible structures seem, by their sturdiness and "unfinished" quality, to reflect the spirit of the great trees from which they were built.

For a complete change in pace, environment, and architectural vernacular, head north along Rio Dell's main street and turn left on Belleview Avenue toward the community of Ferndale. It's a hilly route at first, following the erratic bluffs above the Van Duzen Valley, before the road descends to the fertile plain, dotted with grazing cows and sheep. We're far away from the sear of the sawmills and the bustling 101. Forested hills, bathed in mists, enclose an almost magical land of tiny schoolhouses, exquisite gingerbread bungalows and regal mansions bedecked with all the frills and frimpery of the carpenter-Gothic style. There's a virtual encyclopedia of Victoriana strewn across these pastoral fields—Italianate mixed with Doric details, Classic Revival porticoes on a Gothic facade, stick and shingle mingled with a touch of Tudor.

A total mélange of styles and colors marks the climax that is Ferndale itself. Here at "Cream City" leave the car behind and stroll past the galleries and craft shops on main street, enjoying a flavor that is uniquely Victorian with touches of San Francisco in the bowed and bayed facades. Note the delicate scrollwork around the windows and doors, the stained glass, the gabled and mansard roofs, the arched windows, the beautifully molded cornices, and the hand-carved fans.

Stately mansions, referred to locally as "butterfat palaces," include the 1875 Arnold Berding House on Ocean Avenue, hiding behind a row of oddly shaped "gumdrop trees" and a delicate white picket fence. At the top end of main street is the 1856 Victorian-Gothic residence of the town's first settler, Seth Louis Shaw (based on an approximation of Hawthorne's House of the Seven Gables), and just below the finely detailed Catholic church is my favorite house, an exquisite orange creation dripping with intricately carved trimmings set in a garden of tiny bushes and palm trees.

Outside the village, on the wooded hillside overlooking the plain, are Ferndale's two cemeteries. The Catholic one has an almost Mediterranean flavor, with its walled family plots. Many of the names are Portuguese and Irish—Monetta, Codino, Camepa; O'Leary, O'Hara, and O'Rourke. Over in the other one we find the Scandinavians—Petersen, Rasmussen, Nissen, and Jacobsen. These are all the families who helped develop the flourishing dairy economy that characterized Ferndale in the late 1800s and led to its durable prosperity. Many remain, and social activities in the Danish and Portuguese "Halls" are still an important part of village life.

Before leaving the Ferndale area, take the 5-mile coast drive along a narrow country lane to a secluded stretch of dune-fringed beach, known mainly to the locals. It's a lovely place to rest before the next part of the journey.

The nearby communities of Fernbridge and Loleta, while less elaborate than Ferndale, reflect the cohesion and insular nature of life in this enchanted valley which reluctantly we must leave and rejoin Route 101 into Eureka. Fortunately, though, even this bustling port city has managed to retain part of its architectural heritage. In fact "Old Town" is one of the most convincing examples of constructive preservation on the West Coast. A few years back this motley collection of grimy streets and half-abandoned buildings down by the old docks was ripe for the wrecker's ball. Then with splendid imagination and vigor the city and a body of enthusiastic citizens began a long process of renovation and restoration which results today in this charming neighborhood of cobbled streets, gaily painted frontages, antique stores, taverns, restaurants, and craft shops. Fountains, a plaza, a museum, ornate lamps, newly planted trees, and a delicate bandstand all add an air of permanence and authenticity. Bestowing its haughty approval on the whole creation is the magnificent William Carson Mansion at the end of Second Street. It is known somewhat immodestly as "the most photographed house in America." This gingerbread castle, bristling with turrets, towers, gables,

A Ferndale Mansion

Coast near Trinidad

balconies, cupolas, and porticoes, was built by Carson and his hundred-man army of carpenters in 1885 as a home and showplace for his flourishing redwood lumber industry. Eureka, a city built on lumber, was the obvious place to erect this exotic creation, and the architects, Newson and Company of Oakland, were instructed to weave into their design every subtlety, every nuance, every Victorian variation they could dream up. There can be little doubt that they succeeded—no house in America today can match its flamboyance and unrelenting extravagance. The ceaseless clicking of camera shutters is appropriate homage to this exuberant expression of American capitalism. William Carson died a satisfied man.

Across the bay in the company town of Samoa the lumber industry continues to flourish, and one of its more renowned institutions, the Cookhouse, has been preserved for public enjoyment. I paused for a breakfast here of ham, eggs, and pancakes only to find that, as soon as my plate was empty, a lovely girl would insist on filling it again. An hour later I lurched away from the table with three breakfasts inside me for the modest price of one. Dinners, need I add, are an even more incredible experience in communal family-style dining. In fact, the restaurant has such a fine reputation for satisfied clients that the Chamber of Commerce City Tour features a meal here at the climax of the journey.

Route 255 from Samoa follows the North Spit, a thin strip of dunes between the ocean and

Arcata Bay, to rejoin Route 101 in the pleasant community of Arcata. Once an avid competitor with Eureka for coastal trade, the town, with its unusual main square, seems to have accepted its secondary economic status, and today enjoys a quiet, sedate existence beside the highway.

Route 101 can be frustrating at times, especially when it hides behind the low line of coastal hills, preventing travelers from enjoying views of the ocean. Nowhere is this more annoying than around Trinidad, which boasts some of the most exquisite coastal scenery in California. So, forget 101. Exit at Westhaven Drive and follow signs to Luffenholtz Beach. Here, among jagged cliffs, battered offshore pinnacles, and wind-shaped bushes, one can normally find a quiet cove uncluttered with tourists. Alternatively, follow the winding coast road and turn down Ocean Avenue in Trinidad to the wharf below the Seascape Restaurant. Very often this particular pocket of the coast seems to attract its own fogs, which shroud the pine-topped cliffs and the offshore rocks in a mysterious half-light. The cries of gulls echo eerily in the whiteness. The ocean rumbles and hisses, and the surf booms like threatening thunder against the rocks. This is an enthralling time to stroll the beaches. Most tourists seem to vanish in a flurry of wet towels and sand pails whenever the mists move in. Backroaders, however, will enjoy the seclusion, the Oregon-like character of the empty beaches, and the fleeting glimpses of blue sky through the steaming fog.

Trinidad itself, a one-time supply center for the gold mines, a logging town, and, during the

135

early 1900s a whaling station, has little left to reflect its long and varied history. So continue north on the coast road (not Route 101) through the cliff-top forest to Patricks Point State Park. Although a popular place during the summer, the park offers such a variety of coastal walks and places of interest that it hardly ever seems crowded. The Yurok Indians were attracted to the rocky promontories by the profusion of seafood and sea-lion meat. At the visitors' center there's a small museum depicting the way of life of the coastal Indians and pamphlets showing the various trails, picnic areas, and camping spots in the park. Be careful about going it alone, though. Ironically, in the heart of California's redwood forests this area is a virtual jungle of dense undergrowth among hemlocks, pines, and red alders, through which cavelike paths are carved.

At Orick we leave the coast and begin the long northern loop back to Redding. If you'd like one last adventure in this magnificent scenery, take Route 101 a few miles north to Fern Canyon in the Redwood National Park. This little-known wonderland, a narrow chasm of firs and ferns leading to a tiny cove, occasionally is impassable, so check at the Orick ranger station first.

We begin our return journey east on Bald Hill Road. Immediately there's an abrupt break with docile Route 101 as we climb at a staggering rate up past the Lady Bird Johnson Grove, through an untouched area of redwoods, to a ridge road with views of the coastal range in every direction. As the road surface deteriorates, the views become more and more impressive. On a clear day this is one of the most dramatic mountain drives in the Northwest. There's one rather bumpy 4-mile stretch, but for most of the way the road is adequate if slow. The descent is even more abruptly dramatic than the ascent. Far below you can see the bridge over the Klamath River, and scores of hairpins later we reach its smooth surface, a welcome relief in one way, an anticlimax in another, after those mountain panoramas.

At Weitchpec we're deep in Indian country. This is the combined Yurok and Hoopa reservation, and by the store I paused and talked with a group of dark-skinned, black-haired Indians. They told me that farther down the valley at Hoopa was a museum with exhibits of tribal culture. "It's about all that's left," one of them told me. The others nodded sadly.

At Somes Bar, however, after a drive through the deep cleft of the Klamath River valley, is greater evidence of the region's Indian culture. Close to the ranger station there's a roadside lookout over the Ishi-Pishi Falls. Far below, at the junction of the Klamath and Salmon rivers, in a Japanese watercolor landscape of jagged precipices, wind-torn pines, and churning white-water rapids, is one of the Karok Indians' most sacred places. I talked with an Indian woman of the Karok tribe. "It is part of the trail of the World Renewal Ceremony. We are one of the largest tribes still surviving in California and we keep our ways, our customs. We have to, they remind us that we are Indians." I asked her about the World Renewal Ceremony. "It's difficult to explain, but we believe that every year the earth must be touched and prayed to in certain ways to make sure things will continue as they always have. An old man of the tribe—a shaman—goes out into the mountains sometime around the middle of September, in the dark-moon period, and speaks to all our sacred places along the Fata-Wan-Nun [spirit] trail. While he's doing that he talks to no one and no one talks to him. Then when he's finished there are other ceremonies. It's all carefully done, everything has to be performed correctly. I think they've cut out some of the longer parts of the ceremony but it hasn't changed much. It's hard to understand, though, if you're not an Indian. The Californian Indians were different from other tribes, the larger ones to the east. We lived very simply in houses that were half underground. Our food was mainly salmon and acorn flour. We soon got wiped out, too, when the settlers came—I suppose there weren't enough of us to fight—so there's not very much left today except our baskets. My mother taught me some of the old weaving songs. We sang them so that the things we made would be full of good thoughts—they lasted longer that way."

At Somes Bar there's another choice to be made. Those wishing to continue on Route 96 will follow the Klamath River through Happy Camp, Fort Jones (there's an excellent Indian museum here), and Etna to Callahan. Expect a few unpaved segments south of Scott Bar, but the road is generally smooth, and it's a memorable drive.

Intrepid backroaders (with small vehicles—no trailers) will want to follow the Salmon River road through Forks of Salmon and Cecilville to Callahan. It's a hard narrow route, not too rough but requiring impeccable driving and a willingness to do a bit of backing up in the really tight places. If you have any doubts at all about taking this road, it may be best to keep on 96 or at least check with the rangers at Somes Bar about conditions, particularly on the first stretch, to Forks of Salmon.

Once you have decided to take the Salmon River road, accept it as a slow journey and enjoy it. This is a primitive land. We travel through a winding canyon between the Marble Mountain Wilderness to the north and the Salmon Trinity Alps Wilderness to the south. At times we wiggle our way on cliff roads hundreds of vertical feet above the churning river. It's best not to look down too much if you can help it; even drivers can suffer from vertigo. Use the horn on the tight corners and generally keep a cautious eye open for fallen rocks and oncoming vehicles.

I found this a most exciting drive, one of the few such roads in California. For most of the way the brittle bedrock of the mountains projected in jagged patches through the covering of forest. The river cascaded over rapids and waterfalls, tearing its way between great boulders, cleaved from the cliffs above. This is not the gentle coastal range of the south. We pass through semi-alpine terrain in places. There are signs of old mining camps by the side of the river and up the gulches. At King Solomon's Mine a group of young people have established an unusual commune. Not far away there's a sign nailed to a tree pointing to "The Sacred Society of the Eth, Inc." Unfortunately there was no one around to satisfy my curiosity. In fact, I saw very few people all the way to Cecilville. It was almost with relief that I joined a couple of lumbermen for a beer at the resort there. They seemed glad of company too. The owner told me about the old gold-mining activities in the area. "Hell, the Chinese were up here in the hundreds all along Mathews Creek in the '70s. We still get a few prospectors now and again. Fred Stickle has been mining 'round here for years." He pointed to a display of Stickle's nugget jewelry on the wall. "There's plenty of gold left 'round these parts."

Callahan

The group assured me that "it's freeway all the way now to Callahan." Well, I suppose in these dark, forested canyons anything that approximates a paved two-lane road deserves such a title. I gladly set out on the "freeway" for the 30-mile mountain drive to the beautiful Scott valley and the remnants of Callahan, which I reached in the light of the moon after a long winding descent. The tavern was a scene out of the old West, full of stuffed animal heads, branding irons, saddles, swords, a finely carved Swiss clock, and an ancient nickelodeon. The whole place would have seemed more appropriate somewhere east of Death Valley. The long verandaed building across the street just above the recently restored Callahan Ranch Hotel was built in the 1880s when the town was a major stopping place on the trail from Redding to Grant's Pass in Oregon. Russell Farmington runs the store. The rest of the structure is now empty. His grandfather was a blacksmith here in the 1870s during the height of the gold rush. He came from Bangor, Maine, and Russell delights in showing visitors the old furnace, bellows, tools, and even a few preserved carriages in the shop at the end of the building. Note the branding-iron "test marks" on the back of the door. "I was born just 'round the corner," Russell told me. "That was sixty years ago and I've been here since then. People keep asking me if I'm not ready for a bit of a change. I tell 'em there aren't many places left like Callahan and I've got no plans to leave."

We follow Route 3 south from Callahan over yet one more mountain pass, toward Trinity

Center. Again, it's not recommended for trailers, and there's a road that continues east to Gazelle that provides an alternative route via I–5 back to Redding.

The Scott Museum at the Trinity Center gives an excellent overview of early pioneer life in the region, with displays of Indian artifacts, barbed wire, kitchen utensils of the 1860s, and a few sturdy hand-operated wooden washing machines.

Then there's a lovely forest drive with fleeting glimpses of the Clair Engle (Trinity) Lake to the well-preserved mining town of Weaverville on Route 299. Inevitably the place tends to get a little crowded in the summer, but the famous Chinese Joss House, now a state historic park, and the Jake Jackson Memorial Museum are both worth a visit. No matter where we travel in this region we seem to come into contact with its Oriental heritage. The Joss House is one of the few remnants—and certainly the finest—of Chinese culture in the California mining country. This tiny "Temple of the Forest Beneath the Clouds" has all the aura and mystery of a cathedral. We enter past a "spirit screen," built to keep out evil spirits, and stand in a dark windowless room dominated by a richly decorated altar. Carved wooden canopies shroud the gods of Health, Decision, and Mercy. Long red prayer banners hang from the ceiling beside decorative lanterns. Immediately in front of the altar is a small table covered with offerings of fruit and money left by Chinese worshippers who still regard the temple as a holy place.

At the time of my visit Fred Meyer, warden of the Temple for more than six years, gave a moving description of the statues and other religious objects. He skillfully recreated the scene in the late 1800s when hundreds of Chinese, fleeing rebellions in the southeastern provinces of China, gathered here in the hills to rework old claims. Withstanding the tax on foreign miners and endless oppressions by their fellow miners, they panned the gulches and creek beds, sending most of their earnings home to their families and living a meager existence in the "slums" of the mining camps. The temple was their haven and sanctuary, and it retains that character of proud insularity even today.

Weaverville marks the end of our rather arduous backroading. The journey east to Redding follows the wide, fast 299 through scenic mountain valleys. French Gulch, a delightfully Western-looking hamlet, with its old hotel and stores slumbering by the roadside, is a dainty detour. Also, if it's not crowded, Whiskeytown Lake offers welcome respite for the weary traveler and is part of the rather too popular Whiskeytown–Shasta–Tahoe recreation area. Finally, at the edge of the long descent into the great central valley is the roadside historic park of Shasta, once the "Queen City" of California's northern mining region. The sturdy Shasta County Courthouse has been converted into a museum, but little else remains except a few brick store shells, still with their massive cast-iron shutters. The town grew up at a nucleus of wagon roads from San Francisco and Sacramento. During the early years of the gold rush it was the major supply and trading center until roads to the west and north were improved into the mining country, bringing prosperity to such towns as Weaverville. In the '60s and '70s, bypassed by both stage routes and then the railroad, Shasta faded and Redding took its place. As we reenter Redding it's hard to believe that this pleasant city, with its prosperous commercial strips and downtown mall, was originally known as Poverty Flat and regarded by Shasta residents as a "hot malarious stinkhole." After the long journey it looked more like a little corner of paradise to me.

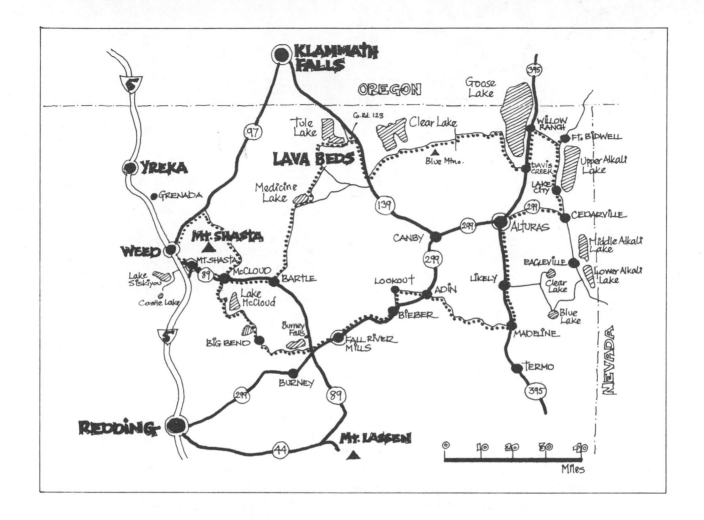

10. THE MOUNT SHASTA–ALTURAS LOOP

Lava Lands and Lemurians

The northeastern corner of California reflects much of the state's history—an era filled with hardy settlers, warring Indians, lumbermen, and staunch individualists living distinctly independent

lives. There's plenty of backroading in this journey, over high mountain passes, across mysterious lava lands, past a haunted lake, into quiet valleys unchanged since the late 1800s, and through little-known canyons, gouged out by the region's turbulent rivers. We'll meet an elderly lumberman and learn about life in a lumber company town, an Indian who claims that intimate fraternizing between natives and settlers helped keep the peace, a lady who has collected a houseful of Indian artifacts, and a representative of one of the more unusual religious cults around the base of Mt. Shasta. Altogether, a very varied journey.

COMPANY TOWNS are usually dull places, but California possesses a couple of lumber-company towns that are among the most interesting I've ever visited. The first is Scotia, way over on the northern coast near Eureka (see Chapter 9, "The Redding/Eureka Loop"). The second is McCloud, set in a forest-filled bowl on the slopes below 14,162-foot-high Mount Shasta. I suppose any town in this position would tend to appear impressive, but McCloud, with its neatly painted clapboard homes, delicate churches, massive high-roofed hotel, old gas lamps, and remnants of a lumber railroad, has a

Mt. Shasta and McCloud

delightful turn-of-the-century flavor.

Look for the town or you'll miss it after that long climb up on 89 from Route I–5, near the village of Mt. Shasta. To be honest, though, McCloud is no longer a company town in the strictest sense. The lumber mill still flourishes and the majority of its residents are employed there, but in 1964, when the company changed hands, the houses were auctioned and most are now privately owned.

I've always wanted to know what life was like in one of these places where the company is sole owner and could, if it so wished, impose an almost dictatorial regime upon its dependent inhabitants. "Well," Ted Kirk told me, "in the old days Mother McCloud took care of everything and most of us didn't mind it too much." Ted worked with the company for most of his life. "I left high school in 1933 on a Thursday, and started lumbering on the Monday. Been with them forty-five years and never been sick once." He began up in the mountains at a logging camp. "It was fifty miles to anywhere, so we stayed in the camp most of the time. We were like a big family, really. At first it was just men, then they allowed wives up later. There were no bars, nothin' like that, and you had to behave yourself or you were out. Single men were kept separate from the married folk. They were

143

strict but usually fair. Once in a while they'd pick on someone but mostly it worked all right. Y'see, in those days men were more proud of their work. We'd log in teams of two—two to a saw. It took a real man to do that kind of work. Even when it snowed we'd stay out there until it was just about impossible to stand. Today you don't get men workin' that way."

When Ted and his wife moved down into McCloud, there were more than two thousand employees at the sawmill, one of the largest in the west. Houses were provided at minimal rents, and they were allowed to "charge" their purchases at the company store. "Company'd get it back out of your check before you even saw it. There was no way you could get out of payin' your bill." Electricity was provided—occasionally. "Tuesday they'd let the power run till ten in the morning so the women could iron Monday's washing. Most days it would come on about six at night till ten. Then you went to bed. There was nothing else to do anyway."

I asked Ted about retirement. "Well, that was one thing I didn't like. When you'd finished working, that was it. You were out—job through and home through—just like that. The Italians used to plan for that. We had quite a few Italians. The girls were always crocheting—towels, sheets, everything for their hope chests. They all looked after one another. We were lucky. We bought our house after the company was taken over so now we can stay here as long as we want."

I had heard that the Hearsts had built themselves a retreat near McCloud and asked Ted about it. "Oh, that was Phoebe, William Randolph's mother. She built some kind of medieval castle and filled it with lots of valuable stuff—tapestries, rugs, paintings, y'know. That burnt down, though. Sometime in the twenties, I think." I checked on Ted's story. It was true, and apparently after the fire the family then built a complete Bavarian-style village of large mansions in the same area, a few miles south of McCloud. In typical Hearst tradition these too are a storehouse of valuable furnishings and artwork but unfortunately are never open to the public.

We leave Ted Kirk and McCloud and drive east on Route 89, arrow-straight through the pine forests, to a scattering of buildings at Bartle. Here we turn north on a narrow paved road signed to Medicine Lake and, after a few initial meanderings, begin the long climb deep into the Shasta-Trinity National Forest. There's an abrupt break in the corridor of trees and Mt. Shasta rears up her eastern flanks, bronzed by the sun. Tempting forest tracks lead off to Porcupine Butte overlook, Deep Crater, and Mud Well. There are signs of old lava flows—huddled grey forms of cinder loom behind the pines, moss-covered and ominous. In one place the road has been hacked directly up the face of an ancient flow, exposing its contorted innards. At Jot Dean ice cave there's a chance to explore a partially collapsed lava tunnel, one of many such subterranean passages through which molten lava continued to pour even after the surfaces of the flow had cooled and hardened. Nearby, half-hidden by undergrowth, are sections of lava casts originally formed around trees felled in the path of the flow and, over the centuries, hollowed out as the wood inside rotted away to dust.

Medicine Lake is surprisingly tranquil, a sapphire-colored body of water in a bowl of lodgepole pine. At its western edge, Glass Mountain lifts its black obsidian bulk above the trees and is reflected in the shimmering waters. This was a sacred place of the Shastan Indians, an initiation ground where warriors of the tribe brought the young boys for the rites of manhood. A month of testing and training followed. During the day the boys exhibited their skills with bow and arrow, riding, spear throwing, running, and wrestling, and in the darkness of the night they listened as the medicine man taught them the long legends of the tribe. I have been here at night too. Under a canopy of moon-bright stars, each one sharply defined against the utter blackness, I could sense the power this place must have had on the vivid imaginations of the young Shastan warriors. Tales of mountain creatures, the gods of the great Mt. Shasta itself, the gentler spirits of the forests and lakes, all take on a persuasive reality in the darkness. Even as I watched dawn approach, the magic remained. The deathlike greys of the first light were slowly suffused with a delicate haze-blue, which turned to pink as the sun edged its way to the horizon. Then the first sweeps of crimson splashed the pine tops and peaks, and night rolled away to the west over Glass Mountain. In the valley below the lake, mists lay like thick woolen blankets on the forests. As the spreading glow of morning warmed them, they began to lift, steaming and writhing. The sun shone like fresh-poured gold through the haze. A faint breeze rippled the water.

Leaving Medicine Lake, we follow an unpaved road to the north, following the signs to the Lava Beds National Monument. From the long winding descent we look over a wide valley edged by dry hills. A sudden change takes place. The thickly forested slopes of the mountains give way to a desert-like landscape of buttes and rounded scrub-covered hills. Below us the valley is a wasteland of lava flats, an ocean of greys and blacks rippled by the now-still waves of lava, broken in places by cones of volcanic ash.

The monument headquarters provides ample interpretative literature on the area, and on the grounds there's the entrance to another lava tube, the Mush Pot Cave. Lanterns are on loan here so amateur spelunkers of all ages can enjoy the thrill of exploring these rotund, smooth-walled passages. If one isn't enough, the cave loop road from the headquarters gives access to eighteen tubes that honeycomb the area. Before setting out, pause to study the display of lava-rock types found in the region—"spatter" stone, volcanic bombs, aa or block lava, obsidian, and pahoehoe. Take time also to drive to Schonchin Butte, one of the largest cinder cones in the region, or follow the trail up Black Crater; both of these overlook the bulk of the flow and an impressive series of fault scarps at the northern end of the valley.

Past the enclosed Bighorn Sheep reserve, where the species is being regenerated under controlled conditions, is Captain Jack's stronghold, an unusually fragmented section of lava full of deep serpentine passages, clefts, and hollows. Here in this brittle wilderness Captain Jack and his band of Indians fought a protracted struggle against the U.S. Army in 1873. The problem was an all-too-familiar one. Time and time again the Indians had been driven from their homes by the insatiable appetites of the white settlers for land. Reservations were often the means to induce their migration from the more favored areas. But gradually the reservations themselves were threatened, and in some instances devious legal maneuvers resulted in Indians' being left homeless with no land of their own. In the case of the Modocs, they had agreed to share territory with their neighbors, the Klamaths, but found tribal differences prevented successful cohabitation. So the Modocs returned to their traditional lands along the California–Oregon border, much to the annoyance of settlers in the area. Even though the tribal leader, Captain Jack, managed to minimize conflicts with the settlers, the cavalry from Fort Klamath arrived in force on November 29, 1872, to return the Modoc to their allotted reservation. At first it seemed the tribe would move peacefully, then a gun was fired, there was a skirmish, and the Modocs fled to the lava beds, leaving one soldier dead and seven others wounded. Here Captain Jack and seventy warriors along with their women and children prepared to defend themselves, and successfully beat off a series of U.S. army attacks during the winter and early spring. However, the murder of General E. R. S. Canby and a priest who had approached the Indians under a flag of truce led to massive troop reinforcements and an eventual routing of the Modocs on April 15, 1873. Captain Jack was captured soon afterward and hanged along with three other Modoc leaders as a warning to other tribes. Nothing was ever heard of the Modocs again.

To the north of the stronghold is Tule Lake, part of the extensive Klamath Basin National Wildlife refuge. Today, following extensive drainage to open up the area for agriculture, only scattered remnants of the original lakes and marshes remain. Yet millions of wildfowl still continue to inundate the area during their spring and fall migrations, and there are few more impressive sights in northeastern California than the great clouds of geese and ducks wheeling over the water against the backdrop of cascade forests and the peaks of Mt. Shasta. Photographers journey from all over the country to capture these scenes, some bringing earplugs to drown out the deafening cacophony of a million simultaneous goose honks!

There's one final surprise here at the Lava Beds, unknown to many visitors. Follow the unpaved road east across the lower end of Tule Lake and turn right near the grain elevator toward a distant line of bluffs. These are actually cliffs, and signs of wave action from the large body of water that once filled the valley can still be seen at the lower levels. Note the petroglyphs thought to have been left here by Rock Indians hundreds, maybe thousands, of years ago. There seems to be little agreement as to the significance of these primitive expressions, but later Modoc occupants of the region regarded them with great reverence, and today's visitors cannot fail to be impressed by their remarkable richness and variety. Unfortunately, heartless vandalism and "souvenir hunting" necessitated the erection of a high wire fence, which makes photography difficult.

The unpaved track continues through the petroglyph area to join a narrow northbound road. Take County Road 123 east to Route 139 and then turn south, passing along the fringe of another lava flow. Immediately after crossing over the railroad, turn left toward Clear Lake, where we begin an extensive backroad adventure to Goose Lake and the beautiful Surprise Valley. Almost the entire route is unpaved but, with the exception of a rather rough 5-mile stretch in the central section, the surface is adequate.

After a gradual climb through an estate-like landscape of dry grasslands dotted with trees, we reach the shores of Clear Lake, a large body of milky-colored water. Like Tule Lake this is also a resting place on the bird-migration flight path as well as an important nesting ground for white pelicans, herons, and terns. But there's something a little strange about the lake. Even on a clear summer day it feels to be a place apart. Some say it's haunted by the ghostly figure of a young woman killed by Indians at the southern edge of the lake, and tales abound of odd occurrences around Fiddler's Green, a one-time livestock watering place way up at the northern end. Hauntings or not, the lake possesses an odd silence. The colors of the water and land seem unusually bleached, like the skin of a long-dead corpse. The only movements are the wraithlike shadows of clouds on the dry hillsides and the occasional slow spiralings of white birds, way in the distance.

Traveling east toward Quaking Aspen Spring and Blue Mountain, we descend briefly into a deep stream-torn gulley and then pass across a high plateau inhabited by grotesque junipers. Many seem to have suffered hard agonizing deaths; their limbs, grey and splintered, lie on the ground around them. Others, still leaved, snatch at the sky with brittle branches. Their gnarled dry trunks are the very antithesis of life, yet they suffer on, snarling at the world. They're hardly the kind of creatures one would care to meet in the moonlight.

At Blue Mountain, a narrow track leads to the 5,740-foot summit, where a lookout tower provides a breathtaking panorama—from Mt. Shasta and Clear Lake in the west the Warner Range in the east. All around pine-covered plains slope away to a misty horizon. It's lonely, empty country.

Following signs to Blue Mountain Spring and Willow Creek, we take a road through woods as far as Mosquito Creek. Then we turn left, and a mile or so past Willow Creek Ranch, we make an abrupt right toward Goose Lake. After a few more miles of woodland driving, we pass an ancient log cabin and soon arrive at the vast blue expanse of water, edged by the forest-covered Warner range.

Washboarding south along the lake, we reach Route 395 at Davis Creek. Cold drinks and snacks are in order at the store before we continue north on Route 395 to the Fandango Valley turnoff near Willow Ranch. Here we end our brief association with the wide highway and head off again into quiet pastoral backcountry beneath the sharp-peaked ridges of the Warner Range. This is early-settler territory. Tales of Indian raids abound, and the sad story of the Fandango Massacre is still fresh in the minds of the valley's older inhabitants. The date was October 1855. A large wagon train of more than two hundred settlers traveling west on the arduous Applegate Trail reached the summit of the 6,100-foot Fandango Pass and caught sight of the bright, wide waters of Goose Lake at the western end of the long valley. It was a hazy day and the weary imigrants were unable to see the hills on the far side of the lake. The cry went up "It's the Pacific!" Even the train leaders believed the end of their journey was in sight, and the whole group flung themselves into an exuberant fandango dance. But their shouts of joy and relief soon turned to terror and despair. A band of Paiutes, concealed in the forest, swooped down and massacred all but two of the settlers. There was no opportunity for self-defense, no chance to save the women and children. For years afterward,

explorers in the area found knives, pistols, lockets, and silverware, left behind after the Indian raid.

And this was no isolated incident. Throughout the dreaded Modoc territory and particularly in the region between Goose Lake and Tule Lake crossed by the Applegate Trail, it is estimated that between 1846 and 1852 more than four hundred early pioneers were murdered by marauding bands of Indians. Bloody Point, a rocky crevasse at the end of the long descent from Clear Lake to the edge of Tule Lake, was one of the favorite places of ambush by the Modocs. People were reluctant to settle in these dangerous valleys until some form of armed protection was guaranteed.

From the top of the Fandango Pass, before the exciting descent, we can pause and look into 65-mile-long Surprise valley. How tempting this must have seemed to weary pioneers, an ideal place to start fresh, to build a new life in an untouched land. But prior to the establishment of Fort Bidwell in 1866 at the northern end of the valley, those who settled here had to put up with a rough life. One of the first arrivals was Captain Townsend, who built his house in Cedarville in 1864, a sturdy log cabin with narrow slit windows. The following year Townsend was killed by Indians and his cabin was subsequently taken over as a trading post by William Cressler and John Bonner. The building still stands today.

Lynchings were commonplace. Official justice tended to be slow and inefficient, so early

Goose Lake

residents settled matters in their own direct way. Socializing was also on rather a crude level. In 1864 the valley's only hotel possessed a pole and brush roof and drinks were served at a bar made from the end gate of an emigrant wagon. Any fraternizing between residents invariably had to be an all-night affair, as no one with any sense traveled between dusk and dawn.

Today it's hard to believe that this tranquil valley, with its old buildings mellowed by a hundred summers, could have seen such arduous times. At Fort Bidwell, the fort has gone and a few Indian families occupy the semicircle of remaining dwellings. I talked to an old man with a face as weathered as a worn leather boot. He told me he was half Paiute and half Irish, and laughed loudly, slapping his thigh. "Don't you believe everything you hear, all those Indian stories and stuff. After a while things settled down and most of us got along pretty well. Heck, I'm not the only half-breed 'round here—and how d'you think we all got here?" He made what one might call an illustrative gesture. "That," he continued, "helped solve a lot of problems. Always has!"

Lowell's 1876 store is usually open to serve the few residents of Fort Bidwell. With its groaning board floors, a ceiling festooned with all manner of odd trinkets, and a group of elk heads, it has all the distinct character and charm of a typical country store. Nearby, Kober's Dry Goods Emporium has more erratic hours, depending on the mood of Elsie Kober, whose father purchased the place in 1897.

South from Fort Bidwell I passed through the deserted remnants of Lake City. It was once an important supply and trading center on the Applegate Trail, but the old store and flour mill are closed up, slowly crumbling into the weeds, and many of the cabins are abandoned. It's the kind of place that photographers and artists love—a creaking corner of yesteryear.

In fact, the whole valley has an air of benign neglect. Large barns lean in the fields that slope down to the dry white lake beds. Mellowed farmhouses, shaded by cottonwoods, peer over the hayfields. Eagles spiral high above the Warner peaks, and in the woods and ditches at the roadside, raccoons, porcupines, and deer ignore the infrequent traveler and continue their foraging with studied intensity. I paused to chat with a farmer. He was sitting in a gutted armchair that had bits of grey stuffing bursting from splits and seams. The shade of his veranda was deliciously cool. "My dad came here 'round 1890. Things haven't changed too much since then. There's a new eating place in Cedarville, and I hear tell someone's putting up a house down at Eagleville. But that's about all. There's a lot of Basques around here, and they don't go in for change too much. They like it like it is. So do I. Now and then someone comes up with a crazy idea for a resort and that kind of thing. I ask 'em, 'Why bother? Who's going to come here anyway?' It's a dead end, this valley, to most people. It don't go nowhere 'less you use the country roads, and most folks seem to like to keep some pavement under their wheels. So—well, these ideas come and go. Don't make no difference. Just a lot of talk." The sweep of his arm extended down the whole valley. "Don't look like much has changed, does it? Well—it won't."

Cedarville, with its line of old stores, is the only community of any size in the valley. A few attempts at modernization only serve to emphasize its sleepy Western character. The thick-timbered Cressler and Bonner store sits by itself in the town park.

Here, in Cedarville, there's a choice of route again. High in the mountains of the southern Warners is Blue Lake, an exquisite place for quiet fishing or just whiling away a warm afternoon. Access by vehicle from Surprise valley is difficult but feasible, following the Patterson ranger station road west into the mountains about 4 miles south of Eagleville and then taking the Harvey Creek–Pit River road down to Likely. If this journey appeals—and it is an opportunity to explore a little-known portion of the Warners—then check first at the Forest Service office in Cedarville for details on road conditions and the best route to follow.

The alternative is to climb west out of Cedarville on Route 299 back over the Warners to Alturas and then continue south to Likely on the 395. For once we'll take this easier route. Actually I must admit to a bias. I had been told that Alturas contained not only an excellent museum but also an authentic Basque restaurant, and I was anxious to sample its culinary wares. Those readers familiar with such establishments will understand why. For those who are not, a brief word of introduction is in order.

The Basques are one of the oldest peoples on earth, thought to be survivors from the Middle

Paleolithic age, forty thousand years ago. Their language, a linguistic riddle even for them, is known as Euskera, and the Basques, in fact, call themselves Euskaldunak. They are a hardy independent race living in and around the Pyrenees along the France–Spain border. Their first significant appearance in America was around the time of the California gold rush, when they joined the rest of the world in pursuit of easy wealth. Later, many remained here as shepherds and farmers. The French Basques settled mainly in California; the Spanish Basques chose Idaho. Nevada received a balance of both.

At first they were subjected to ridicule and scorn for their nomadic lifestyle, following the sheep and the seasons. Then after the end of the open-range days many settled down on homesteads or became valued ranch hands, admired for their honesty and dedication to hard work. Over the years intermarriage and the homogenizing influence of the American "way of life" has diminished their insularity, but they still remain one of the most culturally distinct of western European immigrants.

Fernand and Josephine Larranaga, owners of the Brass Rail Basque Restaurant in Alturas, told me, in still-hesitant English, what it means to be Basque. "We are a very independent people. We like to work for ourselves—all our family likes to work together. It is best that way for us. But we are a very happy, lively people. There's always parties and dances. Last week we were in Susanville. They've got a lot of Basques down there. There was a party in the hotel. Why? I don't know—oh, it was a birthday, I think. Anyway we were there two days—singing, dancing, drinking. We hardly slept at all. And last week there was a festival at Reno. There's one at Winnemucca and the big one at Elko [Nevada] around Independence Day. You can see everything—the weightlifting, pelota games, dancing, bread baking [the shepherder bread] and barbecues—all the time."

The Basques love their food. A typical dinner at a traditional Basque restaurant usually includes a vast relish tray for starters, a tureen of homemade soup with fresh loaves of bread, a huge bowl of salad with a sharp dressing, platters of vegetables served as a course in themselves, possibly with thin slices of cold meat, then usually two meat entrees of lamb, beef, or chicken with thickly sliced fried potatoes followed by dessert, fresh fruit, and coffee. Wine is normally included, and the whole gargantuan affair is often served at long communal tables where everyone becomes "family" for an evening. These invariably inexpensive meals are a splendid way to end a day's backroading.

Before leaving Alturas pause at the Modoc County Historical Museum in the tree-shaded park at the southern end of main street. In addition to the usual plethora of old rifles, photographs, and phonographs typical of many small-town museums, there's one of the most abundant collections of Indian artifacts in northern California. On the far wall the tired face of Captain Jack looks out across a hall brimming with grinding rocks, Indian buckskins and headdresses, axes, straw baskets, and ceremonial drums. "It's a little crowded in here," explained a girl at the desk. She wasn't joking.

Just outside the town, en route to Likely, is the 6,000-acre Modoc National Wildlife Refuge, a popular resting place of the whistling swans during their migratory flights. Canada geese, mallards, gadwalls, and goldeneyes are also conspicuous visitors in the fall. The headquarters, located on the site of an ancient Pit Indian encampment, provides interpretive displays and literature.

South through Likely we travel over a barren landscape of sagebrush plains and eroded hills covered in stumpy pines. At Madeline we turn right for Adin and set off across an even emptier land broken by gulleys. The road is unpaved most of the way. Red dust trails like the tail of a fiery comet. Except for a secluded valley, about halfway along, there's no obvious sign of anyone living in this forgotten corner. Jerry Bath, whose family have been in the valley for two generations, says it's getting a bit too crowded. I looked around and was able to make out one other building a couple miles away against the opposite side of the valley. "Well, there's a few others you can't see hidden away." Jerry stroked the back of his tailless manx cat, Goober, and played with a couple of equally tailless kittens. "Still, it's a good place to bring up a family." He grinned, "School's the only problem. That's twenty-three miles away."

The general store at Adin has the lopsided look of a capsized boat. Inside, a "we've-got-everything" range of foods and dry goods is displayed against crooked walls decorated with scenic murals and stuffed moose heads. One of the customers pointed out the enormous Carey safe. "I remember when they broke into that," she told me proudly and pointed to explosion marks in the door. "It was a Christmas. Everyone was too busy celebrating to notice. They keep it empty now though," she added in a loud voice, in case anyone was thinking of doing it again.

From Adin take the road to Lookout. I'd like you to meet a charming elderly woman who entertained me royally one grey afternoon when I visited the community. I had come to find out more about the 1901 lynching, the last known such occurrence in the state and one of the most notorious. Actually there were five lynchings, all at the same time—four men and a fifteen-year-old boy. They were accused of stealing livestock and other local acts of lawlessness. In fact, they had been a troublesome bunch for some time and the populace was thoroughly sick of them. When a county grand jury failed to indict them, a group of residents raided the Myers Hotel in Lookout, which also doubled as the jail, dragged out the accused men, and hanged them from the Pit River bridge at the east end of the village. Months of investigation ensued, but a conspiracy of silence existed in the tiny town. James Brown, the deputy constable, was the only man ever brought to trial and he was later acquitted. Even today no names are mentioned in connection with the lynching. I chatted with Bob Ober and Joe Fiscella, owners of the village store. "Oh, nobody talks about that—nobody! Many of the families involved still live here, y'know, and there's quite a bit of bad feeling even now." Joe came to Lookout from Manhattan eight years ago and found the contrast exhilarating. "Everybody knows everybody but you can still be as private as you want. People accept you as you are. It's still that bit old-fashioned. Last week one of the young lads came in with a note from his mother saying he could start chewing tobacco and that it was okay for me to sell it to him. Things like that remind me I'm somewhere special."

I found Edith Leventon's house by chance. I was taking photographs of the old blacksmith's shop at the top of the hill and spotted a clapboard house with a garden full of Indian grinding bowls and windows brimming with purple glass bottles.

When I knocked, a thin elderly lady with birdlike eyes opened the door, and I asked her about her unusual garden. "Oh heavenly day, I've been collecting them for years," she told me. "Y'see, no one really seems to understand them—the Indians. They treat them like children. But I love the things they made. They're simple, I know, but they were all they needed." She looked me over carefully and then smiled brightly. "Come in. Come and see my collection." I entered another world. Inside the dimly lit room were hundreds of arrowheads of all colors and sizes laid out in carefully arranged patterns and mounted in frames. On every level surface were more Indian objects mingled with displays of Mrs. Leventon's other treasured possessions—miniature tea services and still-life cameos she'd made from bits of branch and "found" objects. Then there were the bottles, scores of them, from tiny purple vials she'd found in an old mining town to sturdy green liquor bottles. "This is my museum room," she said. "I'm quite proud of it." I spent an afternoon there talking with or, more accurately, listening to this spritely lady. She seemed delighted to share all her treasures with someone from "the outside." "I don't normally ask strangers in," she confided. "The people 'round here think I'm a bit crazy, y'know, 'specially collecting all the Indian things. Well, I told them. When I die I want them to dig a big hole out here in the garden and put me in it and then put all my treasures in with me so I can have them by me all the time. They won't want them."

I left Lookout and headed across the flat Pit Valley to Route 299. The road climbed steadily after Bieber and then began a long descent into a wide fertile valley ringed by mountains. The vast panorama swept southward across the Lassen National Forest and the snow-capped Lassen Peaks. Far below I could see the tiny farms and barns in the wheatfields. It's the kind of landscape that would have sent Constable running for his palette.

At Fall River Mills I paused at the contemporary museum at the top of the hill beyond the town, with its excellent overview of local pioneer life, then continued south toward Burney Falls. At Vista Point there's a startling drop into the Pit River Canyon, a black broken landscape of torn rocks and, hundreds of feet below, the foaming white water of the tiny stream we first crossed way back, near Likely.

Burney Falls is a splendid series of cascades with secondary falls emerging from the basalt precipice. Alas, it's also become a rather popular tourist spot in recent years, so unless you come here out of season, it may be worth only a fleeting visit before you brace yourself for the final segment of the journey back to McCloud.

Again I preface this route with a warning: it's narrow and, in a few places, a little bumpy. So if you've had enough backroading for this journey, if you're pulling a trailer, or if your vehicle is oversized, take Route 89 back to McCloud. Alternatively, if you're ready for one last adventure, let's go.

A couple of miles south of the Falls on Route 89 turn up the fork past a campsite and gas station and follow a narrow oak-edged road along sinuous Lake Britton to a five-road intersection. Here follow the sign to Power House III. (This area is part of a combined power-generating and recreational-land use program administered by PG&E.) It's a tight road, snaking along the upper level of the Pit River Canyon. Keep a watchful eye open for the occasional logging truck. There are plenty of turnouts, and the secret is to drive ahead of yourself to avoid backing-up maneuvers. Fortunately traffic is usually very light, so enjoy this slow journey through primitive mountain scenery and find your own riverside spots for a picnic or an impromptu bath.

About 5 miles beyond Power House IV follow the signs to the Pit-Stop Tavern and Big Bend, the only evidence of habitation until we near McCloud. Check at the ranger station about road conditions through to Lake McCloud. Usually it's best to avoid this area in the rainy season, and certainly if there's any chance of a snowstorm, retreat with dignity! (Take the alternative highway drive to McCloud via 299 and 89.)

The paved road out of Big Bend soon gives way to a gravel surface near Iron Canyon Reservoir, and then for a 3-mile stretch over the top of a twisting mountain pass, the quality deteriorates again, so drive this stretch slowly and carefully.

We descend into a magnificent V-shaped valley, deep in the heart of the Shasta-Trinity National Forest. It's the kind of place you feel you've discovered for yourself. Sparkling waterfalls burst from the darkness of the woods, then dart again like squirrels into rock-strewn chasms. The breeze moves the high branches in a swishing, surflike murmur, and far below the river mumbles, ever present but invisible from the ledgelike road. Then as we continue winding slowly down through the trees, there are flashes of rapids, white water tumbling between mossy boulders, still pools where clear water beckons the hot and dusty traveler.

Abruptly, the great wall of the McCloud Dam looms ahead. We climb up and follow the bumpy road around the edge of the lake until, with a sense of relief, we arrive at a smooth-surfaced highway leading us north through pastoral valleys back into McCloud.

For those explorers still determined to keep on backroading, there's a final drive around the eastern flanks of Shasta from McCloud, highly recommended but, again, a little wearing on the driver. Check for conditions and the exact route at the McCloud Ranger Station. You'll have the mountain and the forests virtually to yourself. It's along this route that you may begin to sense some of the mystery of the mountain, a presence that the Indians felt and worshipped. On certain days a strange lenticular cloud, a whirling disk of whiteness, revolves over the twin peaks. To some it is an interesting climatic phenomenon; to others it is a symbol of the mountain's aura, its polarizing qualities that make it one of the earth's prime "energy" points. The town of Mt. Shasta itself, reached by following Routes 97 and I–5 south after the "behind the mountain" drive, is the home of many unusual religious sects and occult groups with odd-sounding names—the "I Ams," Elan Vital, the Association of Sananda and Sanat Kumura, a Zen mission, the Shasta Buddhist Abbey, and various other organizations that regard the mountain as a base for "the masters." Some claim that

Backroad to Lake McCloud

we all ultimately become "masters," after completing our cycle of reincarnated lives and learning the ultimate mysteries and truth of the universe, and they regard Shasta as a particularly conducive environment for attaining such knowledge. To the uninitiated the community looks normal enough, with its familiar array of supermarkets, restaurants, and tourist stores. But as Jack Moor at the Bicycle Rider store told me, "If you're into it, then you know this is a special place."

There are countless stories and myths about Shasta, about the magnificent golden cities of Iletheleme and Yakatayvia deep within the mountain, with their great bells; about the Elan Vital sect, which communes with "Dugja," the last queen of the Lemurians, who reigns supreme in the mountain with her court. Other groups claim that the survivors of Atlantis exist here in a white marble city set in tropical gardens and work with "chosen ones" on the outside to increase man's consciousness of the great mysteries behind life itself.

I met with Pearl Dorris, one of the more respected sages of Shasta. This sparrow-like lady with startlingly large eyes lives in a tiny rose-shrouded cottage overlooking the town. "One can get very confused with the stories, you know, but most of them reflect similar ideas—that Shasta is a point of power on earth, that many people have experienced very real visions here and that it is a 'home,' if you like, a place to contact the 'masters.'" I asked Pearl if she herself had experienced any visions. "Oh, of course I have. It's very simple, those who are ready will find these things. But it's not the visions that are important, it's the knowledge that one gains and passes on."

She showed me a book she had recently helped write. She smiled enthusiastically. "It was only published last week; isn't it lovely?" I opened a page randomly and read, "Mankind upon this planet all long for the Light. You, as one individual, can assist in giving that Light to them. They need to understand that the presence of the Living God is within them." I looked up. Pearl was answering the telephone. "Look, tomorrow I'm going to be canning some apples. What time do you want to come in for counseling?" As I left, some young people were making their way up to the house to talk with her. She was obviously a person with considerable influence in that small town. But I'm glad she cans apples too.

A final rest is now perhaps in order. Take the road from Mt. Shasta across Route I–5, turn left at the fish hatchery (open to the public and an interesting diversion), and follow signs to Lake Siskiyou, nestled in a bowl of pines. It's a perfect place to end the journey. Or better still, if you'd like somewhere a little quieter, take the road farther south to Castle Lake. Of course for the more active there's always a mountain climb up Shasta. The tourist office in town has abundant literature on trails. For myself I'd love to find that city of gold or meet a Lemurian, but I'll just have to accept the fact I'm not ready for the experience yet and leave my feet where they are, dangling in the cool waters of the lake beneath that mighty mountain.

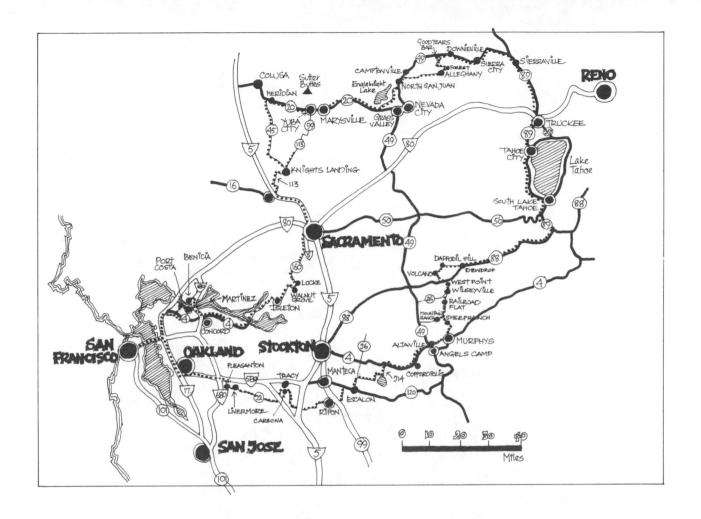

11. THE SAN FRANCISCO-LAKE TAHOE LOOP

Meanderings Through the Mother lode

The San Francisco–Tahoe–Reno route is one of the most popular in California. Most drivers, however, are merely concerned with reaching their destination rapidly and normally rely on

Port Costa

the freeway or major arterials to carry them there as uneventfully as possible. This journey offers a total alternative—slow meanderings through the delta lands and the central valley, up through the foothills of the old gold country, the Sierra peaks, and ultimately the placid Tahoe bowl. We return on an equally rambling southern route, exploring dusty mining towns, strolling by quiet lakesides, and once again sipping the wines at some of the state's more notable wineries. You'll avoid freeways whenever you can after this journey.

Note: We begin this journey at the intersection of I–80 and Route 4. Follow the signs from here to Port Costa.

THE TOWN OF Port Costa, huddled in a niche on the Contra Costa cliffs, rarely appears on highway maps. So thousands of travelers in the bay area whisk by on I–80 or Route 4, blissfully oblivious of its antique charms, its two outstanding restaurants, and the turbulent history of this old Sacramento River wheat port. Bill Rich, a cheerful former beer-truck driver, owns most of main street. "Those bureaucrats are crazy," he told me. "They kept saying the place didn't exist, and here I was with a beautiful brownstone inn, a Victorian hotel, a huge concrete warehouse, and all these lovely clapboard buildings. They said the place was a ghost town. I told them to come and take a look sometime."

Bill and his team of enthusiastic devotees, many of whom live permanently in the port's renovated buildings, have worked for years to restore its faded glory. The warehouse, now containing a popular restaurant, craft and antique shops, and a virtual village of residents on the top floor, was the proud creation of George McNear in the late 1800s. He was for many years California's "Grain King" and helped build the town into one of the largest grain-shipping ports in the world. George was an astute man, always looking for an opportunity to expand his growing empire of grinding and grading mills, retail outlets, and shipping facilities. At its peak his town was a boisterous place filled with "chaw-bacon Irish" from Counties Cork and Kerry. There were only three hundred or so official residents, but during boom periods it expanded to three thousand brawling, bawling dock hands—roaring their way through the taverns, singing, fighting, and generally earning "Port Chaw" a notorious reputation.

"It's a bit quieter today," Bill told me. He may be right, although the restaurant inside the old warehouse, littered with antiques and dripping with bric-a-brac, attracts a hearty crowd of revelers on weekends. Bill himself occasionally retires up the canyon-like valley to the solitude of his tiny lake overlooking the town. From here it's hard to imagine how this cramped little community ever played so important a role in northern California's economy. Yet the facts speak for themselves. From the establishment of a rail ferry between Port Costa and Benicia in 1879 to the opening of the Martinez–Army Point railroad bridge in 1930, most of the grain production of the fertile hinterland flowed through the town. The grain barons made vast fortunes for themselves and then lost them again, usually trying to corner the wheat market. George McNear himself tried in 1900 and, like the others, saw much of his accumulated wealth vanish overnight. Yet Port Costa continued to flourish. It was a favorite haven of Jack London when he was gathering material for his "John Barleycorn." Only the slow diminution of grain acreage and the expansion of rail facilities led to its untimely demise. But then, of course, along came Bill Rich and his crowd. "She's alive again now," he told me, "and she'll stay that way."

Rather than return to Route 4, turn left after the abrupt climb out of the town, on Carquinez Scenic Drive, and follow this narrow road to Martinez. We travel high above the river, wriggling in and out of tight creek valleys. Scrub-flecked hills tumble steeply to the water. Occasional huddles of buildings in the clefts contrast sharply with the open, wind-smoothed landscape. Far below, large ships rest at anchor outside the Martinez docks.

At Route I–680 take a brief detour across Carquinez Strait to the historic town of Benicia, once the capital city of California. Actually its fame was rather short-lived. Thirteen months to be exact. Initially the vacillating legislature chose San José, but the following year reversed its decision and met in Vallejo. Dissatisfied with the town's accommodation, the lawmakers flocked to Sacramento, only to have their ardor doused by the 1852 flood. They tried Vallejo again, but conditions were no better than before, and so it was with almost indecent enthusiasm that they greeted Benicia's offer in 1853 of its city hall for use as a state house. The town's founder, Dr. Robert Semple, also added a supplemental inducement—guaranteed introductions to the town's 20 to 30 marriageable young ladies. That did it. The legislators hurried to Benicia, where an elaborate ball was held in their honor, and for a while everything seemed to be going well for all concerned. The legislators found suitable accommodation and the town experienced an economic boom. The government established its Pacific Coast arsenal on a 250-acre site on the edge of town, and this, coupled with its new status as the capital, gave credibility to Semple's claim that Benicia would be the "Queen City of the Bay."

But alas, its aspirations were short-lived. A year later the legislators declared Sacramento to be the capital and disappeared abruptly upriver with their bags and boxes of records. In 1858 she even lost her status as Solano's county seat, and after that Benicia's fortunes fluctuated erratically. Even as late as 1962 she was brought to the verge of bankruptcy by the closure of the arsenal. Fortunately, enlightened community leaders managed to develop a new industrial estate here, and the town is experiencing a growing tourist trade. Antique hunters ply the old buildings down by the wharves near Jurgensen's Saloon (The Lido), another establishment frequented by "Curly-Headed Jack" London when he lived in his houseboat at the waterfront. There are also plans to establish a large marina, stores, and restaurants along the river. While such schemes will doubtless enrich the town's populace, they may remove much of the quiet charm of a place once described as "a Fibber McGee's closet of a town, bursting with yesterday's artifacts, crammed with undiscovered nostalgia." So before Benicia begins to experience yet another of its spasmodic booms, spend an hour or two here using the town's tour guide as your itinerary (available at the Chamber of Commerce and local stores).

Return south on Route 780/680 to Route 4 and travel east through Pittsburg and Antioch to Route 160. Here, after crossing the San Joaquin River, we leave the docks, the factories, and the traffic behind and head out into that vast expanse of flatlands and marshes known as delta country or, more romantically, the "California Bayou." Sam Goldwyn chose the delta as the prime location for his *Huckleberry Finn* because "it looks more like the Mississippi than the real thing." Immediately the mood of the journey changes. In the early mornings eerie tulle mists drift over the reeds and the masts of boats move through fields of waving wheat. The road rides on a levee, 20 or more feet above the seemingly endless plains, and a lone heron stands single-legged in the shallows, patiently awaiting breakfast. All around, fields and neatly rowed orchards stretch out to hazy horizons. Occasionally a crisply painted farm sits like a doll's house in a cluster of shade trees, its windows reflecting the low sun.

Tourists come here to ride the 700 miles of meandering channels with such odd names as Disappointment, Potato, Whiskey, Hog, and Montezuma sloughs. They hire boats and, like the delta's most renowned devotee, Erle Stanley Gardner, while away languid days fishing, swimming, and eating huge meals at popular riverside restaurants. Gardner himself, creator of the world's most famous lawyer, Perry Mason, wrote a number of books about the delta that did much to increase its popularity with vacationers. Fortunately for the land traveler, though, the roads are often quiet and the small river towns have a snoozy quality that permeates the spirit and makes one reluctant to leave. Take time to explore these places. Walnut Grove and Locke are perhaps the most interesting. Both seem to reflect another era, another time, when the pace of life was slow and "change" was an unfamiliar concept. "Heck, I watch some of the folks that come this way in those modern automobiles an' I don't know how they ever live past being thirty." I was chatting with one of the older residents at Walnut Grove, a delta town of bowed clapboard buildings and dusty bars. "I'm serious." He nodded. "They're always jumpin' and rushin' about, clickin' their cameras and bawlin' at their kids, and then they're off before they've even got here. If that's touristin' they can have it!"

Locke's population is almost entirely Chinese. Many of them are descendants of the Chinese who came here by the thousands, after the completion of the transcontinental railroads in 1870, to build the levees that still restrain the moody Sacramento and San Joaquin rivers. Before the levees the delta was a fragmented hodgepodge of marshes, subjected to constant flooding. Their construction enabled systematic drainage and cultivation, and today these once useless flatlands are the state's richest fruit and vegetable region.

Many of the Chinese stayed on in the delta after the levee building, and during the early 1900s a few of the less accessible river communities developed notorious reputations as centers for illicit pleasures—gambling, drugs, and easy women. But now that's all history. Locke is a delightfully creaking community built on two levels. The top half of the town's clapboard buildings,

Locke

most of them false-fronted, face onto the levee road while the bottom half line the sunken main street. It's a place of deep shade, narrow passages, and sleepy Oriental faces. One store sells a delectable array of Chinese foods and spices, and around dinnertime the smell of wok-fried meats and vegetables wafts enticingly from the homes along the narrow streets.

Find your own piece of riverbank and enjoy the silence of the delta. Better still, make yourself an impromptu fishing line and try to hook a juicy catfish for supper. The delta's "river rats," families that once spent all their lives on the river, often made a good living from snaring fish with their fyke nets. Today it's the turn of "weekend warriors," as the locals call them, to enjoy the bounties of the creeks and sloughs.

Back in the days of the great steamboats, catfish and the like were considered deck-hand fare. The wealthier passengers were beguiled with a dazzling array of delicacies imported from the East Coast and Europe. Competition between the boats was razor-keen. During the 1850s more than thirty side-wheelers plied the rivers between San Francisco and Sacramento. Some even ventured as far as Red Bluff at the northern end of the Sacramento valley. Price wars at one point reduced the San Francisco-to-Sacramento deck fare from $15 to 10¢, and races between matched steamboats became popular excuses for extravagant wagers. "Unfortunately," as Oscar Lewis wrote in 1938, "their saloons were commonly more satisfactory than their engines," and disastrous boiler explosions resulted in the maiming and death of scores of passengers. In 1858, for example, fifty were killed after the *Pearl* blew apart near Marysville following a frantic race upriver from the bay.

This once overpressured artery to California's inland cities and the tumultuous gold-mining regions of the Sierra Nevadas is a tranquil place today, a place for quiet explorations, cat naps along the water's edge, and rambles through faded river towns. Try not to rush this part of the journey.

Unless you intend to visit Sacramento's two main tourist attractions, the replica of Sutter's Fort and the magnificent restoration of Old Sacramento, bypass the center on I–5 and continue west to the remarkable town of Woodland. At first you may consider the place a little mundane. Certainly main street resembles a score of other similar thoroughfares in the state. But turn left and meander along the tree-lined side streets into a fantasy land of Victoriana. Every architectural style and influence is represented here, from the most austere stick and shingle to the overwhelming richness of Italianate and Corinthian mansions.

Much of the town's all-too-obvious wealth was accumulated during the gold-rush era, when farmers and merchants made vast fortunes supplying the Sierra towns with locally grown produce and wheat. At one period money was pouring in so fast that the town claimed to possess more millionaires relative to its total population than any other community on earth. No one, so far as is known, disputed the claim.

From Woodland take 113 north to Knights Landing, a place with much of the flavor of a Mississippi river town, and then continue north on 45 across an unusual area of rice paddies.

At the sleepy community of Meridian, another delightful river town, travel east on 20 to

163

Yuba City and Marysville. We pass alongside the Sutter Buttes, dramatic remnants of ancient volcanoes looking strangely out of place in this flat fertile landscape.

Marysville was another valley town that prospered as a supply center during the mining era of the 1850s and '60s, although its growth was not without problems. In its early years the legendary bandit Joaquin Murietta terrorized the area, and the moody Feather River constantly rolled over its banks into the town's streets. During one particularly severe flood in 1853 the first floor of the resplendent Merchant's Hotel was completely flooded out at the time of the New Year's Eve Ball. Not to be outdone, the hardy socialites rented boats and rowed their way to the second-floor ballroom!

The impact of floods on Marysville can be noted in its architecture. Many of the older homes have their main floor at second-floor level, linked to the sidewalks by ornate sets of steps. The richness of the architecture also reflects the wealth of its early citizens. A miniature castle, once the home of the Aaron family, is particularly notable and contains an excellent overview of life in the town during the late 1800s.

Following Route 20 east along the Yuba River valley we begin our initial ascent into the oak-covered foothills of the Sierras, on the fringe of the mother-lode country. Take the road with the sign to Englebright Lake, just beyond Smartville.

It's a lovely place to pause once again. Ahead we have some exciting driving, so rest awhile by the water, watching the brightly colored houseboats meandering up the narrow, mountain-bounded lake.

Those unfamiliar with California's gold-mining country should continue east of 20 to Nevada City and explore this well-preserved mother-lode community. A one-time tent town, Nevada City gradually emerged as the region's most prosperous community, boasting an ornately detailed hotel, extravagant Victorian mansions, and three firehouses to protect it from the conflagrations that were a constant hazard in most hastily built clapboard mining towns.

Inevitably, the charms of the place attract a hearty tourist trade, and backroaders may find it a little too crowded during the peak-season months. So a rewarding alternative is to take Mooney Flat Road east from Englebright Lake to Lake Wildwood and then turn north (left) on Pleasant Valley Road, following signs to the covered bridge at Bridgeport. This is a narrow winding road, unpaved in places, and a splendid introduction to the real Sierra mining country. Remnants of communities at French Corral and Birchville are reminders of the 1850s, when every creek and stream had its own flurry of panning prospectors seeking easy wealth. They came from everywhere. They left their homes and businesses in the coastal cities (San Francisco, Benicia, and Sacramento were virtually devoid of a male population during the early euphoria of the rush), they deserted the ships and steamers, they flocked in from virtually every nation on the surface of the globe. They surged their way across the wide valley on steamers, mules, wagons—anything that moved—and tore their way up the steep Sierra hills with their sacks of flour, sides of bacon, and placer pans. A diarist of the time gave an eloquent description of the gold fever that brought tens of thousands of fortune seekers to these sun-scorched hills:

> Lawyers, doctors, clergymen, farmers, mechanics, merchants, sailors, and soldiers, left their legitimate occupations to embark on a business where fortunes were to be made in a few weeks. Villages and districts, where all had been bustle, industry and improvements, were soon left without male populations. Mechanics and merchants, and magistrates were alike off to the mines. Vessels are left swinging idly at their anchors, while both captains and crews are at the mines.

Inevitably the huge demand for food, clothing, and equipment and the lack of an equivalent work force to make and transport the goods to the hills led to startling inflation. Eggs often sold for more than $1 each, boots that could be purchased in Boston for 75¢ went for up to $50 in the mines, and liquor, particularly brandy, was recorded as high as $48 a quart! Yet even our objective diarist found it hard to restrain his enthusiasm after visiting the mines himself:

> I went to them in the most skeptical frame of mind, and came away a believer. From all that I can learn as to similar deposits of gold elsewhere, I believe these to be the richest placer mines in the world. Many instances are known of persons having obtained $800 to $1000 in a day. I saw six men, in six days, get ten and a half pounds of gold. Two others, with a party of indians, removed $17,000 in two days. From another dry ravine, within a few rods of the last mentioned, $30,000 were collected in three days.

With this kind of news being headlined in newspapers around the globe, it is hardly any wonder that these scorched, dry hills were soon as crowded as the great port cities of the East Coast. According to our diarist, conflict and disorder soon became the natural state of affairs:

> In the solitary recesses of the Sierra Nevada are little clusters of men, with nothing but the trees for their covering, and no protection but their own vigilance and strength. Many of these people are known to possess very large amounts of gold (sometimes as much as $20,000), wrapped in their blankets. Is it strange, when the temptation is so great, that the robber and assassin should be abroad among the mountains? Many robberies and some murders are known already to have occurred; but little attention is excited by these events, where all are in the eager pursuit of wealth. No one can conjecture the extent of these outrages, for living witnesses are not at hand, and "dead men tell no tales."

At North San Juan on Route 49, a line of worn brick buildings look out across the cemetery, shaded by walnut and locust trees. What a truly international community this must have been when its peak population of over ten thousand assembled here during the rich hydraulic mining period of the 1860s on the San Juan ridge. Headstones memorialize "natives of" Switzerland, Germany, Devonshire, and Wales. Others reflect a strong Cornish contingent, often referred to as the "Cuzin Jacks," whose prime aim seems to have been to amass sufficient capital to pay the passage to America of the rest of their enormous extended families. The only visible remnant of their presence today is signs for "Cornish Pasties" usually found in local taverns and restaurants. These spiced meat, potato, and onion concoctions baked in crisp pastry are truly delicious with cold beer.

There's an interesting detour east from north San Juan to the Malakoff Diggins State Historic Park. Take Oak Tree Road, turn left on Foote Crossing Road, and follow the signs after 5 miles, down to the 1,600-acre pit, gouged out of the hillsides by enormous hydraulic monitors between 1866 and 1884. This was the largest hydraulic operation in the world, and today the ghostly buttes, cliffs, and gullies remain a mute memorial to that frantic era. Several of the buildings at North Bloomfield have been restored, and there's an excellent museum here. It's worth a detour. In fact for truly intrepid backroaders it's not really a detour. Back up on Foote Crossing Road, a mile north of the turnoff to the Diggins, is one of the most awesome backcountry drives in the Sierras, along the notorious Foote Road to Alleghany. The sign at the entrance to the road reads "One lane road. Last turn around. Narrow road. No turnouts. Proceed own risk." I've tried it, and to be honest, unless you're driving a small vehicle and don't mind some jarring and the possibility of having to back up on the edge of 500-foot precipices, you should avoid it. If you do decide to risk it, I guarantee it will be an experience you will never forget and the basis for a fine travel tale. But, once again, err on the side of caution.

An easier but equally scenic route to Alleghany leaves Route 49, 3 miles north of north San Juan, and weaves its way along a ridge, hundreds of feet above the churning waters of the middle Yuba river.

Alleghany is one of those mountain towns that just never seem to change. At Casey's Place a few of the town's sturdy women were playing pool. Adeline O'Donnell, whose husband Phil owns the still-active Dreadnought Mine, took long pulls at her beer as we talked about life in this hidden mining community. "They got $50 million in gold from this valley," she told me. "The big mine, the Original Sixteen to One, got more than half of that. It kept going until 1965 and could have gone on longer too. There's still plenty of ore left down there. The place was loaded with it. Someone once picked up a sixteen-pound nugget—one hundred percent solid gold!" All that remains of the mine today is a few boarded-up buildings. The rest of the town, though, clutching to its almost vertical hillside site, seems determined to endure. Cords of split wood are piled under the wide verandas of the steep-roofed houses. "We're set for a hard winter," Adeline told me. "Road's usually closed for much of the time, so it gets pretty cozy here." The others in the bar looked up. "Cozy's the word!" said one of the women, waving her pool cue, and they all laughed together. I asked if there were any stories or events for which the town was famous. "Nothing printable," bellowed the girl behind the bar, and the whole place broke into giggles and guffaws. She was right, too!

It's possible to travel east across the Sierras from Alleghany to Lake Tahoe via Henners Pass, but again, unless your vehicle is exceptionally sturdy and you can withstand arduous miles of washboarding, head off north through the weathered mining camp of Forest and follow the signs to

Downieville

Goodyear's Bar and Downieville. It's a memorable drive. The unpaved Mountain House Road climbs up to the top of the ridge beyond Forest, and incredible mountain vistas stretch in all directions. To the north we look directly into the Yuba River valley, a thousand feet below. That's where we're heading, so take a deep breath, test your gears and horn, and start the long winding descent. If you're not used to driving narrow mountain roads, this is an excellent opportunity to learn!

Downieville, nestled in a shaded bowl below the towering pine-covered ridges, is one of the mother lode's most attractive mining communities. Even the tourists browsing through the trinket shops do not detract from its authentic pioneering character. It's a place to be enjoyed leisurely. Stroll the winding streets, visit the museum, and if you meet an old-timer who likes to talk, listen as he tells you stories of the old mining days when this was a town of more than five thousand inhabitants. The creeks here were so rich that what may sound like fictitious tales turn out to be based on solid fact. Gold was found everywhere, in the bellies of salmon hooked from the Yuba river, in the rocks used to surface Main Street, and under the floorboards of a restaurant, which was immediately dismantled so that its owner could start excavating the site. At the nearby Tin Cup Diggings the three owners filled a tin cup every day for weeks with gold dust. Farther up the valley one prospector found a 100-pound nugget in 1860, later sold for $25,000. Where the town's movie house stands today was the site of a theater graced by such notables as Edwin Booth, Lotta Crabtree, and Lola Montez. The culture-poor miners showered them with gold dust after each tumultuous performance. Even the Chinese who arrived after the first rush had peaked still made fortunes as they reworked the old diggings and placer claims. The stories are endless. Some are humorous, like the tale of a man caught stealing a pair of boots in 1850. Rather than jailing him, an impromptu court of miners ordered him to buy drinks on the house in the local saloon and indulged themselves riotously at his expense until late into the night, only to find the wily character had quietly disappeared without paying the bill—and had even taken the boots with him!

Other stories have a more somber flavor. It was here that a Mexican dance-hall girl, Juanita, was lynched by a fiery mob after she stabbed a miner to death. The girl claimed she had been molested constantly by the man, but the mob thought otherwise. The story of the lynching spread around the world, and it took the town many years to live down its unsavory reputation.

The remnants of Sierra City, a few miles east of Downieville up the canyon-like ascent along the Yuba River, straggle by the roadside. High above the pine slopes rise the jagged peaks of the Sierra Buttes. The road continues to climb over the 6,701-foot Yuba Pass and then, with startling rapidity, zigzags down the east slope of the range. The views are dramatic and surprising. After those miles of arduous switchbacking across pine-covered ridges, we suddenly find ourselves looking out over a dry, desert-like landscape of dusty plains and eroded mountains. On the horizon are the great wastelands of Nevada. We descend to scrub-covered fields and broad spaces. Sierraville, a scattering of bleached buildings at a crossroads, seems an odd contrast to the tight, huddled villages of the mountains—a contrast, however, that is short-lived. Soon Route 89 is carrying us back into pine-covered hills as we climb over to the sturdy lumbering town of Truckee. Smoke and steam rise from scores of chimneys, and Main Street is a jumble of honking cars and jaywalking pedestrians. Restaurants and bars are abuzz with tourists, and Lake Tahoe lies a few mountainous miles to the south. The first half of the loop is complete.

Return Journey: Lake Tahoe to San Francisco

While there are a few backroads over the Sierra ridges south from Lake Tahoe, I don't recommend any of them. Stick to the main road until you're across the range.

Take Route 89 up over 7,740-foot-high Luther Pass and then follow Route 88, twisting westward through the mountains toward Sutter Creek. It's a thrilling drive. Resort development and the like is minimal, and the road is far less crowded than Route 50, a few miles to the north.

At Dewdrop, we leave Route 88 behind and begin our backcountry explorations meandering along the Fiddletown–Silver Lake Road. Look for signs to Daffodil Hill. Six miles west of Dewdrop take the left fork on Shake Ridge Road, and after 3 more miles you'll come across a series of immaculate gardens in a farmlike setting. If you can arrange to visit in spring (end of March to the third week in April), you'll appreciate the appropriateness of its name. The land around the "old homestead" contains more than 200,000 daffodil bulbs in addition to acres of crocuses, tulips, violets, hyacinths, and lilacs. The McLaughlin family have tended their garden here since 1887 and welcome visitors warmly to their color-brimmed creation.

The Ram's Horn Grade from Daffodil Hill to Volcano is a fitting reintroduction to the mother-lode country. For many miles now, in fact all the way to Copperopolis on the edge of the San Joaquin valley, we'll be switchbacking over ridges, twisting and weaving through narrow valleys, and exploring lesser-known gold-mining towns snuggled in cozy mountain bowls. It's a hard, exciting drive—but slow. Mileages are misleading. One 12-mile stretch of ridges and valleys took me almost an hour. So accept that you'll not be moving anywhere very quickly and enjoy the steady, quiet spirit of the forests and hills. Of course, if you're the impatient type you won't be reading this book anyway.

Compared with many older mining towns, Volcano is a tiny place with only a handful of historic buildings. Yet it's one of the most charming communities in the region. The short remnant of main street shaded by lopsided trees, the proud 1862 St. George Hotel, and the cannon used by the "Volcano Blues" during the Civil War are convincing reminders of its importance as a gold town. If you'd like a self-guided tour of the town, pick up the handout sheet at one of the stores.

Hydraulic monitors were used here in the 1850s, and estimates of total ore output exceed $90 million. But not only was the town rich, it was also one of the more culturally oriented communities, claiming the first library, theater, observatory, law school, and debating society in the mother lode.

Store—Railroad Flat

    I strolled through the high-ceilinged lounge of the hotel, with its massive stone fireplace and deep armchairs. Sarah Gillick, the stout, smiling cook, was making fresh dinner rolls in the kitchen, and we talked about the town. "It's not got spoilt y'know like the other places, specially those on the 49. We get quite a few people here but they're a quieter bunch." She was kneading a huge mound of dough as she spoke. From the oven came the smell of baking pies. I asked how long she'd been at the hotel. "Since the place was built, I think," she laughed. "Actually I started when I was a college student, weekends and vacations mostly. Then I sort of came and stayed and I'm still here. Volcano's like that, it's a hard place to leave."

    But leave we must, following signs to West Point across Route 88. To the right just outside Volcano is a short detour to the Indian Grinding Rock. This large flat expanse of out-cropped limestone is pock-marked with hundreds of mortar holes used by the Miwok Indians for grinding acorns. According to the trail guide there are 1,185 holes here in addition to scattered petroglyphs. A veritable factory!

    After the dog-leg crossing of Route 88 we make a long descent into the Mokelumne river canyon and an equally arduous climb up along an old pioneer road to Route 26. At West Point, turn right and roll downhill again along the false-front main street south toward Wilseyville and the

lopsided general store at Rail Road Flat. This wonderful, rambling edifice founded in 1868 by Edwin Taylor, from Yorkshire, England, was the focal point for workers at the nearby Petticoat Mine. Across from the store is a rusty mule-drawn ore cart memorializing the mine and the Black Fever epidemic that decimated the population in 1880.

Ten miles to the south, take a short detour west from the Rail Road Flat–Sheepranch Road to the sturdy, if somewhat ramshackle, community of Mountain Ranch. Few tourists come here except those who have heard about Marge's famous homemade sausage at Das Wurst House on the outskirts of town or the interesting antique showroom in the stone Dughi building. The 1856 Domenghini General Store was one of the town's first structures and is still in active use today as a store and beer bar. Take a stroll inside. Nothing has been prettied up for visitors. It's a basic gold-country tavern with barrel tables, a large wood-burning stove occupying the center of the room. If some of the locals are around (and they usually are), have a glass of beer and eavesdrop on their tall tales, rambling anecdotes, and rustic humor. This is real Sierra backcountry.

Sheepranch's lovely old store is now used as a post office and real-estate office. Outside, an ancient hand-operated gas pump reads "18¢ a gallon." At the far end of main street is the town's verandaed hotel, now owned privately. "It's fantastic inside," a young man in a wide-brimmed

Stetson hat told me. "Three families from Marin own it. They've kept it just like it was. They should open it really, it's not right to keep it all locked up, 'specially when they're hardly ever there." George Hearst, father of William Randolph, is said to have slept occasionally in the hotel after he purchased the Sheepranch mine in 1875. It was a highly profitable venture for the already wealthy man, and even when it was sold after his death in 1898, the mine kept on producing until 1942.

The drive south to Murphys takes us through real Bret Harte country. The writer roamed for many months in these hills collecting material for the gold-country stories that so delighted Eastern readers. Today the scene is little changed. The narrow road wriggles and bounces through a contorted landscape of oak-studded hills, pine forests, and tight valleys. It's not hard to imagine the time when every gully and creek around here had its contingent of rock-turning, earth-scratching, pan-swirling prospectors arduously seeking those elusive specks of yellow metal that could bring instant wealth and a lifetime of indulgent comforts. Occasional vistas look out across the twisted landscape. Thick woods soften its broken outlines, but the scorched-white grasses and bare patches of cracked earth give an indication of the torrid conditions in which these early-day dreamers toiled.

We pass Mercer Caverns (an interesting tour) and descend into the welcome shade of Murphys' locust-tree-shaded main street. The "Queen of the Sierra" is one of the mother lode's best-preserved mining towns. Relative isolation from Route 49 to the west has enabled it to maintain its physical integrity and charm. The place attracts a fair share of tourists during the peak months, usually en route to walk among the giant sequoia redwoods in the Calaveras State Park, 15 miles north on Route 4.

The town's most notable building is its hotel, built in 1856 and still adorned with an elaborate balcony and thick cast-iron shutters. In its heyday it rivaled the finest hotels in San Francisco, and the register lists such renowned guests as Horatio Alger, Jr., Ulysses S. Grant, John Jacob Astor, Jr., John Pierpont Morgan, and even Will Rogers, who starred in a movie here in 1934. Only its sturdy construction saved the hotel from a series of devastating fires in 1859, 1874, and 1893, when, on each occasion, most of the central part of the town was destroyed. Today the profusion of iron shutters, brick, and stone suggests that the citizens finally learned to build a durable community.

When it was first settled by John and Daniel Murphy in 1848, the town was nothing more than a huddle of tents and brush shelters. Later, as prospectors realized they had found some of the richest placer diggings in the country, the population expanded rapidly and merchants began establishing businesses. The local Indians provided much of the early labor, and a visitor in 1849 described the arrangement:

> The camp of Mr. Murphy is in the midst of a small tribe of wild indians, who gather gold for him, and receive in return provisions and blankets. He knocks down two bullocks a day to furnish meat. They respect his person and property in part due to the fact that he has married the daughter of the chief.

Using this form of cheap labor Murphy is said to have amassed a fortune of more than $1.5 million. Other Americans also made a lucrative living up here in the narrow creeks but resented the presence of "foreigners," particularly the Chinese and Mexicans. The Foreign Miners' Tax reflected this resentment by requiring any miner who was not a U.S. citizen to pay a monthly fee of $20 for the privilege of operating a claim. Other legislation also made sure that such foreigners found it virtually impossible to obtain citizenship. There was no way they could win. It is said that the notorious bandit Joaquin Murrieta began his career here in 1850 after his brother had been unjustly sentenced and hanged for horse stealing and Joaquin himself flogged. Many other Mexicans in the gold country also took to a life of crime when they realized they would never be allowed to make a fair living.

Unless you have an overwhelming desire to ride the wide highway after all those miles of weaving backroads, avoid Route 4, and take the old Murphys grade (it begins on French Gulch Road) alongside the lovely Angels Creek to Altaville. Angels Camp to the south has an excellent museum and some interesting remnants of an old mine if you wish to make a slight detour, but be ready for the crowds and traffic jams typical of Route 49.

Continuing west on 4 from Altaville through a desolate landscape of dry hills and deep gullies, pause briefly at Copperopolis to explore the remnants of what was in 1860 one of the richest copper-producing towns in the United States. By 1863 the population was in excess of ten thousand. Many of the impressive buildings were constructed of brick brought from the Mother-lode town of Columbia, which frantic miners were literally tearing apart to get at the rich gravels beneath. Today there's little left to reflect its importance except the old armory at the south end of town, a brick church now used as a community hall, a couple of rather run-down taverns, and a lone palm tree, the latter being perhaps the most notable remnant in the landscape of oaks and pines.

Route 4 takes us slowly down to the lonely dunelike hills at the edge of the great central valley. There are few trees here. Farmhouses huddle in the folds, and the only prominent objects are the wind pumps—brittle silhouettes against a burnished sky.

Take Route J14 south to Woodward Reservoir Regional Park, a welcome stretch of cool water surrounded by shade trees and picnic tables. Weekends tend to bring the valley residents scrambling up into the hills for some relief from the heat, but at other times, it's a delightfully quiet spot to rest awhile before driving on to Escalon.

There's ample excuse for relaxation here also. At The Cadlolo Winery, Ray and Theodore Cadlolo offer tastings of their mainly generic wines, and farther down the street the recently developed "Old Winery" complex provides wine and cheese samplings, restaurants, stores, and even a theater, all designed to appeal to a weary traveler. Then 5 miles to the west on Route 120 is the Franzia Winery, whose modern tasting room features an interesting range of varietal wines. So, by the time you leave you should be well and truly rested up. Set off across the flat fields and orchards to Route J2 on your way to Livermore and more wine tastings.

As usual there's a fast and slow way, the former through Manteca and Tracy and the latter south to Ripon and then west across the quiet part of the valley. Backroaders will prefer the slow way, so head south to Ripon ("Almond Capital of the World") on Murphy Road near the Franzia Winery, and follow signs from Ripon to the Caswell Memorial State Park down by the Stanislaus

River. This lush overgrown wilderness is an odd contrast to the regimented orchards and furrowed fields all around. The Indian chief Estanislao made a stronghold here during early conflicts with the Mexicans, and in the late 1800s the rancher Minnie Elizabeth Poe described this area as part of a vast hardwood forest stretching all the way along the river. Today there's an interpretative display on the park's ecology and an oak-forest nature trail. It's an unexpected and welcome surprise.

Retracing our route for a mile or so, we turn left on Melton Road and pass an odd assortment of old wagons, cartwheels, and wrought-iron concoctions at a farm called Petticoat Junction. I talked to the creator of this remarkable piece of indigenous "folk art," Manuel Tosti. "Ah, it's just a hobby," he told me in a thick Spanish accent. "I don't know why I do it. I just got a lot of wheels and stuff I don't know what to do with, so, well, I did this. People seem to like it, so that's nice. Some people think I'm crazy though. That's not so nice!"

At Manteca Road, turn left and follow the curving road to Airport Way. When I was last here, a regional park was being developed alongside the river by the Durham Ferry Bridge. Cross the river at this point and continue east on Durham Ferry Road until it ends at Chrisman Road. Turn right to Linne Road, and after 3 miles, left on Corral Hollow Road (J2). And that's it. We've completed our somewhat meandering but pleasant wander across the valley.

The J2 immediately plunges up an eroded canyon below Black Butte into an odd landscape of noduled hills and exposed rocks pockmarked with indentations and holes. At the Carnegie Cycle Park, tire tracks scour the hillsides where motorcyclists have taken advantage of the rollercoaster terrain to test themselves and their spluttering machines. Then abruptly the land flattens out into a rolling plain littered with ranch houses. White painted fences line the roadside, and Stetsoned characters ride paints and palominos across dusty fields. In the distance are the vineyards, miles of them, as we enter the famous wine-producing region of the Livermore valley. The soils here are similar to those found in the Garonne River district of Bordeaux, and many of California's finest wines, particularly the whites, are produced in the locality at such well-respected wineries as Concannon and Wente, both of which we pass on Route J2 and both of which offer daily tastings and tours.

We're now approaching the bay area. If you intend to head toward its southern end, around San José, then include a visit to Mission San José and the nearby Weibel winery, famous for its champagne. Alternatively, if you're aiming for San Francisco or Oakland, take Route 84 for a short distance south from Livermore, then turn right on Vineyard Avenue (a new winery has recently opened up here) and on into Pleasanton. Here, as a final indulgence, sample some of the more unusual Italian-influenced wines at Villa Armando in the center of town, before joining the freeway into the frantic hullabaloo of the city-rimmed bay. Welcome back.

12. SAN JOSE TO SANTA BARBARA
The Quiet Way

The coastal route between these two cities is one of the most heavily traveled in the state and should be avoided by backroaders in the summer months. Instead take this inland route through quiet oak-shaded valleys and over little-known mountain passes. We'll spend time wine-tasting (again) at a huddle of wineries near Gilroy; visiting an old mission; exploring quiet forested canyons, eerie talus caves, and a deserted mining town with most of its buildings still intact; and meeting the residents of a religious community established at the turn of the century. Of course we can't ignore the coast altogether, so we bypass the tourist spots in favor of hidden beaches and coves where we share the solitude with butterflies and sea lions.

THE BREAK WITH suburbia is abrupt. Traveling south from San José, the Almadén Expressway (G8) cuts a swath through an all-too-typical rash of shopping centers, fast-food outlets, and stockaded townhouse developments with guarded gates. The profusion of exotic landscaping contrasts oddly with the bare mountain ranges. Then suddenly the wide highway narrows to a country lane. Median strips, traffic lights, and the bright shiny trappings of conspicuous abundance give way to small orchards, horse ranches, and grey-green pastures dotted with cows. Route G8 makes an abrupt turn and meanders past Calero reservoir south through a landscape of woods and low rounded hills. The bustle of the bay seems far behind.

There's a small sign at the roadside to Uvas Canyon County Park. It's a 4-mile detour, and the last mile is hardly wide enough for one car. "We don't get too many people up here," one of the rangers told me. "It's mainly the locals who know about it. Most out-of-staters are too busy heading for Monterey to come up around these hills." Too bad. They miss the tiny waterfalls, the strolls through silent oak and fir forest, and a chance to experience the California of yesteryear. Indians from the coast and valley used to travel to the canyon to fish and collect acorns. Later there were sporadic attempts at quicksilver mining, followed by logging forays, which removed many of the redwoods and Douglas firs. But much of interest still remains. Take the nature-trail walk, about an hour of easy woodland strolls, and enjoy the variety of trees and shrubs growing in these steep valleys. If you'd like the place virtually to yourself try to visit on a weekday.

Now, a good walk in these woods makes one thirsty. So let's move a few miles farther south through rounded valleys and indulge in a little wine tasting. Close to the junction of G8 with the 152 west of Gilroy we enter one of California's lesser-known wine-producing regions. The low hills and valleys are blanketed with vines from which hang the plump bunches of ripening grapes—Pinot Noir, Zinfandel, Cabernet Sauvignon, Barbera, and Grignolino. At Kirigin Cellars, Nikola Kirigin

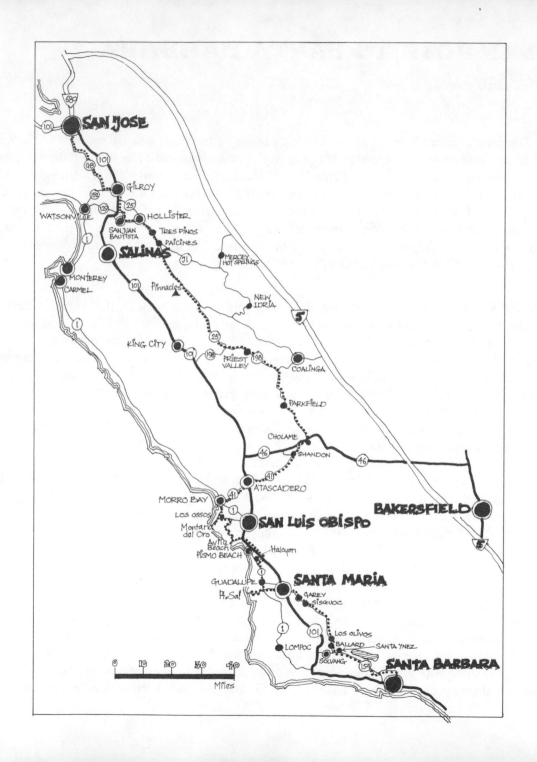

Chargin and his family warmly greet visitors to the tasting room and provide an interesting description of the winemaking process while serving glasses of some of their more unusual creations—Sauvignon Vert, Malvasia Bianca, and Opol Rosé. Although Nikola recently purchased the winery from the Bonesio family, winemakers here since 1916, he is no newcomer to the art. Several generations of his family were engaged in winemaking in Croatia (Yugoslavia), and Nikola gained his degree in oenology at the University of Zagreb before spending many years with the San Martin and Almadén wineries, both famous establishments in California.

Ernest Fortino, owner of the nearby Fortino winery, also comes from a long line of winemakers. When he took over the place in 1970 he immediately abandoned the old bulk-processing traditions of the winery and began preparing a more limited range of high-quality varietal wines, including his Petit Sirah, a sturdy wine that has received much attention in the bay area.

Members of the same family own the adjacent Hecker Pass Winery and feature an interesting Zinfandel and other varietals in their tasting room.

Thomas Kruse and his wife Susan operate the smallest winery in this area, but from their 33 acres of vineyards, they produce eight wines for commercial distribution, including Zinfandel, Grignolino Rosé, and an interesting champagne. Tom's dislike of the excessive wine filtration and "polishing" techniques used by many of the larger wineries means that his wines, particularly the reds, contain small amounts of sediment and possess a distinctly bold character. "They're traditional in the best sense of the word," Tom told me.

At the Live Oaks Winery, Peter Scagliotti presides behind the bar of his attractive tasting room, which is adorned with stuffed birds, animal heads, and old sepia photographs. His father founded the place in 1912 after working with the great Miller and Lux organization, the biggest cattle barons of the western states. He even managed to maintain operations during the Prohibition era by producing sacramental wines, and today Peter's primary problem is creating enough of his "Premium Burgundy" to keep loyal customers happy.

If you've got some picnicking to do along with the wine tasting, pause at the Bertero winery. You can't miss it. The oldest and largest oak tree in California stands nearby, and down past an ancient water tower there's the new tasting room where Angelo Bertero and his sons offer samples of their notable Barbera, Grignolino, and Sauvignon Blanc wines.

For those accustomed to wine-tasting expeditions, these six notable establishments may well provide an adequate introduction to the region's wines. Other more hardy oenologists can continue this exploration in nearby Morgan Hill and south of Gilroy, where a further four wineries welcome both the casual traveler and the connoisseur.

Gilroy itself is an unusual valley town with a main street boasting a number of splendidly ornate buildings. Take the old city hall for example. Where else but in California could one expect to find such a magnificent Flemish-Oriental-baroque creation complete with Spanish-styled pantile roof and a brick, stone, and stucco exterior. Somehow this odd mélange of architectural influences

works, and even though it ceased to function in its official capacity in 1965, the historical society managed to generate enough local enthusiasm to ensure its preservation and possible future use as a restaurant. There was talk of putting the museum here, but that honor was bestowed instead on the sturdy little Carnegie Library building at Fifth and Church streets (weekdays, 9–6; Saturday, 1–6; closed Sunday and Tuesday).

South of Gilroy we pass through a region of cherry orchards and then head off on Route 129 to San Juan Bautista, one of the state's most beautiful historic communities. Admittedly, during the summer one has to share its charms with a disproportionate number of camera-wielding tourists, but it remains an essential element of any itinerary in this region.

The tiny town consists of two distinct sections. Third Street is the commercial center, a western-flavored collection of restaurants, antique stores, and tearooms. Many of the buildings date from the 1860s, and Dona Guadalupe Vásquez, mother of the infamous bandit Tiburcio Vásquez, operated her popular Spanish restaurant in a building on the west side of the street between 1863 and 1867. The plaza area by contrast is a broad stretch of lawn shaded by old pepper trees and dominated by the large adobe mission building, founded in 1797. A walk through its porticoes and inside the church, with its leaning pillars and earthy frescoes, is a reminder of California's Spanish heritage. The other buildings around the square—the hotel, the stables—reflect another era, a later period when the great ranchos, the religious fathers following in the footsteps of Father Junipero Serra, the

Valley Scene—near Hollister

Indian mission schools, the vaqueros, the seasonal fiestas, were eradicated almost without trace following the secularization in 1834 and the subsequent defeat of the Mexicans by the United States in 1846. By 1850, when California became a state of the Union, there was little left of that tranquil era except the empty mission buildings themselves. The gold rush, the ceaseless tide of settlers, the Indian wars had destroyed a whole way of life in a few brief years. So take time to wander through the cool rooms and patios of the mission. Look over the fence into the old burial ground, where more than four thousand Indian converts are interred. Try to capture the flavor of life here in the early 1800s. Remember that California didn't start with a bunch of gold-crazy miners. There was a flowering culture here, a delicate relationship between the Indians, the Spanish, and the land itself— a simpler life under the protective gaze of a loving God. San Juan Bautista is a place apart, a place in which to remember a lost heritage.

At Hollister we turn south on 25 and travel through an immaculate landscape of rounded oak-dotted hills and crisply furrowed fields. There's a feeling of timelessness here, a feeling that we shall experience again and again before we reach the coast. The valleys seem insulated from the outside world, there are few indications of "development," few signs of change.

Tres Pinos, an old shipping town with large lopsided warehouses, a tavern, and a small clapboard fire station, seems much the same as when it emerged alongside the railroad from Hollister in the late 1800s. The "Holy Hill of Tres Pinos," a pine-shaded grove adjoining the

179

Catholic Church, which is filled with statues and memorials, reflects the intensely religious attitudes of the valley's Portuguese- and Spanish-speaking inhabitants. In an increasingly agnostic world such devoted expression of belief and faith seems anachronistic and yet somehow appropriate for this quiet rural backwater. The people lead simple lives, tied to the rhythm of the land and the steady ebb and flow of the seasons. Recent agricultural expansion in the valley, including the extensive new Almadén vineyards, "the largest varietal vineyards in the world," assure plenty of work for the valley's inhabitants, even for their sons and daughters, so they stay on from generation to generation, telling their tales in the taverns.

Events that occurred decades ago sound as if they happened last week. One man told me about Tiburcio Vásquez's robbery at the nearby Paicines store. Although he kept referring to the 70s I almost felt he was discussing events of this century, not an escapade that occurred more than a hundred years ago. Vásquez apparently robbed the store in August 1873. It still stands today at the junction with the New Idria Road. In a rather uncharacteristic manner, the bandit killed three people, the first a deaf man who didn't hear Vásquez's orders, the second a Portuguese resident who couldn't understand English, and the third the hotelkeeper, who was shot dead by a bullet through a two-inch-thick oak door when he refused to open it. This cruel episode so angered the local populace that a huge posse set out to find the bandit and eventually dragged him back to San José for his subsequent trial and execution in 1875.

Lloyd Neilson at the store told me, "Oh there's all kinda tales like that 'round this area. The old-timers love to keep telling them. Today must seem pretty dull in comparison." I asked Lloyd about the road up to the famous New Idria Quicksilver mine, which I'd heard was an interesting remnant, way in the backcountry southeast of the town. "Well, the road's fine as far as the mine, but Clear Creek Road, that's the one that gets you down to the Coalinga Road, isn't usually advisable 'less you got a four-wheel drive. Course you got other problems too. Those people up 'round there don't take too kindly to strangers, you might say. Been known to shoot off a few blasts at anyone they thinks snoopin' around a bit too much. Troublesome bunch." Yet the temptation to go there was strong. The place is largely intact, with its schools, stores, dormitories, and mining gear still standing. In the 1850s it became one of the most famous quicksilver mines in the world, immortalized in Bret Harte's "Story of a Mine." By 1861 miles of tunnels had been driven into the mountainside, and the needs of its more than three hundred miners generated a flourishing agricultural economy in the Hollister region. Mining activities actually continued until as late as 1972, when the demand for mercury finally diminished.

The 50-mile drive out to the mine passes through the fertile grasslands of the Panoche valley and then follows the old "wiggletail" road alongside Tres Pinos Creek before climbing over Panoche Pass and continuing southward to the town. There's an unusual detour en route. Journey a few miles north on J1, after its junction with the New Idria Road, to the Mercey Hot Springs. Here for a reasonable fee one can bask in the 115-degree mineral waters before being steamed and toweled and emerging like a newborn babe, devoid of all aches, pains, and twitches.

Of course a visit to New Idria means a long return journey if the Clear Creek Road is impassable. It's best to check with Lloyd at the Paicines store first, although this may not be as easy as it sounds. The day I visited, each of Lloyd's three friends, all wearing Stetsons and chewing large wads of gum, had a different opinion about the mutual suitability of my vehicle and the road. If his friends are still there when you arrive (they seem to be almost permanent fixtures), it may be best to call the county road office from the store.

Assuming you manage to negotiate the Clear Creek Road, continue south on Coalinga Road to Coalinga, and take Route 198 west to the Parkfield Grade Road, where we'll meet for the continuation of the journey.

Of course, if you take the New Idria drive then you'll miss the magnificent Pinnacles National Monument. These unusual clusters of eroded spires and steeples, rising from behind low ranges of chaparral-covered hills, were described by George Vancouver on one of his inland explorations in 1794 as "most extraordinary mountains which presented the appearance of a sumptuous edifice fallen into decay." Had he known their geological history he might have been doubly impressed. More than 23 million years ago these rocks were formed as part of a large volcano located due east of what is today the city of San Luis Obispo. About the same time a collision of the Pacific and North American tectonic plates led to the creation of a 600-mile-long rift known as the San Andreas Fault. The fault line passed through the center of this volcanic region, and gradually the Pacific plate slid northward, carrying a portion of these ancient lava flows on its back. The movement of the plate has been consistent, and today the old volcano, worn and eroded into spectacular pinnacles, is more than 195 miles north of its original location! What's more, it's still moving at the rate of about an inch a year, and some geologists think that in 6 million years (give or take a year or two) the fault rift will have widened to such a point that the pinnacles will have become a prominent coastal feature of a new offshore island. Of course, by that time there may not be too much left of the unusual rock formations. All this moving about has resulted in considerable fragmentation of the strata, and massive segments have already collapsed into the two deep canyons on either side of the peaks, creating some of the most startlingly beautiful talus caves in the country.

The Bear Gulch caves located a mile or so above the visitors' center are particularly impressive. I spent more than an hour slowly climbing and squeezing my way up through their eerie passages. A torch was essential in places, but many sections were bathed in a ghostly light that permeated through the cracks and chinks between the massive boulders above me. The air is always cool down in the darkness, although the excessive heat of the summer months tends to discourage much hiking outside the caves. And hiking is what makes the pinnacles popular during the spring and fall. This is no place for the autobound. Leave the machine behind, pick up the printed trail guides at the center, and set off up the canyons to enjoy this unique place. It's the only example of coast-range chaparral in the National Park System, and nature lovers will find the numbered markers helpful in

The Pinnacles

identifying the Mexican manzanita, buckbrush, and chamiso, the three primary shrubs of the chaparral group. In addition look out for the red-barked madroño (similar in color to the manzanita), blue oak, holly-leaved cherry, juniper, and black walnut. In shady moist dells you'll occasionally find groups of ferns, loved by affluent gourmets for their delicate "fiddlehead" shoots (similar in taste to asparagus and delicious in hot butter sauce).

If you take the short Bear Gulch or Moses Spring Trail, you'll arrive, after a steep climb up steps cut into rock, at the tiny Bear Gulch Reservoir. Rest here on a rounded rock by the edge of the water. This is one of the most delightful mountain lakes of the coastal range, a tranquil place to pause before the return descent.

We continue south on Route 25 through a gentle landscape of soft, rounded hills. The grass, bleached by the summer sun, is neutral-toned, a kind of faint beige. Under a clear midday sky it becomes silver, and at sunset it is transformed into fiery fields of golds, bronzes, and scarlets. A bright moon can introduce an ethereal ghostlike quality. The stubby oaks that speckle the slopes become contorted creatures, writhing and rolling in the half-light.

This is a silent, empty land. There are no communities by the roadside, only infrequent homesteads and barns. Occasionally someone has tried to impose a little of himself on the emptiness. For example, at Lewis Creek there are twelve brightly painted automobiles, all without wheels, all early '60s vintage, implanted in an even row, parallel and equidistant on the banks of the stream. One wonders who, in this endless realm of tiny valleys and dunelike hills, decided to exhaust his energies creating this unsigned statement. What symbolism was intended by the creator? Maybe after all it was merely someone saying, "Hey, I came here and did this just so someone would ask daft questions."

At Route 198 we turn left and immediately begin a long climb up into a region of deep eroded valleys, delicately pastel-colored. At Priest Valley I paused at the store to chat with the owner. Up the road a barnlike building creaked and snapped as the sun heated its corrugated walls. The sign over the door read "Dance Hall." For whom, I wondered? Who came here dancing in this bleak wilderness? "You'd be surprised," the lady at the store told me, with an enchanting smile. "It may look pretty lonesome 'round here now, but when there's a dance goin' they come out of the creeks 'n' gulches like jackrabbits from a bush fire. Quite a crowd comes up from the valley too, 'round Coalinga." She motioned to a large painting on the wall. The scene was an old saloon filled with caricatures of its regular clients, dozens of them. "That was done by one of my friends down there. She runs a saloon. Most of those folks get up here sometime or another." I looked at the painting. It bubbled with life, full of grinning, grimacing faces. You could almost hear the hullabaloo, the crashing of glasses, the raucous laughter, the rolling rumble of good friends having a good time. Then I looked at the empty store. Outside the sand devils scurried across the sagebrush. The gasoline sign creaked in the wind. The lady must have read my thoughts. "Well, it keeps you company, y'know, when it's quiet." Those people in the painting were her friends. I wondered how often she saw them.

Ten miles or so farther down the long descent, take the Parkfield Grade Road south toward Cholame. Drive slowly. This is a steep and, in places, a rather rough road back over the mountains. But what a drive! On a clear day you can see across the torn bleached hills around Coalinga, across the broad, blue-green San Joaquin Valley, across the eastern foothills, right to the very peaks of the Sierras beyond Yosemite and Kings Canyon. There are perhaps easier ways to reach the coast, but none even begin to compare with the majesty and drama of this drive.

At the crest of the ridge there's a final vista over the central valley and then we're switchbacking downhill, past odd-shaped basalt pillars, back into a pastoral landscape of oak woods and grazing land. Parkfield slumbers in a cocoon of deep shade and vine arbors. A rusty truck stands outside the dozing store. Farther down, the valley flattens and widens, and the final 10-mile stretch to Cholame is an arrow-straight road across range land reminiscent of the great spaces of northern Montana and central Texas. It's a marvelous opportunity to polish your cylinders with a bit of cleansing speed after all that mountain hopping.

Cholame at first glance seems to consist of a gas station and a tiny 9-foot-by-9-foot post office. But look again. Opposite the post office, around a large Tree of Heaven, is a strange memorial to actor James Dean, who was killed nearby in a motor accident on September 30, 1955. It is a rectilinear structure of stainless-steel shafts. Everyone who stops here seems to be more curious about the man who erected the monument than the person it commemorates, but Seita Ohnishi, a wealthy Tokyo businessman, doesn't seek publicity. He was merely one of Dean's devoted fans and wanted to express his admiration for the man's lifestyle and philosophy. Note the horizontal figure 8—the symbol for infinity—on the side of the stainless-steel shaft that mirrors the bend in the road where Dean was killed. Mr. Ohnishi has certainly done his bit to ensure the actor's immortalization.

From Cholame we follow Route 41 west through Shandon and then south through another odd stretch of dunelike landscape toward Atascadero. There are signs just outside Shandon warning of the road's narrow, winding characteristics. If your vehicle is somewhat oversized, it's best to heed the advice and take 46 west, rejoining the 41 in Atascadero.

After a long hairpinning descent from the high rolling plateau, we enter this odd little town with its palatial civic center set at the eastern end of a long expanse of landscaped lawn adorned with fountains and naked nymphs. A sign informs the curious visitor that the layout was patterned after the Taj Mahal and was part of Mr. E. G. Lewis' concept for a perfect Californian community. Lewis purchased the Atascadero Rancho in 1913 and immediately assembled a group of nationally prominent experts to help plan his visionary metropolis, covering 40 square miles. Many of the elements of his project were farsighted, including zoning ordinances based primarily on terrain and soil characteristics, elaborate public buildings and open spaces, an enclosed shopping center, a lake, a zoo, and even a 3-mile stretch of Pacific beach, 16 miles away, exclusively reserved for the residents and linked to the town by a dramatic mountain highway. Unfortunately for Mr. Lewis the town's growth was less than spectacular, although today the resident population has reached sixteen thousand and that journey (Route 41) across the coastal range to the beaches is as impressive as ever.

Morro Bay, with its famous collection of seafood restaurants, snack bars, charter fishing boats, and Museum of Natural History along the Embarcadero, all under the shadow of Morro Rock, is one of the most popular tourist centers on the California coast. For that reason, unless you have an urge to mingle with the crowds after those miles of driving through a people-less landscape, continue south through the beautiful Morro Bay State Park (also invariably overcrowded) and follow the signs to the largely undeveloped Montana de Oro State Park. Admittedly even this splendid area of rugged headlands and cozy coves attracts its fair share of visitors, but there are so many paths and coves to explore that it's not hard to discover a quiet niche to while away a day by the sea. If you visit in late fall or winter, you'll find the eucalyptus groves here filled with the fluttering of millions of tiny wings. This is the home of the monarch butterflies, which migrate from colder northern climes to spend a few months comfortably ensconced along various parts of the coast, from Pacific Grove on the Monterey Peninsula to Pismo Beach and Ventura. It's a very unusual sight.

If, however, you would prefer a place even farther removed from traditional tourist routes, then continue southward toward Guadalupe and Point Sal. As usual there's a hard and an easy route, the former following the Los Ossos Valley Road to the 101, the latter traversing yet another segment of coastal range after turning south on Prefumo Canyon Road, just by the Laguna Golf Course (on the Los Ossos Road). A word of warning—this is a slow, steep, bumpy road with unpaved segments on the higher portions, but the views back over the Bay and eastward across Black Butte and over Santa Margarita Lake make it all worthwhile. Toward the end of the drive, past the Sycamore Mineral Springs, you can either join Route 101 or take a short detour to Avila Beach and Port San Luis by turning right on San Luis Bay Road and right again on Avila Road. The nuclear power plant here welcomes visitors, in case you like to combine a little education with your relaxation.

From Route 101 take Route 1 south through Pismo Beach and Grover City toward Guadalupe. As the road approaches a dense grove of eucalyptus, note the sign to Halcyon. Here in 1903 a group of followers of the Wisdom Religion, an integral part of the Theosophical Movement, founded the Temple of the People, based upon "an ancient body of spiritual lore." They lived their lives according to "the Golden Rule" and built their philosophy upon "Religion, Science and Economics—the foundation stones of the Temple." Unlike many idealistic utopian settlements, Halcyon continues to flourish because, as its current head, Harold Forgostein, explained, "we never set out to be an exclusive community. People live here who are not part of the Temple and we get on together fine. There are some aspects of our teachings—such as those that deal with occultism—that are rather complex to grasp. When I say occultism, I'm not referring to witches and all that gobbledegook; I mean those forces of nature not normally perceived through the five senses. Essentially we believe in absolute self-responsibility and the continual improvement of each individual's spiritual character through reincarnation. We believe that we keep returning to this life until we finally grow to become part of God, what we call a master. All the prophets were masters—

Pt. Sal

Jesus, Buddha, Krishna—even Hiawatha was also a very important master." Harold, who was once an art teacher in San Luis Obispo, showed me a series of twenty-three large paintings he had done of Hiawatha's life (in the University Center, usually open on Saturdays, 2–4, or on request). Eight of them, entitled "Indian Legends" and "The Four Winds," were particularly outstanding, exploding from the wall in frantic sweeps and swirls of color. Harold was modest. "Oh, I did those a long time ago."

At the post office I talked with Eleanor Shumway about the community. "We're not very big now, only about a hundred members. But I think all human beings need to belong to some group, need that identity. This is my community. I can understand the basic tenets of the philosophy—the karma, the reincarnation—it explains a lot of life's injustices and foibles. It just seems to make sense." As we talked, people came in and out of the post office and I noticed an almost family-like relationship between them, very warm and responsive.

The Temple of the People is open to the public. Every day at noon there's a short meditation service that combines elements of Christianity with the Temple's own teachings. Also nearby, notice the exotic Victorian mansion surrounded, most unfortunately, by a mobile-home park. This is the Coffee T. Rice house, named after the businessman for whom the house was built. It was purchased in 1903 by the Temple for use as a sanatorium, and until the late 1920s it was this aspect of the Temple's work that attracted many of its earlier members.

186

The temple itself, hidden behind bushes and trees at the northern edge of the community, is an unusual triangular stucture surrounded by a continuous pillared portico. According to Harold, its shape symbolizes the trinity of God-powers in all systems of religion, and also the heart of man, source of the higher self.

At first this straggle of cottages in the woods hardly seems worth investigating. But that's what backroading is all about, looking a little more closely at places most people miss. Guadalupe, nearby for example with its Spanish-style church, Mexican restaurants, and brightly painted main street, is reminiscent of Tijuana. Old men, dark-skinned and mustached, squat in the shade or huddle in the dark bars over glasses of beer. The pace is slow. No one hurries in this sun-baked town. Even the dogs are too weary to snap at passing heels.

On both sides of the town there are access roads to the vast arc of dunes that curves northward to Pismo Beach. Unfortunately the dune buggies seem to have taken over, and for much of the year the beach is a very inhospitable place for sunbathers. So, continue on to what I think is the finest stretch of unspoiled coast in the region, at Point Sal. Admittedly, the 9-mile access road, with its unpaved sections, is quite a scramble as it switchbacks over the ridge and careers down the other side to a tiny parking area perched above a broad sweep of bay. But it's all worth it, especially if you give yourself a day here. The beach is usually uncrowded, and you can walk for a mile or more on golden sands beneath the dark, chaparral hills, watching the sea lions and enjoying the silence of latter-day California.

Just one word of caution. Close to the turnoff from Route 1 there's a sign reminding those heading to Point Sal that the beach is within the Vandenberg Missile Range and the road can be closed at any time the Air Force authorities wish. Fortunately they use their powers sparingly, and access is normally unrestricted.

After returning along the same road from Point Sal, continue across Route 1, through Betteravia (tours of the sugar factory here are usually available), over Route 101, and east on Route 176 toward Garey and Sisquoc.

Following the Santa Maria River, we enter a wide fertile valley resplendent with vineyards and budding wineries. Rancho Sisquoc, at the time of my visit, was not yet a bonded winery but produced an interesting Cabernet Sauvignon [call (805) 937–3616 for an appointment]. Farther south near Los Olivos is the Firestone Winery on Zaca Station Road (tastings 10–4 daily except Sunday), one of the most recently established wineries in the state and devoted to estate-bottled premium varietals.

Alongside the road we pass old country stores, the lovely little white church just outside Sisquoc, and the 1886 Mattei's Tavern at Los Olivos, once a stage and railroad terminal and still an extraordinarily popular restaurant. The village itself is slowly being "discovered" as a center for crafts, fine arts, and health foods. As you follow Ballard Canyon Road south from Los Olivos, look for a small cluster of buildings on the left-hand side behind the trees. This is Ballard, home of the little red schoolhouse. Now a historic landmark, the school has been in continuous operation since 1882. In fact the village itself was the first settlement in the Santa Ynez valley and contains a number of old homes, a delicately detailed Presbyterian Church, and most unexpectedly, a charming restaurant located in the old village store. It's run by John Elliott, a Brooklyn-born chef who worked at Manhattan's Lüchow's, Sardis's, and "21."

A mile or so down the road, past the well-preserved Santa Ynez mission, is the tourist town of Solvang, where the Old World flavor of Denmark has been superimposed, quite convincingly, on the original Spanish architecture. There are temptations galore for the gourmet, including the splendid array of bakeries and restaurants featuring inexpensive smorgasbords. Inevitably such an unusual community attracts a continual stream of tourists, but if you've never been here, at least one visit is recommended.

Route 154 east from Solvang is a fast leg of the journey to Santa Barbara, passing Santa Ynez, a surprisingly authentic Western-flavored community, and the usually crowded Lake Cachuma Recreational Area. These are not places for the backroad explorer, but the drive itself, up over the San Marcos Pass, is a scenic route full of variety and contrast. If you're not quite ready yet for the Spanish-style urbanity awaiting us below, make a detour on the Old Stagecoach Road, past Cold Springs Tavern, nestled in its wooded glen. Then cross directly over the 154 and follow the East Camino Road over the ridges of the Santa Ynez Mountains and down through Rattlesnake Park to join Route 192. This is a road known mainly to the locals and a rewarding final experience before entering the shady streets of Santa Barbara.

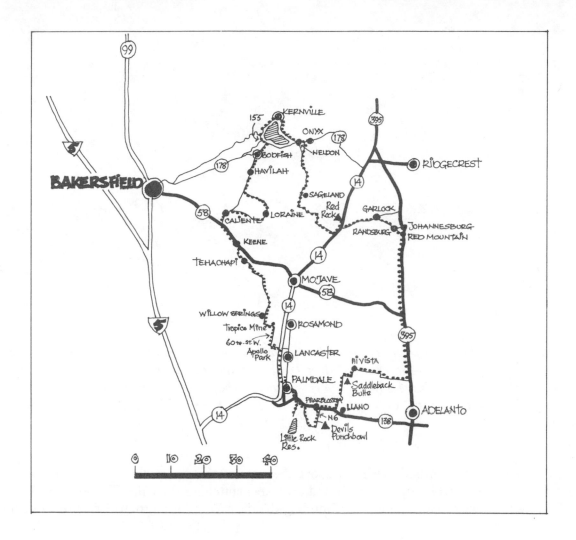

13. THE PALMDALE LOOP

Roaming Through the Desert Gold Country

Leave the smoggy suburbs far behind. Come exploring the fascinating backcountry of the Mojave desert and the gorge-threaded foothills of the southern Sierras. We wander past old gold

Tropico Gold Mine

mines and through ramshackle mining towns, pause at a lovely lake high in the mountains, sample the home-cured ham at a store unchanged since the 1850s, and discover the little-known charms of the Antelope Valley itself. There's history in this journey, the hard history of mining men, coupled with glimpses of the desert's brilliant beauty, its flourishing wildlife, and its ever-changing harmonies of color.

IT WAS 6:30 A.M. The sun had just risen above the edge of the desert and the Joshua trees were silhouetted against the gold dawn—furry-fisted creatures clutching for light. The air was chill and clear. There was no wind. Nothing moved. Nothing, that is, except for a group of fishermen with red noses.

Fishermen! In the desert?

It's true. All around, the parched sands stretched away to hazy infinities but here, at the landscaped lakes in Apollo Park (a sign points to it off Route 14, just north of Lancaster), a hardy bunch of anglers stood with rods rampant and thermos bottles by their sides, waiting for the first bites of morning. Just another one of those anomalies of life in southern California.

The park is named in honor of the first Apollo moon flight that transported Edwin "Buzz" Aldrin, Mike Collins, and the giant-step-for-mankind spokesman, Neil Armstrong, to the moon in July 1969. There's a replica of the space module near the parking area, and each of the three lakes is

named after one of the famous astronauts. Nearby, on the fringe of the airport, are the beginnings of the Antelope Valley Air Museum.

The park is a celebration of the future. The Tropico Mine, on the other hand, at the northern end of the desert valley at Sixtieth Street W., is an acclamation of the past. A huddle of worn clapboard buildings below the shattered bluffs of Tropico Hill tells of a time when the only inhabitants of the Mojave desert were transient miners, burrowing into the ocher buttes for gold. Visitors here can explore the old shafts with a guide (daily, 10–4; closed Tuesday and Wednesday) and browse through the mining museum. As was the case with many of California's richest mines, gold was discovered here accidentally in 1894, when Ezra Hamilton, owner of a Los Angeles pottery, found signs of ore in the fire clays sent him from the Rosamond area. Surreptitiously he began his own explorations in the hills at the edge of the desert and finally discovered the lode. His Lida mine flourished, and the ore was of such exceptional quality that it was exhibited at the 1904 World's Fair in St. Louis. Ezra was soon a wealthy man. But he had other plans. He sold his mine and established a sanatorium and health spa at nearby Willow Springs in an old stage station. Later he added cottages, bathhouses, and a hotel, all massive structures of rock and cement, and experimented with silkworm rearing and winemaking in the verdant estate surrounding his resort. Today Willow Springs is a sad remnant, worn by the winds. The ponds and shade trees are gone, along with most of the buildings.

On the outskirts of the abandoned settlement, Jim Russell has his International Racing

Driver School at the race track here, which twists among the sandy foothills. Occasional trials and competitions bring some life back to the area, but for most of the year it's a silent niche in the desert inhabited only by the Joshua trees, odd plants often growing to more than 20 feet in height. On the Tehachapi–Willow Springs Road near the famous Cactus Silver Mine I noticed an area where they were forest-thick in a profusion of knobbly limbs and spiky trunks. Half-close your eyes and you'd swear they were moving toward you with evil intent. Yet come in early spring, when these distant relatives of the lily family sparkle with creamy blossoms and you'll enjoy the gentler side of their nature.

The road winds its way laboriously over the Tehachapi Mountains with incredible views back across the desert, and then drops sharply down to Highline Road. Turn left here and then right after 5 miles, on to Backes Lane. Look for signs to the Tehachapi Mountain park, a delightful detour to picnic areas and campgrounds in a rocky glen below Woody's Peak. Follow the bends and continue north on the Tehachapi road through clusters of white-fenced ranches. Pretty girls ride exquisitely groomed mares across the bleached pastures, and ranch houses peer out from oak knolls. Beyond are the Sierra mountains, brooding and ominous. We climb up through Piñon Canyon and begin a winding descent.

A mile or two before Keene, where we join Route 58 briefly to the Caliente turnoff, look out for the world-renowned Tehachapi railroad loop, built in 1876 under the direction of Southern Pacific's remarkable engineer, William Hood. The track here does a complete 360 degree turn. As the plaque explains, a 4,000-foot-long train will cross over itself 77 feet above its rear cars. I was disgruntled: a train had looped through here a mere three minutes prior to my arrival.

From Caliente I moved up a craggy gorge filled with torn cottonwood trees. The stream bed was dry, but something, wind or water, had obviously given the valley a recent battering. Broken limbs hung dejectedly from the leaning trunks. A tiny clapboard cabin stood roofless at the edge of the road. I'd heard talk of windstorms that reached hurricane proportions in the mountains where they funneled through the clefts. I stopped to talk with an elderly man in a wide-brimmed Stetson walking by the roadside. "Oh yeah, it got us last week. There's 'nother one comin', so I hear. Bad time of the year, this, for winds." I asked him about the roofless shack. "That's Luke's place. He's away right now. He's a prospectin' man. Got a mine up in the hills someplace. He's goin' to have a hell of a shock when he gets back!" His face broke into a hundred leathery wrinkles as he laughed. "Still from what I hear he won't be needin' it now. They say he's found himself some good ore up there. He's a lucky one. I've known fellas live round here five, six years and never found more'n an ounce or two. You never can tell. Yeah, Luke's sure a lucky one."

I left him smiling at the roadside and continued on up the canyon to the fork with the Bodfish Road. During the dry season this paved shortcut over the Piute Mountains is one of the most exciting drives in the southern Sierras. If there's any likelihood of wind or rain, though, it's best to avoid it, as landslides are commonplace; take the Twin Oaks loop around Harper Peak instead. It's a lovely ramble through dramatic gorges and quiet valleys. The occasional cabin peers up from behind the scrub bushes and a couple of gold mines have been reopened in the area. I paused at the Sand Canyon store to find out more about local mining activity. Country music played from a squeaky radio and a rotund lady stood behind the counter regarding me curiously. "We don't get too many strangers 'round this way. Where you headin'?" I told her I was traveling north to Lake Isabella. "Well, you sure picked the hard way, It's pretty, though," she added.

The ceiling of the tiny store dripped with old bits and pieces of guns, holsters, branding irons, and spurs. "They've been here twenty years or more. I remember them when I was a kid. People are always wantin' to buy 'em but the boss says they've got to stay put. They're part of the store almost." I asked about the mining. "Why, you thinkin' of trying?" She chortled. "Hell you wouldn't be the first to come up here fresh and find gold. There's still plenty left. The big mine, Mammoth and Eureka, that's doin' pretty good now and there's talk of openin' up a few of the other old places." I asked if there was anything for visitors to see. "No, no, they don't want people around. Folks in these parts are pretty secretive about things. You find that in most mining places. Always a lot of rumors and tales, but those that know what's goin' on just shut up and shovel!" She laughed loudly. "That's what they say y'know, just shut up and shovel!"

A little farther up the valley we pass "Lizzie" McGuirk's ranch in a clump of trees by the roadside. Lizzie was a prototype pioneer. She arrived here in 1876 and eventually came to own and operate the Gwynne gold mine, the store, the hotel, and the stage station. The plaque erected in her memory also adds the titles of cattle rancher, Indian agent, and postmistress to her remarkable list of accomplishments. Her spirit lives on in the valley. This is still very much pioneering country.

At Walker Basin, an exquisite bowl of grazing land surrounded by dark mountains, we head north over a steep pass into the Havilah Valley. The town itself, once the county seat of Kern County, is the sleepy remnant of a flourishing past. Gold mining attracted a large population in the 1869–80 period, and local history buffs have erected signs and plaques at regular intervals along the town's short main street. Little actually remains, though, besides the first Kern County Courthouse and a concrete plinth marking the original school site. Still it keeps its country charm and is a pleasant place to rest awhile under the shade trees.

After another climb, this time north out of the Havilah valley, we suddenly face the majestic panorama over Isabella Lake and the Sequoia National Forest. What a view this is! Far, far below resort communities huddle alongside the blue waters and sneak up into the canyons. At the northern end the Kern River curls its way down through a wooded valley and pours into the lake near the tiny community of Kernville. High above, clouds scurry across Black Mountain and the Baker Ridges, their shadows dappling the dark hillside.

Unfortunately, the scene is somewhat less appealing when we have completed the spiraling descent and slip down the final slope into Bodfish and Lake Isabella village. Tacky stores and real-estate offices dot the roadside, and hamburger stands attract a jostling crowd of weary adults and shouting children. But escape is at hand. Take Route 155 across the river and immediately turn left on Keysville Road to the last silent remnants of an old gold-mining town. There's not too much to see, but it's a lovely valley here below the Greenhorn Mountains. Alternatively drive around the lake through Kernville and look for your own private cove along the eastern shore. Finally, if you have plenty of spare time and you'd prefer to do something really crazy, drive the unpaved Greenhorn Mountain ridge road down to Bakersfield (take the Saw Mill Road off Route 155 just past the Boulder Gulch Campground, and then travel south on Rancheria Road) and dine at one of the town's splendid Basque restaurants. Return up the tortuous Kern Canyon Road (178) and rejoin the route at the eastern end of the lake, where we continue on to Weldon.

Here's another of those almost forgotten communities. The large white store stands at a road junction, empty and ghostlike. Across the fields in an unfortunate state of decay is the old Brown and Co. Flour Mill with some of its intricate machinery still intact. In contrast a few miles farther down the road is the noble Onyx store, a place usually full of life and laughter. During summer it's almost smothered by the colossal cottonwoods guarding the front entrance. Inside are squeaking floor-boards, stuffed animal heads, antlers, and bits of saddlery dangling from the high ceiling. Conversation is always abundant, and the owners love to tell strangers of the store's remarkable history. It was supposedly built in the 1850s by a local rancher, William Scodie, in conjunction with an adjoining hotel. Often the haven of Hollywood stars, the hotel's register reveals such names as Charles Chaplin, Jean Harlow, Douglas Fairbanks, Jr., and Mary Pickford. The store itself was robbed by none other than Tiburcio Vásquez, the infamous California bandit who helped himself to the money and merchandise and left poor Mr. Scodie bound in a chair behind the counter. Today, however, things are a little less hectic, and the store's main claim to fame is its homemade sausage and cured hams, which seem to attract customers from all over the state.

At Onyx there's a choice of route. If you'd enjoy a fast scenic drive back over the Sierras and down into the desert, then take the Walker Pass Road (178) to Route 14 and turn south to Red Rock Canyon. Alternatively, there's an exciting backroad journey on the Kelso Valley Road south through an old mining area to Jawbone Canyon on Route 14. The central section of about 19 miles is unpaved, but a good surface carries us safely through impressive mountain scenery. Unless rain or windstorms are likely, this is the best route for backroaders.

Return a couple of miles from the Onyx store to the Kelso Creek Road and take it south, joining with the Kelso Valley Road after 4 miles. Here we begin the slow ascent up past the site of Sageland, once the trading center for the miners in these hills. The road off to the right climbs into the Piute Mountains. Most of the mines are now closed, their names ringing with the sound of the '90s—the Lone Star Mine, the Waterhole Mine, the Alaska Mine, the Iconoclast Mine, and the Gwynne Mine, once operated by tough Lizzie McGuirk, whose ranch we passed near Walker Basin. There's plenty of opportunity for detouring up here, and it's a favorite haunt of the more avid bottle hunters. If you're uncertain about the ability of your vehicle to negotiate some of the rougher parts,

Onyx Store

though, keep on the Kelso Valley Road to Jawbone Canyon Road and then begin the long descent to the paved section at Blue Point. This appropriately named mountain is a glorious riot of turquoises, in a canyon glowing with purples, bronzes, and golds. The towering rocky monolith facing you as you make the last winding descent is a mass of color writhing in the heat waves. It's a wonderfully desolate place.

Just before the junction with Route 14 note the remarkable Jawbone Siphon, part of the aqueduct system carrying water from high in the Owens Valley all the way to Los Angeles. Constructed in 1912, the individual steel sections for the pipe, each of which weighs 26 tons, were hauled in specially built wagons with steel wheels, pulled by teams of fifty-two mules. Today it's still a remarkable feat of engineering, not to mention art. The bold uncompromising sweep of the 7-foot diameter black and white pipe, down one side of the canyon, flat across the bottom, and then swooping way up and over the other side, is aesthetically comparable to recent examples of large-scale "environmental art."

A few miles to the north is Red Rock Canyon, one of the most interesting geological formations in the Mojave desert. Here one can wander for hours among strangely eroded rocks, pastel-colored and wraith-shaped, appropriately named the Towers of Silence, Temple of the Sun, Buried City, and Shrine of Solitude. The best way to explore is to take 14 up through the canyon first and then double back on Abbott Drive, pausing at the ranger station to pick up a pamphlet with suggested trails. After that it's up to you. There are scores of mini-canyons to investigate, and if your vehicle is four-wheel-drive, you'll find an abundance of routes into the valleys east and west of the park itself.

The area is rich in fossils. The soft sedimentary rocks were laid down in the Pliocene era sea, and evidence suggests that during that period, prior to the formation of the Sierra Nevada and El Paso ranges, camels, antelopes, saber-toothed cats, rhinoceroses, and mastodons roamed in the chaparral hills around this inland lake.

The canyon itself has always been an important thoroughfare. Nomadic Indians passed through here, and petroglyph evidence suggests that more than fifteen thousand years ago the area was inhabited by the "Old People." In the 1850s miners moved through on every conveyance imaginable up into the Sierra gold-mining country, and later, during the 1890s, the canyon even attracted its own little gold rush at the same time that the adjoining El Pasos were being inundated by claim seekers. The town of Ricardo sprang up to serve the miners. Later, when the rush had peaked (it's rumored that more than $10 million of gold was mined in the canyon alone), a few buildings remained for many years as a stage stop. The ranger station is all that is left on the site of Ricardo today.

To the east the gold rush had a more marked influence. Four-wheel-drive vehicles may be able to negotiate the tortuous tracks over the El Pasos, passing such interesting remnants of the mining era as Schmidt's Tunnel, but most backroaders would be wise to take the Red Rock–

Randsburg Road east along the Fremont Valley. Garlock, a group of dilapidated structures by a bend in the road, was the site of a large stamp mill built in 1896 for processing the ore from the famous Yellow Aster mine, high on the slopes of the Rand Mountains across the valley. But such was the mine's wealth that by 1898 a 130-stamp mill operation flourished in Randsburg itself, and the town developed from a straggle of grubby tents to a flourishing community of hotels, restaurants, saloons, whorehouses, and even a church or two. Unlike most other places in the region, Randsburg kept its mines and its 53 miles of tunnels open for almost fifty years, producing more than $16 million in gold. And even then the town didn't die, but along with its sister cities Johannesburg and Red Mountain, experienced two more "booms"—one for tungsten and the other for silver. It's claimed locally that the Kelly Mine at Red Mountain produced more than $20 million in silver before being closed in 1947.

Today the rugged hillsides, torn by the vicious Mojave winds, are littered with the debris of the ore booms. Yet, surprisingly, there are few abandoned buildings up here. Most of the homes in the three communities are occupied, although many seem held togethor by tin sheets and batten boards and look as if a good blast of breeze through the high mountain pass will send them cartwheeling through the scrub.

Randsburg has a distinct personality. From a distance, the scattering of flimsy shacks with peeling paint resembles an abandoned film set. But along main street there's life and action. Two museums present displays of mining equipment and other more intimate glimpses of life in a mining town. A few antique stores, authentically museum-like themselves, attract weekend trade from the cities to the south during the cooler months. The old false-front barbershop is now a small art gallery, and the woman at the soda fountain in the general store seems just as comfortable serving curious outsiders as locals. "We don't need tourists," she told me, "but we don't mind 'em, so long as they don't go messin' around all over our lots. Heck, let's face it, 'cept for a few old-timers we're all from someplace else anyway. A few of us came for a day and just stayed on. Well, you could pick up a house for a couple of thousand a few years back, sometimes you could just walk in free, and there's no taxes and no hassle here. Police never bother us. We handle our own problems."

Randsburg is one of the most authentic mining towns in California. Although its antique stores and art gallery rely on outside trade, there's no self-conscious "twee-ness," no attempt to create a Calico with false-bearded prospectors and gold-era saloons. "Hell, for all we know, this place might just come alive again," Gary Parker, owner of the Bottle Shop, told me. "There's often talk of new finds. If the price of gold keeps goin' up, we may be back in the boom days. Happened in the Depression, y'know, when everybody was starvin' to death, that's when this place really lived. People in the cities were workin' for a dollar a day, these guys here were makin' seven dollars. We're just restin' now, waiting for the next one to come." Gary smiled. "It's a good life. The saloon is where everybody meets. Nobody cares how you drive up to the bar, don't even care if you drink or not—so long as you come. There's none of that status nonsense 'round here."

Red Rock Canyon

From Randsburg my plan was to follow the 20 Mule Team Parkway to California City, one of the desert's new "planned" communities, and then go south through the Edwards Air Force base to Saddleback Butte State Park. Unfortunately, the base was closed to through traffic and, from all accounts, looked as if it would stay that way for quite some time. So there's little choice but to take the lonely, fast 395 south to Adelanto and then west to the Butte. If this 60-mile stretch of highway gets a little monotonous, head off right on Shadow Mountains Road (10 miles north of Adelanto) to Hi Vista and then south on 200th Street to Saddleback. It's a good road, and you'll pass through some wild desert scenery as you travel west through the El Mirage Valley.

Saddleback Butte was created as a state park in 1960 to protect one of Antelope Valley's finest rock buttes and to preserve the native Joshua tree woodland that flourished on its slopes. Interpretative material is limited here, but visitors are free to roam where they wish across the broken hillsides or follow the trail to the 3,651-foot peak. The views from here are impressive in the spring, when the whole desert bursts into a gushing bloom of color. To the north, south, and west are extensive areas of wildflowers, some of which have been declared official sanctuaries.

A short distance from the butte (south on 170th Street and west on Avenue M) is one of the region's most fascinating museums. Initially founded by artist H. Arden Edwards in 1928, this odd jumble of Tudor-influenced steep-roofed buildings huddled below Lovejoy Butte offers splendid displays of southwest Indian artifacts. Baskets, soapstone, carvings, quiltwork, jewelry, and mats from the Hopi, Navajo, Zuñi, and Apache tribes are included in the collection, thanks to the diligent efforts of Grace Oliver, who coordinated the museum's expansion and maintenance. Try not to miss this place—it's charming and totally unexpected in this bleak scrub-covered wilderness.

Continuing south of 170th Street, we pass another of those rather pathetic new desert communities that invariably come equipped with lake, restaurant, sales office, and smatterings of brilliant green turf. One can't help feeling that eventually people may well settle by the hundreds in the Antelope Valley and its wildflower sanctuaries will ultimately be buried under a plethora of pools and parking lots. Fortunately, though, progress is quite slow. Most of these "new towns" are still a planner's pipe dream. Some, in fact, have already been and gone, as is the case with Llano del Rio at the junction of 165th Street and Route 138. Here in 1914, the socialist visionary and exponent Job Harriman founded a utopian community on these parched acres. He and his nine hundred followers, each of whom paid an initial fee of $500 to live here, proceeded to develop an elaborate system of cobblestone water channels, and within a short time the community was growing most of its own food and making a small profit selling its products and handicrafts to the outside world. In 1916 a lavish hotel was built out of large river boulders, and the town was featured in some of the nation's prominent magazines as a prototype of future communities. Then, alas, the valley experienced a long drought, and by 1918 the place was virtually deserted, returned to the desert by Harriman's disgruntled followers.

Today, near the tiny real-estate office, there's a sign stuck in the sand that reads "Town for

Main Street—Randsburg

Sale." "Yeah, that's right," the agent told me from behind a big cigar. "You wannit?" He pointed to the thick pillars across the road, all that was left of the hotel. "Foundation's solid as a rock. Wouldn't take too much to build that up again." He looked at me expectantly. I left wondering what Mr. Harriman would have thought of the agent's sales technique.

From Llano, continue south of 165th Street up Halcomb Ridge to the Devil's Punchbowl County Park. This little-known area of strangely eroded sedimentary rocks in a chaparral bowl provides some excellent nature trails and exciting canyon walks for the curious traveler. The place abounds with wildlife—snakes and lizards of every type, horned toads, grey foxes, red-tailed hawks, tarantula spiders, scorpions, and cute big-eared Piñon mice. Pause first at the interpretative center, where there are excellent displays on the Punchbowl's geological origins and its flora and fauna. When I was there I found the profusion of "Jesus" signs among the exhibition cases a little distracting, but the park rangers were a helpful if somewhat effusive lot. One of them wished me a beaming "God be with you" as I set out on the Piñon pathway.

There's one final stop before reaching Route 14 at Palmdale. Return along Route N6 to Fort Tejon Road, turn left, and rejoin Route 138 at Little Rock. Three miles farther on, at Four Points, follow signs south to Little Rock Reservoir, a narrow stretch of water in a steep-sided valley.

There are campsites for those reluctant to return to Palmdale and the parched sands far below, and picnic areas for others content to spend a few hours lying by the lake watching the eagles spiral above Mt. Emma, or listening to the breeze in the chaparral.

Enjoy.

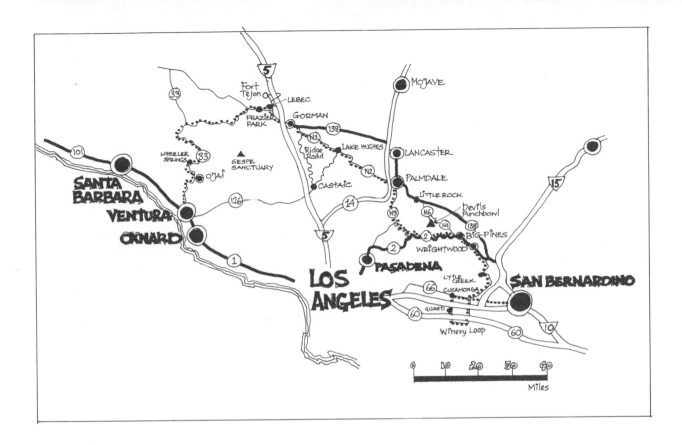

14. VENTURA TO SAN BERNARDINO
The Great Los Angeles Bypass

Why suffer the interminable anxiety of freeway driving through the heart of the Los Angeles basin, when there's a splendid alternative?

Assuming your intent is to move from east to west, or west to east, across that endless sprawl of single-family homes and cloverleaves, the best idea by far is to bypass it all! This chapter will not only tell you how to do this but also introduce you to many hidden delights en route, including old Indian hot springs in a forgotten valley, vistas over the wilderness of a condor sanctuary, a fort once famous for its camels, an abandoned Irish castle, and a hair-raising switch back along the crest of the San Gabriels. After many miles of quiet ramblings on narrow roads we explore a hobbit land of rounded rocks, meander along the towering slopes of a wide, river-torn canyon, and reenter the bustling basin to enjoy a little wine tasting. It certainly makes a change from freeways!

OUR JOURNEY really begins north of Ojai. To the south the state beaches at Ventura and the San Buenaventura Mission attract a disproportionate crowd, and Lake Casitas is invariably smothered by admirers. Ojai itself, once a sleepy Spanish-flavored community snuggled in the Los Padres foothills, has now attracted all the accouterments of twentieth-century affluence. Overheated autos snail along main street and parking lots occupy the old orchards, a predicament all too familiar in contemporary southern California.

But a mere mile north of town on 33 we enter dark-green groves of citrus trees and climb steeply into the chaparral-covered mountains. The bustle of the valley is far behind. Hawks wheel over the scoured hills and breezes blow fresh and clean. At Matilija Hot Springs Park, below the dam, a stream gurgles between rounded boulders and a family prepares lunch at a barbecue pit. In Madame Sophie's antique store the tiny woman with sparkling eyes tells me in a Spanish-flavored accent, "we're hidden away here. Not too many people come, mostly the same people. They go to the bath and then sit by the water just like the Indians used to." Apparently the hot mineral springs were a favorite resting place for the Chumash Indians. In 1871 a Mr. Wilcox developed his health resort here, adding cabins and a hotel in 1873. Not surprisingly in this narrow cleftlike valley, a flood destroyed most of the buildings a few years later, but in typical pioneering tradition the place was quickly reestablished on an even grander scale with bathhouses. Today the modest facilities include a pool, indoor baths, Jacuzzis and an array of massage treatments for the true enthusiasts.

After Wheeler Springs, another valley spa restored following the 1969 flood, we enter a bleak gorge of broken rocks and vertical precipices. The narrow road snakes its way up through three short tunnels to the open hillsides beyond. Pause near the crest and look back down the long valley, out across the ocean, to the Channel Islands along the horizon. This is true southern California. These are the vistas that led one of the early missionaries to write in his journal: "This is a fearful place, lonely and apart. Yet God is here in the canyons and across the mountain tops. The natives know God in these places. They know he is here."

A few miles to the east is the larger of two condor sanctuaries, more than 53,000 acres, originally established in 1947 as a haven for these giant birds. According to a recent report there are less than fifty of these creatures left today. Patient watchers may see the occasional twosome slowly spiraling up the mountain air currents, their wings outstretched to more than 10 feet, their tip feathers splayed like fingers. Close up they are hardly attractive creatures, resembling overgrown turkey buzzards. In the mid-1800s they were hunted for their huge flight feathers, the quills of which were used as gold-dust containers by the early miners. Gradually the species began to disappear. The female lays only one egg every two years, and, unlike the more protective birds, will often abandon her nest if she senses danger. In 1901 concerned naturalists sponsored statutes to ensure the condor's protection, but their numbers still continued to diminish. As civilization encroached upon the coastal ranges from Oregon to lower California, the great birds moved from their traditional nesting places in search of more reclusive habitats. Today the Sespe Wildlife Refuge and a smaller area near Sisquoc are the only places they occupy on a regular basis. Access in both cases is restricted, but the U.S. Forest Service ranger station in Ojai will provide information on hiking routes and regulations. If you're intending to take photographs, make sure you have telescopic equipment. These creatures are extremely reluctant subjects and seem to delight in tantalizing shutter-happy travelers by flying the spirals to such a height that it's hard to distinguish them from dust spots on the lens.

After the tight squeeze through the air-bubbled sandstones of Sespe Gorge we follow a long, level valley westward past the Pine Mountain Inn. A garage mechanic in Ventura had reacted with great enthusiasm when I told him which route I was taking over the mountains. "Oh, you'll see pine trees up there," he gushed. I hadn't the heart to tell him that I'd just come back from the Oregon mountains and had seen more than enough of pine trees. "Yeah, near the top, there's whole bunches of them." I suppose in this endless wilderness of scrub and chaparral, a few pine trees do attract attention. And he was right. As I traveled alongside Sespe Creek I noticed small clusters of pines in hollows on the north slope of Ortega Hill. An elderly man was busy taking photographs. I wondered if I was missing something. "It's very rare to see pines in these hills," he told me with the same kind of enthusiasm as the garage mechanic. I looked again. They seemed rather small and scraggly. "Wait till you get to the top of the hill over there." He pointed to the road where it climbed steeply up the hillside at the end of the valley. At Pine Mountain summit I understood his point. The view north was bleak. A series of parallel ranges stretched away to a hazy horizon. Those in the foreground had a light covering of scrub on ocher-colored flanks, but each successive range had less and less vegetation and exposed more and more of its eroded skeleton to the elements. In the far distance the ranges were light-lemon-colored, like sand dunes. I felt parched standing there. Turning around, I could see the verdant chaparral hills tumbling away to the ocean and understood why people treasured those pines so much. Their quiet, cool shade offered a sanctuary from the great empty wilderness of the Cuyama badlands beyond—nature providing a hospitable haven before the long descent.

And what a descent it is! The road switchbacks down the dry hillside, gullied by a recent storm, and gusts of hot wind send the tumbleweed bounding across the road. Groups of them huddle, creature-like, in ditches, moving and shifting ominously, and then leap out, blown by the wind through the scrub. Sand devils scurry across the hillside like desert wraiths. Down in a boulder creek a clapboard shack crumbles into the creosote. Bits of fencing still mark the boundary of the hardscrabble homesteads. A pile of rusting cans half-covered by sand suggests someone actually tried to make a life out of this place once, a long time back.

Past the ranger station at the bottom of the descent we turn east along the Lockwood Valley Road to Lake of the Woods and Frazier Park. A sign warns that the road is subject to flooding and closure. Frequent dips into sandy washes give it a switchback feel, but it's a comfortable drive. There are trees again, and at the Owl's Barn, a bunch of locals gather for a few beers and a discussion on last week's square dance. "We don't get too many strangers through here. Usta once, y'know, but not so much now." From the ceiling dangle a score of owls, glass ones, plastic ones, string ones, and a wooden one that winks. Fat jars behind the bar contain pickles and hot sausages. A radio plays country music. The conversation murmurs on. Outside the wind bustles down the valley, sending more sand devils scurrying across the dry pastures and abandoned lots.

At Route I–5 there's a detour north to Fort Tejon, located in an oak-shaded meadow alongside Grapevine Creek. From the original complex of more than twenty buildings only two remain, but the interpretative displays are so effective that one can sense the flavor of the place during the fort's active period, 1854 to 1864.

"The Troopers," so a sign reads, "guarded miners and Indians, chased bandits and gave band concerts." One has the feeling that maybe the concerts were accorded highest priority here, for this was no humdrum camp of raggle-taggle soldiers but the home of the elite First U.S. Dragoons. The caliber of these men was such that in the upcoming Civil War, fifteen of the officers who served at Fort Tejon later became generals, eight with the Northern forces and seven with the Southern. The Dragoon uniforms were the most elaborate in the army, and they were the only soldiers permitted to

Sespe Sanctuary Country

wear mustaches and grow their hair long. They knew they were special, and a spell at Fort Tejon was considered one of the fringe benefits of an elite army life.

The Fort is perhaps best known for the camels brought here by Edward F. Beale under the direction of U.S. Secretary of War Jefferson Davis in 1857. These ungainly creatures performed magnificently, each doing the work of four mules, and plans were made for their more extensive use throughout the southwest. However, the outbreak of war terminated such schemes, and the camels were removed to Los Angeles in 1861.

The museum here, in addition to presenting an overview of the fort's role in early California history, also contains a small exhibition of the Chumash and Yokut Indians, and a display of the Peter le Beck story. This gentleman, of whom little is known, was supposedly killed by a bear in 1837 and buried near a large oak tree in what later became the fort's parade ground. There are a few interesting theories about le Beck's actual identity and his reason for being here at such an early pre-gold-rush time, but none have been verified—so the man remains a mystery.

Take Route I–5 briefly over Tejon summit to Gorman and then follow the Gorman Post Road and Route 138 past Quail Lake to Route N2. Alternatively, if you're still a frustrated condor seeker or fancy a little real backcountry driving, return from Fort Tejon on the service road through Lebec to Peace Valley Road (paralleling the freeway) and follow this for about 2 miles to Hungry Valley Road. Here turn south into a pastoral valley of grazing land for 5 miles, and then follow signs to the

Gold Hill ranger station, where it's best to inquire about road conditions for the loop drive around the summit of Alamo Mountain. At certain times of the year, especially after rain, the roads can become a little too rutted for standard automobiles. This is lonely country up here, but the views from Alamo are among the finest in the Los Padres National Forest, especially to the south over the Sespe Condor Sanctuary. If you don't see any of those birds from here, then you're really out of luck!

Rejoining our route at the western edge of the Antelope Valley, we climb up the slopes of Bald Mountain to Pine Canyon Road (N2). Immediately to the south is the infamous Ridge Road, a 48-mile stretch of hairpins, which, in its original form, provided drivers with almost 40,000 degrees of turn. When it was first built in the 1914–19 period, it was classed quite justifiably as "a miracle of modern engineering" and attracted a memorable array of gas stations, tourist cabins, snack bars and the famous Sandberg's resort. The sign says "Not a through road" and warns about lack of maintenance. This inaccurate information is really a test of driver resolution. It's actually a splendid, if slightly jolting, drive, and those intrepid backroaders wishing to embark on this slow journey into yesteryear should rejoin our route by taking the scenic Lake Hughes Road north from Castaic to Lake Hughes. Detourists should be warned, however, before embarking on this journey, that it is rather time-consuming and tiring.

Those taking the basic route will continue east along Pine Canyon Road (N2), meandering through oak- and scrub-studded hills with occasional vistas over the desert-like Antelope Valley far below. The road follows the line of the San Andreas Fault, although there are few indications of this at ground level. Odd signs at the roadside point up rough tracks leading to the Running Well Ranch, The Land of Oz, and Niavarna. One reads pointedly "Hermit—keep out." The land has a reclusive character. There are few houses in view, yet one feels that people live here, hidden in little niches up narrow rocky valleys.

At the Three Points we turn right, continuing along Route N2. The road is wider and faster and there are more signs of habitation. The occasional ranch appears with white-painted fences, and even a few mobile homes have crept surreptitiously into scrub-covered lots.

Lake Hughes, a place of modest cabins and sleepy motels, has a pleasantly old-fashioned resort atmosphere. The town store and tavern has received an ambitious facelift of river-rock arches. An attractive young woman behind the counter complained of lack of trade because of the drought. "There's hardly any lake left," she lamented. Elizabeth Lake, a mile or so farther down the valley, has actually vanished. One disappointed fisherman stood dejectedly looking over the dry grasses and bits of soggy marsh, once a favorite haunt of anglers. "I didn't believe them," he told me, "they said it had gone but I thought they were joking."

Near the eastern end of the lake there's the narrow Munz Ranch Road that meanders off to the left. If you're in the mood for yet one more detour, follow it for a couple of miles and then take the unpaved road to the left with the sign to Fairmont Reservoir. Look for the bleak mansion set against the hills. This is "Shea's Castle," once the home of John and Ellen Shea. John was a

The Old Ridge Road

prosperous Los Angeles realtor who designed his residence based on some photographs he'd collected of fourteenth-century Irish castles. Surrounding his estate of 1760 acres, he had 8 miles of fencing erected and for a few brief years lived a truly baronial life until the stock market crash of 1929 eradicated his fortune and he was obliged to sell out and move back to the city. According to the legend, he later committed suicide off Santa Monica pier with his wife's cremated remains tied in a leather bag around his neck.

Today the castle is deserted. There's been talk of opening the estate to the public, but the ornate gates still remain locked, and notices attached to the high fence warn visitors of guard dogs. The place retains its aura of sadness and mystery.

Back on Route N2 follow the first sign to Green Valley and then bear left to Leona Valley and Palmdale alongside the quiet Amargosa Creek down into the flat desert of the Antelope Valley. Palmdale is one of those nondescript communities with a main street lined with junk-food establishments and gas stations. The only notable building is the new library, a Spanish-style edifice with an interior sunken court and kingly chairs. Some claim all this will soon change, though, and that a few years from now the great tidal wave of Los Angeles overspill will come roaring through the San Gabriel canyons and flood out across the Antelope Valley in a surf of single-family homes. So far, however, there's little sign of this. Although the desert is etched with a gridiron pattern of roads and highways, Joshua forests flourish undisturbed and shattered buttes peer out over the gray-brown wilderness, unpeopled and empty.

At Palmdale there's another choice of route to be made. The Pearland–Little Rock–Wrightwood Road (Fort Tejon Road and N4) climbs slowly out of the desert into the northern foothills of the San Gabriels and the Big Pines recreation area. En route, travelers can pause at Little Rock Reservoir, south of Pearland, and the Devil's Punchbowl Park (both of which form part of the Palmdale loop; see Chapter 13).

Alternatively, for a change of pace and perspective take Route N3 (Sierra Highway) south from Palmdale. We're soon out of the subdivisions and climbing steadily up the Angeles Forest Highway toward 4,910-foot-high Mill Creek summit. Here the canyons to the south were the scene of an 1880s gold rush. Mines such as Monte Cristo, Black Crow, and Gold Bar have left their legendary folklore in these hills. Somewhere down there, so the story goes, is the fabled Los Padres Mine, which supplied the mission fathers of San Fernando with thousands of dollars of gold dust, millions according to some, prior to the 1833–34 secularization period. A few brief decades later, miners swarmed up the gulleys searching for the lost mine but it remained a mystery, and even today the odd prospector can still be found groping his way up the canyons, tapping the rocks, examining tailings, and believing with all his heart that the next boulder he moves will reveal the secret tunnel.

At Mill Creek summit we turn left on an unpaved road past the ranger station and immediately begin a hairpinning 15-mile journey across the crest of the San Gabriels. Take it slow and use the horn on the sharper bends. The views after the initial ascent are incredible. To the north the vast ocher-colored Mojave desert stretches into a haze of beiges and whites. The Greenhorn, Piute, and Tehachapi ranges rise dark and ominous from the sandy flatlands. In late fall the snow-flecked peaks of the Sierras often peer above the haze, and there's a mountain that looks remarkably like Mt. Whitney more than 150 miles to the north. In the other direction we look across range after range of San Gabriels and way over to the Los Angeles basin and the Pacific. If you happen to be here on one of those rare days when the air is pure as crystal, you'll also catch a glimpse of Santa Catalina and San Clemente islands.

There are frequent turnouts to pause and enjoy these vistas and the narrow road leapfrogs on either side of the ridge. One moment we're looking over the Mojave wastelands, the next, deep into the forested canyons beyond Round Top mountain. For the truly energetic there are trails signed to Granite and Pacifico Mountains, where you can view the 360-degree panorama from the wind-whipped summits. Except for the occasional weekend traffic, you'll normally have the road and the mountains to yourself.

We join the famous Angeles Crest Highway a few miles below Waterman Mountain ski lift and begin a long drive back over the ridges to Wrightwood. There are few roads anywhere that can match its splendor, yet I have met scores of southern Californians who have never even explored the southern tip leading to the Mount Wilson observatory. While hardly a backroad, the Crest Highway is usually quiet during the week and one can again enjoy the dramatic panoramas from almost empty turnouts.

At Vincent Gulch Divide there's a signed detour off to the Devil's Punchbowl (left-hand fork). If you've never visited this unusual geological zone of sandstone canyons, then follow the road west below Pinyon Ridge to Holcomb Canyon and walk the trail up the rear entrance to the park. At the western end there's an interpretative display (details in Chapter 13).

Big Pines and Wrightwood are both popular recreational areas, so unless you have a strong desire to share the lake, the forests, and the campsites with scores of others, take the Lone Pine Canyon Road one mile east of Wrightwood. Here we journey along a quiet mountain-rimmed glen filled with towering yucca plants.

The narrow road descends the mesquite slopes until, without any warning, we enter a fantasy land of rounded sandstone bluffs and boulders, similar to the Devil's Punchbowl but more whimsical in shape and character. These are the Rock Candy Mountains. Leave the car and take a stroll through sensuous canyons where the pink-beige stone bulges like a Buddha's belly. Odd protuber-ances and rounded hollows, gnome-sized, add to the mystery of the area. One feels to be in a dreamlike world, a hobbit land of hidden passages and secret tunnels. A mile or so to the east, the freeway hums, but here all is quiet among the fleshly folds.

The final leg of the journey presents three options. Weary travelers can take I–15 south into the basin; those who missed the Angeles Crest detour and fancy some moutain driving should follow Route 138 east to Silverwood Lake and then travel over the San Bernardino Mountains via Crestline.

Finally there's the real backroad way, into the valley via Lytle Creek, which we'll take by retracing our route up Lone Pine Canyon about 1½ miles from the Rock Candy Mountains. After a sharp bend, follow the track to the left, off across the mesquite-covered floor of the valley. At the cattle grid there's another track to the right, leading over the low range of hills to Lytle Creek and Scotland. It's a bit rough in places on the one-mile upslope but take it slow.

Lytle Creek, a splendidly rugged canyon in places, and the adjoining Grapevine Canyon were the scene of gold mining in the 1860–90s period until a major flood in 1891 ended most activities here. Today it has an empty, desolate feel. It's hard to believe the vast expanse of the Los Angeles metropolitan area lies just beyond its southern entrance. Even the elevated freeway at the end of the canyon cannot destroy the wilderness quality of the valley. We move along the widening wash to the flatlands beyond.

At Summit Avenue there's a chance for one last detour if you're in no hurry to reach San Bernardino—an opportunity to sample a few wines at four of southern California's wineries.

Nonresidents are often surprised that the smoggy basin can support establishments of any merit. Back in the early 1800s, however, this was California's prime wine-producing region, and although vineyards are now slowly being buried under patios, porches, and pools, enough remain to ensure continued high-quality production.

Take Etiwanda Avenue south from its junction with Summit Avenue. Continue over the San Bernardino freeway (I–10) half a mile to the Filippi winery (at Jurupa Avenue; tastings 8–6 daily), half a mile or so north of Marlay Avenue. Joe Filippi now has more than six tasting rooms in

southern California and his label features some interesting premium varietal wines, including Gewürztraminer, Barbera, and Cabernet Sauvignon.

To reach the San Antonio winery (daily, 1–7, except Monday), famous for its unusual Almondoro, Carinale, and fruit wines, continue south on Etiwanda Avenue to Riverside Avenue, turn right, and, after two miles, right again on Hammer Avenue to a complex of pink roofs and old wine barrels.

Brookside, one of the largest of southern California's wineries, is particularly revered for its flor sherries, which can be sampled at its Guasti tasting room by continuing west on Riverside Avenue from Hammer Avenue and then turning north (right) on Archibald Avenue into the heart of Guasti.

Four miles to the north, in Cucamonga, is the last winery in this loop detour. Situated on Foothill Boulevard (66) a mile or so west of its junction with Archibald Avenue is the renowned Thomas winery, which claims to be the oldest producing winery in California. It was founded in 1839 by Tiburcio Tapis on a land grant from Governor Juan Bautista Alvarado and in 1967 was purchased by the Joseph Filippi Company. Two years later a disastrous flood swept down from the mountains, destroying many of the vineyards and some of the original buildings. Fortunately, there's still plenty to see here, and visitors are encouraged to take the self-conducted winery tour (daily, 8–6).

There are a few other wineries in the area, but four is usually enough for any tasting session. So enjoy your trip home, or better still, join me for the next and final journey through the beautiful San Diego backcountry.

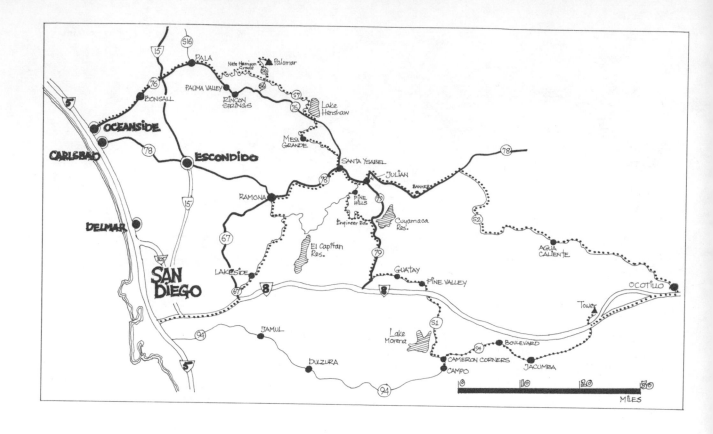

15. THE SAN DIEGO BACKCOUNTRY

Missions and Mineral Spas

    On our final journey we explore the mountainous backcountry of San Diego, rich in mission and Indian history. We hear tales of a lost treasure, visit four asistencia missions, all still in active use, talk with Indians on their reservations, and trace the remnants of early stage routes across the notorious Anza-Borrego desert. But that's only the beginning. Gourmets will relish the bakery where more than twenty kinds of bread are baked fresh each day and remember the tiny country candy store with its homemade hand-dipped chocolates. Others will enjoy a trip to the Palomar observatory, strolls along the Western-flavored main street of an old gold-mining town, a plunge in hot mineral springs, and some of the best backcountry driving in southern California.

Note: The journey begins in the tiny mission town of Pala, and there's a choice of access from the north. First, avoid Route 15. It's not a pleasant journey. The most scenic approach is via Route 74 to Elsinore and south through Murrieta, Temecula, and the twisting S–16. A faster route follows 76 east from Oceanside through San Luis Rey (pause at the mission here) and Bonsall.

THE GREAT CHAPARRAL-COVERED mountains slope steeply into the valley of the San Luis Rey River. To the south, the flatlands and parts of the lower mountain slopes are covered in dense groves of orange and lemon trees, bottle-green blankets speckled with brilliant color. To the north the S–16, always an exciting drive, snakes down Pala Creek from Wolf Valley and the once-quaint pioneer town of Temecula.

Here at Pala it's a hot, silent day. The white-painted mission of San Antonio de Pala, restored in its authentic Spanish style, peeps from behind a grove of trees at the edge of the square. It was originally founded in 1815 by Father Antonio Peyri as an asistencia for the San Luis Rey Mission, one of the sequence of twenty-one coastal missions that stretched all the way from San Diego to Sonoma.

The courtyard is shaded by an array of fir, palm, pepper, and fruit trees. A fountain splashes softly. On a hot day it's a delightful place to seek shelter from the sear of the valley. There's a tiny museum nestling in a niche by the church (Tuesday through Sunday, 10–3), and for restless children, a collection of birds and rabbits in a small compound.

The church itself is a long, low building, always dark and cool inside. Simple frescoes in bright colors adorn its uneven walls, and roughly carved benches face the altar on either side of the central aisle. Outside, by the graveyard, is the mission's unusual campanile, said to have been styled after a similar tower at Juárez, Mexico. The 1916 flood demolished the original tower, and an identical new one was built by the Cupeno Indian "neophytes," whose love for this simple huddle of adobe buildings has led to its retention as the only Californian mission still ministering to Indians.

It has always been a peaceful place. In 1820 the presidente of the California missions wrote of the Indians at Pala, "whose Christian docility and joyful aspect gladens the heart." One of the few incidents that marred understanding between the missionaries and the Indians occurred in the early 1900s during the regeneration of the ministry after the chaos of secularization in 1833–34. The bishop inadvertently appointed a priest unfamiliar with the history of the mission and even less informed about the local Indians. One day soon after his arrival he decided the inside of the church needed brightening up and without consulting anyone proceeded to whitewash over the intricate murals the Indians themselves had created. They were understandably incensed. The priest feared his gross error might lead to a resurgence of the rebellions of the late 1700s, when many coastal missions were destroyed in a series of tumultuous holocausts instigated by Indians against the insensitive and arrogant padres.

Fortunately for the priest, he was given an opportunity to make a hasty departure, and the Cupeno immediately set to work replacing the wall paintings. "There are many stories like that," an elderly Indian told me as we stood together in the pepper-tree-shaded cemetery. "The padres could be cruel. Here we were lucky. We had good men and we all worked together to build the town. In other missions the Indians were treated like slaves, and if they ran away they were whipped— sometimes they were even killed to scare the others." I asked him what happened during the secularization period, which destroyed the missionaries' domination of "alta California." "Well, the Indians were suddenly told they were 'free.' Just like that. Some of them were very happy at first. If they had learned a skill, a trade or something at the mission, maybe shoemaking or tanning or soapmaking, they went out to get work and set up a home for themselves. But most of them didn't know what to do. The padres had always told them what to do in the past. Now there was no one. A lot of them started drinking. Some others went back into the hills and tried to start their tribes again. It was a very difficult time. The Mexicans said they were doing it for the Indians. That wasn't true. They wanted to get hold of the mission land and the church gold. And they did. We were just a nuisance to them."

Following secularization the Indians were decimated. It is thought that by 1860, a mere twenty-seven years after the decrees were issued by the Mexican government, the Indian population of California had been reduced from over 120,000 to less than 30,000. John Frémont, one of the founding fathers of American California, was a notorious Indian killer. One of his men recorded: "We killed plenty of game and an occasional Indian. We made it a rule to spare none of the bucks."

The rest of the story is all too familiar. Spasmodic Indian resistance to the increasing flow of settlers was classified as "uprisings," and massacres of whole villages and even tribes ensued. The original 7.5 million acres set aside as Indian reservations in the early treaties of the 1850s soon dwindled to a mere 500,000, much of it unproductive mountain land.

Nowhere is this more evident than in the San Diego backcountry, which is dotted with tiny reservations, some occupying less than 2 square miles. In many instances, the land is unfit for habitation, with virtually no access and no services. "One thing's for sure," my elderly informant told me. "If the land was any good we wouldn't own it."

I looked out across the dusty square in front of the mission. Dark-skinned Indians were chatting quietly under the broad shade trees. Inside the church, two women were cleaning the rough floor. I could hear Indian children playing outside their classrooms on the far side of the courtyard. It was a peaceful scene. I found the sad history hard to believe.

Up the Pauma Reservation road off Route 76, I talked with a young Pauma Indian and heard the same pathetic stories. "We're luckier than most tribes in these mountains, though; we can grow oranges here." He indicated the straight lines of dark-green-leaved trees bent with bright fruit. "Those belong to us. But some reservations, about all they're any good for is acorns and Christmas

Pala Mission

trees." He laughed. "Yes, didn't you know that? Indians get a free Christmas tree. It's one of the perks!"

We were standing near the reservation's tiny whitewashed church. The Indian's long black hair flowed down his back and his dark eyes shone brilliantly as he spoke. "I'm not sure exactly when that was built. I know my grandfather helped on the construction when he was young. He's eighty-four now." He pointed to a new community center. "When that opens up, we may start to feel like a tribe again." I asked him if any of the other regional tribes had regular celebrations and festivals. "There's a couple of big ones. The Pala Reservation has a Corpus Christi fiesta in July and the Rincons have their fiesta in August, 'round the twenty-fourth sometime. We'll perhaps organize something too when the center gets started. We're not much like a tribe at the moment."

A mile or so farther down Route 76 is the Nate Harrison Grade Road up to the Palomar Mountain State Park and the famous mountaintop observatory. The man for whom the road is named was a freed southern slave. He originally came to California with his master during the gold rush and then later settled in a cabin high up in these mountains, raising pigs in the lush meadows. Normally the unpaved surface is reasonably smooth, and it's an exciting, scenic drive up through the chaparral to the shady woods and campgrounds of the park. Avoid this steep climb, however, after a rainstorm and take Route S6 instead. The profusion of white Coulter and Jeffrey pines, incense cedar, and big-cone spruce gives this area a flavor of the Sierras and Cascades farther to the north.

Following secularization much of the region was granted by the Mexicans to Juan José Warner (actually a Connecticut Yankee whose real name was Jonathan Trumbull). The community of Warner Springs a few miles to the east and the sad remains of the adobe Warner's Ranch near the junction of Route 79 and S22 are all that memorialize his brief reign. Relationships with the local Indians were at best tenuous. He used the Cupeno as stock hands for a monthly wage of $3 and was a little too agile with the whip for their liking. In 1851 they drove him off his estate and reoccupied their old homelands for a few decades, until being forcibly moved to the specially established Pala reservation in 1903.

Today much of the area is in public ownership, although Palomar observatory itself is owned by the California Institute of Technology, a privately endowed research organization. Most of the $6.5 million required to establish the complex was donated by the Rockefellers, and the huge 200-inch telescope, for years the world's largest, took more than ten years to grind and polish in a specially established workshop at the Institute. "It's not the biggest now. The Russians have one that's 235 inches." So I was informed by one of the maintenance men as I stood gaping at the incredible machine in the twelve-story-high dome. "There's a problem, though." He chuckled. "It's crooked! Last week we had four Russian astronomers here and they told us this is a much better telescope than theirs. They've started to build another one, but it'll take fifteen years. You've got to get the mirror right, you see. If it's not ground perfectly it's not really much good."

I asked him if he ever worked on the telescope itself. "Oh no," he told me. "No, none of us can touch it. There's one man specially hired to clean and oil it. We wouldn't go near it. Last week, though, one of the scientists asked me if I'd like to look at the moon. First time anyone asked me. And y'know it scared me to death. I looked right into all the craters, right inside them like I was just floating there. Heck, I told him, you can have your moon. I'm staying here on the ground." He laughed. "The moon is nothing to them. It's like next door. They can see Lord knows how many billions of miles with that thing!" According to the observatory brochure, records have been made of galaxies more than 15 billion light years away (one light-year is equivalent to 6 trillion miles).

Even though this windswept hilltop attracts a disproportionate number of visitors during the warmer months, it's a place that should not be missed. In addition to the visitors' gallery in the dome of the 200-inch telescope, there's the Greenway museum of impressive astronomical photographs and a series of walking trails around the complex. Access to the observatory's three smaller telescopes is usually limited to staff and visiting scientists.

We follow Route S7, winding our way down the ridges to a broad valley and Lake Henshaw. When the lake is full, it's a lovely place to pause for a few hours.

A mile or so on 76 beyond the southern end of the lake, take the turnoff to the right to Mesa Grande (there's a small store near the junction and a sign for Lake View Resorts). After a steep twisting climb we enter a pastoral region of rolling oak-covered hills and cow-studded meadows. An old bathtub sits in a field and is used as a drinking trough by the cows. There are few buildings up here.

The second mission church of our journey can be found down a gravel track that swings off to the right, just before an abrupt turn in the road leading to the now-abandoned Mesa Grande Store. Perched on the hillside overlooking a narrow valley is a simple, sturdy structure, white-painted, with a wooden campanile beside it. Inside it's dark and a little dusty. Rough pews face a simple altar. A crudely painted sign nearby reads "St. Dominick's Chapel," and gives the time of the once-a-month service. In contrast the adjoining cemetery is ablaze with flowers and decorations on the plain, often unnamed, crosses. Down the valley a cow gives out a melancholy moo and a warm breeze rustles the leaves in the branches.

Erected in 1818 as an asistencia of Mission San Diego, the Santa Ysabel Mission, a few miles farther east, is a lively place full of displays and historic plaques. There's even a small picnic area here under a group of shade trees for travelers. The church itself was restored in the 1920s, and while it is one of the least historically authentic in the region, the adjoining museum contains a wealth of Indian artifacts and gives details of two mysteries connected with the mission. The first relates to more than $5 million in gold, diamonds, and emeralds collected by the Padres of Santa Ysabel from other missions for safekeeping following secularization. The "Treasure of Santa Ysabel" was subsequently mislaid, and local legend has it that the Indians know its whereabouts and ensure its protection with "a pillar of light and a necklace of human eyes." Equally intriguing are the missing church bells. There were two of them, and long after secularization, when the church fell into ruins,

Julian

they were mounted on a framework of logs and rung regularly for services conducted by the Indians themselves. They were said to be the oldest bells in California, cast in 1723 and 1767 respectively. Then in 1926 they disappeared and nothing has been seen of them since. Some say the Indians have them hidden along with the lost treasure. The padres wait patiently for them to be returned.

Down the road, opposite the Santa Ysabel general store (founded "1870—I think," says the sign), is the town's most notable establishment, Dudley's Bakery. Even if you've just had lunch at the mission picnic area, you'll find it hard to resist the enticing aromas wafting through the ever-opening doors. People come and go in droves, clutching tightly wrapped packages of breads—potato, raisin nut, German black, round sheepherders, New England hearth, Irish brown, Norwegian pumpernickle, the list goes on. An official "Bread-Baking Schedule" sheet indicates the availability of each type on each day of the week. There are twenty-three different kinds listed, but the lady behind the counter told me, "We can make just about any kind of bread you want if the order's big enough."

Dudley Pratt, founder of the bakery, died recently after twelve years' devoted service to the region's bread lovers. An ode on the wall sings his praises, and the steady stream of customers pays continual homage to his memory. "We still use his recipes just as he wrote them," a young woman baker told me. "They're like the Bible. We wouldn't dare change them."

On the long climb out of Santa Ysabel toward Julian, pause at Inaja Park, which was created as a memorial to eleven fire fighters killed during the 1956 forest fires. Take a stroll along the self-guide nature trail. It's well signed and provides a thorough explanation of the rich chaparral covering most of the Cleveland National Forest mountains. Then continue the climb up past the charming Spencer Valley School and the region's famous apple orchards, into the Western-flavored town of Julian. Except for main street, with its false-front stores, bowed verandas, and raised wooden sidewalks, much of the community is built on incredibly steep slopes. The place has a durable spirit. Even a smattering of recent developments does not detract from its authenticity. At the eastern end of main street is the 1887 Julian Hotel, founded as a stage stop on the Yuma–San Diego route by the Albert Robinsons, freed Georgia slaves, who first arrived here in 1870 during the town's brief but lucrative gold-mining era.

Mike Julian, along with his cousins, James and Frank Bailey, all ex-Confederate soldiers from Georgia, founded the town after initial discoveries of placer gold in 1869. The following year saw the beginning of mine opening, and for almost a decade the place was a tumult of activity. More than $15 million in gold is estimated to have been claimed from the lode here before the big strike at Tombstone, Arizona, left the little town slumbering peacefully, devoid of most of its residents. It may well have faded altogether, but its emergence as the center of a remarkably rich fruit-growing area gave it a second and more lasting lease on life. There's still abundant evidence of its two-pronged past. The Julian Museum (weekends, 10–4) and remnants of the Eagle Mine (daily, 9–5) give visitors an insight into the early mining era, and stores selling fruit jams, cider, and delectable homemade pies are a constant reminder of the town's flourishing economy today.

Anza Borrego Desert

Before leaving, take a short drive around the community. Note the delicate library building, originally a school and brought here in one piece from nearby Witch Creek. In the rear gardens, tall water towers rise on stilts high above the rooftops, and on Second Street, look out for the trees in the middle of the road!

From Julian we wind along Route 78 through shaded forests and then abruptly begin a dramatic descent through a cleft in the Volcan Mountains to Banner. The tall trees are gone. The steep mountain flanks, evenly covered in dark-green chaparral, resemble the folds of a velvet gown. The view ahead looks out over the western edge of the largest state park in the country, encompassing most of the notorious Anza-Borrego desert. Joshua trees, yuccas, and scrub oaks compete for scarce water on the dry plains and up the narrow creek beds.

At Route S2 we follow the old Butterfield Overland Stage route south down Earthquake Valley, another segment of the San Andreas Fault. Immediately the desert begins, the vast horizons and panoramas, the infinite stillness and silence of a land devoid of people, of towns, of wide highways. Yet for all its emptiness, this was once the corridor of California's history. Through here passed the Spanish explorers under Pedro Fages in 1772 and Juan Bautista Anza in 1774, legendary trailblazers like Kit Carson, General Stephen Watts Kearney and his dragoons, bound for the fateful battle of San Pasqual in 1847, and the famous Mormon Battalion under Colonel Philip St. George Cooke, hacking its way up Box Canyon in the same year. Then, after the discovery of gold in

northern California, came the endless stream of settlers on the Southern Emigrant Trail in their creaking Conestoga wagons, pioneers looking for a new beginning in an almost mythical paradise. They all came this way, scores of thousands, leaving their tracks in the sand and scars on the bedrock of the desert. Only after the completion of the transcontinental railroad in the late 1800s were these routes abandoned and the wheel tracks left to the elements.

Today, with the exception of a few historical plaques and the restored stage station at Vallecito, little remains of that frantic era. What the traveler may enjoy instead is a wonderful sense of space and utter timelessness here in the emptiness of the broad valleys and deeply eroded mountain ranges.

Pause at one of the campsites and pick up a pamphlet on the desert. This is a rich region, full of unusual sights and experiences. If you have a high-clearance or four-wheel-drive vehicle, devise your own detours to strange lost palm groves hidden deep in mountain canyons, areas inhabited by the bulbous elephant trees, natural cactus gardens, and the mysterious canyons of Split Mountain.

Those intending to remain on Route S2 will find much of interest on the long drive to Ocotillo and Route I–8. Pause at the 1852 adobe Vallecito Stage Station, and then continue south to bathe in the hot mineral pools of Agua Caliente Springs. At the ranger's office here is an excellent display of desert cactus and flora. Look for odd-shaped succulents as you drive south—the saguaros, prickly pears, devil's fingers, fish hooks, hedgehogs, jumping chollas, staghorns, beaver tails, and pin cushions. Note also the remarkable array of bushes and trees—ironwood, palo verde, Joshua trees, mesquite, saltbrush, creosote, and smoke trees. Come here in the spring and you'll move across multicolored carpets of scarlets, purples, and bronzes when the tiny desert flowers burst into bloom.

Those unfamiliar with the desert might assume that little of any significance inhabits these torrid wastelands, but nothing could be further from the truth. Long dry spells will often bring the bighorn sheep down from the peaks and ridges into the valleys in search of water. Here they mingle with mule deer, antelopes, coyotes, foxes, jackrabbits, kangaroo rats, and bobcats. Even the occasional mountain lion has been recorded in the more remote parts of the wilderness, and over 150 species of birds live in or pass through the park.

One of my favorite haunts is the Carizzo Badlands overlook halfway between Agua Caliente Springs and Ocotillo. At the edge of a steep drop into a torn canyon, one can look across a wilderness of eroded mountains, pastel-colored and etched by rivulets. Take a stroll down the sandy slopes. Soon the road seems far behind. There are no sounds. The heat of the day stills the breeze and the air shimmers. A lizard darts from behind a rock in a flash of scarlet and then vanishes as if by magic. Find a patch of shade and sit and listen to the sounds of the desert. Don't bother to think. Be silent and let the desert tell you its secrets. You'll return refreshed.

At Ocotillo we join Route I–8 for a few miles to climb the parched eastern slopes of the Jacumba Mountains. The odd Desert View Tower at the summit of the pass was constructed by Bert L. Vaughn during the 1920s as a monument to the region's pioneers and was later opened by Dennis Newman as a vista point and tourist attraction, complete with a collection of old wagons, a museum, a trinket shop, and a viewing platform. In the cool spring and fall months the roaring wood fire and comfortable armchairs provide a welcome haven for chilly travelers. The last time I was there I saw a notice in the museum offering the place for sale. "I've had more than thirty years here," Mr. Newman told me. "It's been fun but I'm ready to retire now."

Following signs to Jacumba on Route 94, we pass through an upland landscape of odd boulder-studded hills and thick chaparral. A few homesteads huddle in the narrow valleys, and the area has a bypassed quality to it, a characteristic even more pronounced in the once-fashionable stucco resort of Jacumba. The town was founded in 1852 as a stage post on the main road between Yuma and San Diego.

Following the discovery of hot mineral springs, the Jacumba Hot Springs and Health Spa was opened in 1927 and for many years attracted an enthusiastic clientele from the coastal cities. When I visited, the place was still operative, although Henry Lazare, owner and head physiotherapist, was trying to sell it. He also owned most of the town and was hopeful that someone with regal aspirations would relieve him of his rather bleached kingdom.

Before leaving Jacumba note the strange collection of Oriental-flavored buildings on the rocky hillside above the town. The residence is known locally as the Chinese Castle, and its owner, determined not to be pestered by curious tourists, has attached guard-dog notices to the high fences. You can get a good view of the place, though, from the track leading off from the main road.

224

We continue across more of this boulder-and-scrub landscape through the tiny community of Bankhead Springs, whose main claim to fame is its Chateau Basque restaurant, renowned for gargantuan family-style dinners.

At Boulevard, the quaint, arbor-shrouded Wisteria Candy Cottage offers a marvelous array of hand-dipped chocolates and exotic candies to the sweet-toothed traveler. Unless you have a will of iron, avoid this place. Once inside, Mrs. Brown will beguile you with her array of coconut clusters, chocolate creams, pecan rolls, brittles of every kind, chocolate fudge, and seventeen different kinds of divinity. She is the fourth owner since the store's founding in 1921 and claims to use the original recipes. Every day she makes fresh batches of delectables in her enormous copper kettles and told me the job that really tires her out is spreading the peanut brittle. "It's very popular now because of President Carter, I suppose. But you've got to work fast to spread it while it's still hot. You've got no idea how difficult caramel is to spread when it starts to harden up."

At Cameron Corners take a short detour to the Campo Store, founded in 1868 by the Gaskill brothers. These chaparral hills were at that time the haunt of scores of Mexican banditos, who made frequent raids to the north and then evaded their pursuers in this borderland wilderness. The Gaskill brothers knew there would ultimately be trouble with the bandits and laid in enough guns and ammunition to withstand a lengthy siege. On December 4, 1875, Pancho López, one of the original Tiburcio Vásquez gang, made his move and along with six gunmen took the store by surprise. The Gaskills responded quickly and a furious gun battle ensued, in which most of the López gang was wiped out. The rest turned and fled, and Campo, from that day on, remained undisturbed in its rocky hollow beside Campo Creek.

At this point those ready to return to the comforts of the coast can continue west on 94 through Dulzura and Jamul. It's a dramatic drive across more of this mountainous wilderness, relieved by the occasional ranch or quiet resort. At Jamul, backroaders should take the Proctor Valley Road down to San Diego rather than follow the main highway—it's a much more enjoyable drive.

Alternatively, if you have plenty of time, take Route S1 north from Cameron Corners to Route 79, near Guatay. On a weekday or out of season, pause at the delightful Lake Morena before continuing on into the Cuyamaca Rancho.

This large state park is a varied upland region of oak and pine forests, quiet meadows, streams, and waterfalls, with a desertlike section in the northeastern corner. While it attracts a considerable flow of coastal residents on weekends and throughout the summer season, more than 75 miles of walking trails provide plenty of space for everyone. Pick up a pamphlet from one of the ranger stations and devise your own hike.

Before the gold rush of the 1870s transformed this pastoral landscape into a flurry of camps and creek claims, the Kumeya'ay Indians lived an independent existence in these hills, oblivious to the influence of the missionaries. Even when part of their land was included in the 1845 Rancho

Cuyamaca Mexican land grant, they successfully resisted attempts by the whites to fell the forests in the region by staging "a kind of revolution," according to the rancho's disgruntled owner.

At the park headquarters, there's a sensitively designed exhibit on the region's Indian culture that captures the rhythm and spirit of tribal life in these hidden hills. A member of the Kumeya'ay tribe gives this sad summary of the inevitable takeover of their lands and the destruction of their culture by the white settlers:

> As time went on strangers opened up more of our land, they cut down our trees, scared away the animals. They built roads where our trails had been, fenced in areas where we sowed our grass seed. Now he digs big holes in the earth, in search of gold and runs machines that drown out the voice of the land.

Stonewall Mine, of which a few traces remain near the northern edge of the park, was the largest operation in the region. By 1872 and before its closure in 1892 it produced more than $2 million. The pleasant resort community of Cuyamaca today, however, is very different from its rip-roaring predecessor during the gold days.

Here we have a choice of route to the valley town of Ramona to the west. Route 79 wriggles its way through mountain forests to Julian, where it joins the westbound 78. It's a pleasant drive and particularly advisable if you're traveling with a trailer. However, if you'd prefer a bit of backroading, take Engineer Road off to the left just past the dam wall at Cuyamaca and follow its snaking contours through the forests to the 78/79 near Julian. There's one more option: If you'd like a real backcountry adventure, look for the unpaved road off to the left near Pine Hills, 3 miles north of the junction of Engineer Road and Boulder Creek Road. This travels west past the Eagle Peak Sportsman Club and the El Capitán Reservoir to join the Wildcat Canyon Road at San Vicente valley, and it is one of the most exciting mountain drives in the region. Try to get some advance information on conditions, though, before attempting it. Usually a ranger or someone else in Cuyamaca will be able to help.

At Ramona we turn south on San Vicente Road and travel across the pastoral Barona Ranch Indian Reservation. Look for the charming Barona Mission, a white twin-towered structure that unfortunately is normally closed to the public. Then we're suddenly out of the valley and heading down narrow Wildcat Canyon. Enjoy this last taste of unspoiled backcountry before the freeways and sprawl of the San Diego suburbs far below.

Of course the shock of contemporary urbanization may be too jarring after the silence of the mountains and desert. So detour to the Santee Lakes, a chain of six small reservoirs 3 miles west of Santee, and pass the remainder of the day island-hopping on pulley-operated raft ferries. Maybe when you leave it'll be dark and you won't see those interminable miles of sprawl around El Cajon.

Of course, you can always retrace your steps back up Wildcat Canyon and start backroading all over again.

INDEX

Page numbers in italic refer to illustrations.